# Sex Is *Not*
# A Four-Letter Word!

PATRICIA MARTENS MILLER

# Sex Is *Not* A Four-Letter Word!

*Talking Sex With Your*

*Children Made Easier*

CROSSROAD · NEW YORK

1995
The Crossroad Publishing Company
370 Lexington Avenue, New York, NY 10017

The publisher wishes to thank SIECUS for permission to reprint material from "When Children's
Sexual Behaviors Raise Concern," *SIECUS Report* August/September, 1991, 19 (6), Copyright
1991, The Sex Information and Education Council of the U.S., Inc.

*Library of Congress Cataloging-in-Publication Data*
Miller, Patricia Martens.
  Sex is not a four-letter word! : talking sex with your children
made easier / by Patricia Martens Miller.
    p.    cm.
  Includes bibliographical references (p.        ).
  ISBN 0-8245-1437-8 (pbk.)
  1. Sex instruction.  2. Sexual ethics.  3. Parenting.  I. Title.
HQ57.M55  1994
649'.65—dc20                                      94-29499
                                                 CIP

*To Mom and Dad*

# Contents

# Acknowledgments

I would like to express my deepest gratitude to the many people who gave me the support and encouragement to help this book become a reality.

A big thank you to my readers: Lois Martens, S.S.N.D., Gene Martens, S.J., my sister and brother who have shared so much wisdom and are always there for me. For providing the "first time" parents' perspective: Diane and Terry Heitman and Gene and Jane Schmittgens. Also to "seasoned parents" Barb and Rick Huelsing and Nancy and Greg Stockmann. To Christine Pawleck, Lynette Aldapa, Michael Lauzon, Rick Watson, Jake Varela, and Jim Gatson: a huge thanks for your insights. To Milton Fujita, M.D., for keeping me grounded, and to longtime friend, Richard Ready, M.D., for medical correctness.

Thanks also to busy colleagues-heroes of mine—Michael Garanzini, S.J., Charles Bouchard, O.P., Mike Henning, Jim and Evelyn Whitehead, and Louis D. Peters, Ed.D., who all *made* time to review chapters of my work; offered guidance, expertise, and thus improvement; and who model dedication and excellence for me. To Nancy Schillinger, Millie Steffe, Alexandra Birke, Ann Tuxbury, and Sandy Lauzon—good friends and loving mothers—for practical advice and shining examples. To my dear friends Jan and Carl Rossow for the telephone and recreational therapy that helped me finally reach the end. And to Dee Ready for prodding me and asking provocative questions.

Thanks to Gail Schmitt for her always available secretarial skills and to my friend Rick Meyer for generously providing me with a peaceful and inspiring place to write. To Jeanie Donovan for working so tirelessly and unselfishly to help me with the many technicalities. Peace and all good things to Jenny Boulais for keeping my body going and my mind clear. To Stef Vergara, heartfelt thanks for expertise as a reference librarian and enabling support as a treasured friend. Thanks to my former students, to the gays and lesbians I have worked with, as well as their parents, who have been willing to risk sharing so that I and others might learn. And last but always first, to my children Niki, George Jr., and Jeff for their valuable advice, continual encouragement, and most of all, for their nonstop hugs.

# Introduction

I have been involved in education for over thirty years now. Many of those years have been spent teaching human sexuality to students of all ages and levels of schooling. I have trained teachers and lectured to parents all over the United States. No matter where I go, no matter what the educational, ethnic, or cultural background of the parents, I am always asked the same questions. This book is an attempt to answer those questions I am most frequently asked and to share some experiences in my own life as a mother, and the experiences of those parents and students who have shared stories with me over the years. I hope these will be helpful to young parents just starting out as well as to parents who find themselves facing the challenging teen years.

Parenthood should be fun. If you are not having fun raising your children, you could be. If you do not view children as a blessing and a source of joy in your life, then your children will pick up on your feelings. As they become more and more aware of your discomfort or uneasiness, they may feel that they are somehow responsible for your discomfort. This often contributes to feelings of low self-esteem and attitudes of low self-worth. Owing to a lack of understanding, the results are often experimentation with drugs and alcohol, possible addiction problems, and/or abuse of sexuality on their part. These symptoms often manifest themselves as the child begins the teen years. By this time patterns of behavior are set in place, and because they are difficult to change, become lifelong entanglements causing disappointment, difficulties in relationships, and stress for all involved.

This need not be the case. With a lot of love, conscious effort, and many careful choices on your part, raising children can be fulfilling and gratifying. Parenthood can and should be one of the greatest sources of joy in your life.

Being a parent, however, will not always go smoothly or be without serious strain. If you are going to be a good parent, you must be willing to give up many years of your life to do so. Being a good parent takes a lot of work. It is *not* something that comes naturally. Unfortunately, in the American culture, we do not prepare people to become parents; we just let it happen! We insist that our young men and women go to school and carefully train for any other career they wish to undertake, but in one of the most challenging and important areas of life, parenthood, we provide no education or preparation at all.

This is not to say good help is not available. There are excellent programs and various other assistance, yours for the asking, but *you* must want and seek this help. An effective parent does just that. The conscientious parent seeks out and takes advantage of courses, lectures, books, and programs that offer assistance in the many and varied aspects of parenting. Time is limited for today's parent. Many parents are filling both the role of mother and father. But the reality is that you have only *one chance* to become a good parent, and raising children is one of the most important tasks of your life. So parenting must become a priority in your life.

I assume that because you are reading this book you *are* a concerned parent. I further assume you are a parent who loves your children and wants to help them, as much as possible, to grow up happy, mentally and physically healthy, and spiritually grounded. It is my desire to aid you in this task by offering suggestions and information that may help you as you begin to talk with your children about sex.

*Sex is not a four-letter word!* Nor is it a bad or dirty topic that should be avoided or left to chance. When we ignore the sexual development of our children and the questions they have as they grow and change, we risk giving our children the message that sex is some undesirable, secret thing that no one should talk about. By avoidance we imply that someday—miraculously—our children will suddenly and instantly know all about sex and have a mature, healthy, and satisfying sex life, and will be able to handle any problem or complication that arises, without ever needing help or guidance. But sex is a *learned* behavior and if we do not discuss it with our children, we miss the opportunity to tell them just how wonderful and beautiful sexuality really is. We forgo the chance to guide them toward a spiritual approach to sexuality and to teach them how to respect and treasure this God-given gift.

Please do not avoid this topic with your children. Resist the temptation to ignore questions about sexuality because they make you feel uncomfortable or ill at ease. Don't assume that your children will pick up what they need to know somewhere along the way. Don't take for granted they will "get it at school."

All of us are sexual beings from the moment we are conceived, and you and I have been learning, formally and informally, about sexuality all of our lives. Who better than ourselves to pass on to our children the knowledge we possess from a lifetime of experiences, successes and mistakes, strengths and weaknesses? Many of us had no role models in this regard. We are exploring new territory with our children and that's a little scary. We worry we might say the wrong things, or tell our children too much too soon. Be assured, there is no evidence that indicates children are harmed by knowing "too much too soon." They tend to brush off too much information about sexuality with a shrug of uninterest, just as they do with other issues they are not yet ready to assimilate. On the other hand, there is plenty of evidence that indicates children are harmed *greatly* by learning too little too late!

Besides, if we leave this job to the world, our children will indeed learn about their sexuality, but it may not be within a framework of spirituality, values, morals, and loving relationships found within truly faith-filled families. Instead, they might gain the mistaken belief that sex is easy, uncomplicated, engaged in for pleasure only, with no strings attached; a learned sexuality that could become selfish and cheap, and carry with it lack of responsibility or commitment; a sexuality that is not God-centered, but self-centered.

I don't believe that this is what most parents want for their children. I think the problem is simply that since many of our parents didn't talk to us about sexuality, we don't know how to begin. At the time we were growing up, it wasn't expected of our parents. Sex simply wasn't discussed. Many of our parents were able, to some degree, to protect us from the immoral and demeaning practices our children are faced with today, such as certain TV programs and easy accessibility to explicit movies, pornography, and music that often glorify sex, drugs, and alcohol. I could go on and on, but you are aware of the negative influences facing our children today, and you know that most of us did not face these same influences to the same degree that our children do.

We all do our best to keep our children from what is harmful, but we are not with them all the time. In fact, with many single families and families with both parents holding down jobs, our children are left to face many important choices and moral decisions on their own, often without any preparation.

Some parents try to guard against negative influences by refusing to have cable TV, by monitoring music and movies, or by trying to provide adequate and responsible day care. These are very important things to do, and a good start. But our children are often influenced by what their friends do, and many of their friends' parents are not as concerned about these negative influences as we would hope. No longer is sexually explicit programming restricted to cable TV. Regular TV channels carry programs, and even commercials, which demean the very faith and morals we are striving so hard to instill in our children.

Our best recourse is to develop open and honest patterns of communicating with our children about sexuality and morality. Such communication is a *must* if we truly want children to understand and enjoy their sexuality and treat it with the respect and honor it deserves.

This book is designed to help you begin a process, a process of communicating and learning with your children about sexuality. The suggestions in it come from gospel principles, from educators, doctors, counselors, parents, students, and many others who work with youth. What you will be reading, then, are simply suggestions and options for you to consider. Then you must decide for yourself if the material will be helpful in your household. No one knows your children better than you do, so you are the one to decide if one suggestion will work better than another one. If you feel that you don't know your son or daughter very well, then this will be a good opportunity to begin the process of getting to know him or her better. Remember there are no perfect answers, no perfect formulas, no perfect programs or books that will tell you absolutely everything you need to know.

Just do the best you can. You love your children. *Be sure they know you do.* Making an effort to provide opportunities for communication and understanding will be another step that they will come to see as an expression of your love, your concern for them. Trust yourself and pray for guidance. Begin with them whenever they ask their first question. Begin with yourself right now.

# Chapter 1

. . . . . . . . . .

~

# The Fantasy and the Fact

Both as a parent and a teacher, I often hear kids and parents say things about sexuality that are based on rumor, myth, fantasy . . . call it what you will. Sometimes parents will use these as excuses to avoid talking to their children about sex. Because many of these fantasies have been repeated so often, people believe them to be true. They unwittingly hide behind them rather than face their ignorance or embarrassment regarding sexuality. Listed below are some of the more common of these fantasies. Before we can begin to seriously approach the topic of sex education and children, we need to dispel these myths.

*Fantasy #1: Kids today are so sophisticated. They already know everything about sex.*

FACT: Kids ask some of the same questions you and I did. What they see on TV is not a complete picture of sexuality. Often what they see is two people, meeting for the first time in a bar, having a drink and a few laughs, and then going home together and jumping into bed. All this in sixty minutes or less. There is so much more! Television programs seldom show the enhanced joy and beauty attainable through the mature spiritual dimension of a sexual relationship. They seldom see a positive attitude portrayed in the sexual relationship between a husband and wife. (Good sex is usually only between unmarried persons or persons married to someone else!) Often these programs neglect dealing with the fear and shame of many lonely people who use sex to ease their pain; the humiliation of being used in a sexual relationship; the broken marriages; the unintended pregnancies. Programs usually show what sells. Uncomplicated sex sells! Time constraints prevent dealing with the complexity of many issues and often result in oversimplification or trivialization. True, our children have more access than we did to the media, movies, and magazines, but is it teaching them to be responsible, loving, and committed married adults who have positive and healthy sexual relationships?

*Fantasy #2: If we talk about it, they are going to try it.*

FACT: The research does not bear this out. In fact, the most recent studies show that kids who are better informed about their sexuality are *more likely* to make responsible decisions regarding it and postpone intercourse longer than those who lack such knowledge. More complete information is a deterrent to premarital sexual activity, not an incentive. Those most likely to engage in sexual activity at an earlier age are those who do not talk to their parents about sex and have not been educated about their sexuality at school. Generally speaking, too much information about sexuality is better than too little when it comes from a parent. The best solution, according to recent studies, is to augment parental discussion with education courses in human sexuality given by schools. Both are important.

*Fantasy #3: I don't know how to begin; I would be too embarrassed.*

FACT: Of course, there will be times when you will be embarrassed, but that doesn't mean you can't do a good job. In the beginning, it is natural for there to be some awkward moments for all of you, but as time goes by you will find that it is not so threatening after all. You will find you are simply relating what you know and have experienced. It is also OK to tell your child that you are a little nervous or embarrassed. You might say, *"No one talked to me about sex, so I feel a little nervous and I may get embarrassed sometimes. But I feel this is very important and I want you to get correct information from someone who loves you. So just bear with me, I'll get over it!"* Before long, your son or daughter will be comfortable asking questions and bringing up personal topics because you will have given permission for them to talk to you about a sensitive topic and created an atmosphere of personal trust, a loving bond. If we want our children to have a balanced view of sexuality, we have to take the necessary steps to allow this to happen. In so doing we can help them avoid some of the hang-ups our generation has had. What a wonderful legacy to leave the next generation!

*Fantasy #4: I am divorced. How can I possibly talk to my child about a good relationship?*

FACT: If we could talk to our children only about areas we have never had any problems with, there would be little, if any, conversation in our homes! You have much to offer your son or daughter from what you have learned in your life and from your own personal situation. If you can talk with them about some of your own frustrations and problems and how you handle them, they can learn much from you. You can teach them that they can have a serious problem, resolve it in some way, and get on with their lives. What a tremendous gift to give your child!

*Fantasy #5: I didn't have anyone to talk to and I made out OK.*

FACT: Given the reality of AIDS, sexual abuse, date rape, and the epidemic proportions of sexually transmitted diseases rampant in the teenage population of society today, this is a particularly dangerous attitude. Our children deserve our very best efforts. Withholding critical information about sexuality from them, because we are too uninformed or embarrassed to deal with it, can cost them their very lives. Suppose you had a huge pile of sand you had to transport from the bottom of a hill to the top of a hill. Would you use a shovel, a wheelbarrow, or a truck? All of them would do the job, but certainly the truck would be easier on you and do the job most efficiently. If we have resources at hand that can ease some of the troublesome situations that confront our children today, does it not make sense to use them? Your child may not be as lucky as you. Why take the chance?

*Fantasy #6: My child does not want to talk about sexuality with me. He or she never asks any questions.*

FACT: There are many things our children may not want to talk about with us: cleaning their rooms, shoplifting, curfew, alcohol, and so forth. But as concerned parents, we know that they *need* to talk and we *need* to listen and talk with them. Sometimes it is a matter of giving them permission to talk about it, saying in effect, "It's OK for us to discuss sexuality, we can handle it." There are many "teachable moments": a friend of the family is pregnant or watching a show that condones teenage sexual involvement. We need to use these situations to provoke questions or comments: *What do you know about natural childbirth? How do you feel about kids fourteen or fifteen engaging in sexual activity? What have you heard about AIDS?* By using these moments to break the ice, we have given them permission to ask their questions or express their opinions. It is not necessary to give long lectures or discuss sexuality every day. And be sure to avoid questions that can be answered with a simple "yes" or "no." Instead, use open-ended starters like "what," "why," "how," and "if."

*Fantasy #7: Wait till they are in high school. That will be soon enough!*

FACT: Education in sexuality should begin as soon as the child is old enough to ask a question. In actuality it begins even earlier in the womb and continues as the child begins to observe others, long before he or she begins talking. Education in sexuality is a lifelong process, from the cradle to the grave. If children can ask questions as they need, then sexuality education becomes a normal and natural part of their lives. If you wait until a child is sixteen or seventeen, you are not going to get many questions. They will have already found answers, perhaps dangerously incorrect, from their peers, magazines, from experimentation, or from other sources. Unfortunately, if you do not start the process of talking with your child about these important matters while they are young, it will be more difficult for you to start it later.

Studies today show sexual activity is starting at a much earlier age. We have a significant number of elementary school children engaging in sexual intercourse and other sexual activities. According to a 1992 survey by the Center for Disease Control, by the ninth grade thirty-nine percent of our young people have engaged in sexual intercourse. We need to prepare our children well in advance of the time at which they may begin to become sexually active. Sexuality education should begin at home at a very young age, continue in grade school and high school, and in religious instruction programs, be followed with instructions before marriage and, hopefully, continued after marriage with programs such as Marriage Encounter, parenting, and self-help groups, community and university programs, and the like.

*Fantasy #8: Sex is natural. They will pick up what they
need to know.*

FACT: Sex is a *learned* behavior. We give children messages about what it means to be male and female constantly, both verbally and nonverbally. From our messages and those gleaned from friends, television, and society, they learn what it means to be a sexual person and how to live out their sexuality. Some of the messages they receive encourage dysfunctional and/or unhealthy behavior. Some messages may even result in dangerous behavior. Sexuality is a complex part of our personhood, one that undergoes changes, adjustments, and new understandings throughout our lifetime.

Our children deserve to be informed by the most current and accurate information available from the physical and social sciences, so they may learn to make wise and careful decisions, decisions that show respect for their sexuality and for the sexuality of others. Withholding this kind of information—information that will affect them directly and/or indirectly the rest of their lives—is tantamount to raising them with one arm tied behind their back. One day they will recognize our refusal to deal with reality and hold us responsible for this undeveloped and misformed area of their lives.

We can find all kinds of reasons for avoiding something that is uncomfortable for us. I am sure you have heard all kinds of excuses from people as to why they do not want or need to talk with their children about sexuality. But the truth is, if we want our children to have responsible, accurate, and Christian-based information about sex, we parents have to be the ones to give it to them. It is simply not enough to hope that they will pick it up along the way or learn it in school.

The school should support and enhance our educational efforts in sexuality and provide the more formal assistance we rely on from them in other subject areas. But we parents have the primary responsibility to educate our children informally, at home, in this very important area of their lives. If refuse to do so, we will have to accept the possibly unpleasant and potentially disastrous consequences of our failure to do so.

# Chapter 2

. . . . . . . . .

~

# Are You Comfortable with Your Own Sexuality?

Before we begin with suggestions for discussing sexuality with your children, we need to bring up the question of your personal comfort level with the topic of sexuality. Many of us grew up in families where sexuality was not talked about. This was often because no one ever talked to our parents about sex. Coming out of a period colored by Victorian attitudes, American society in general did not discuss sexuality, so it is not surprising that our grandparents ignored this topic as well. They lacked accurate information about the body and understood little of the human sexual response. A cycle of ignorance and avoidance was set in place.

To make matters worse, most Christian religions viewed sexuality with suspicion. The important influence of Platonic philosophy on the thought of Augustine combined with the widespread influence of the Stoic and Gnostic philosophies to lay a foundation for the way Christians would approach sexuality for centuries to come. Augustine, linking intercourse to original sin, had a great distrust of sexual pleasure, while the Platonists, dividing body and soul, sought rigid control of all bodily functions, in particular, intercourse. Indeed, we are just now, entering this twenty-first century, coming to understand sexuality better and to appreciate it as a God-given gift!

The problem with avoidance is that you can never understand something you refuse to investigate. It is time for us to break the avoidance cycle. I assume most of us would like to see our grandchildren have an easier time of things than we did. One way to facilitate that possibility is for us to talk to our own children, openly and honestly, about sex.

This means giving our children permission to ask questions, to explore issues, to disagree, to challenge and be challenged, and to do so with comfort and the confidence that we will be able to see our way through these discussions. In so doing, we are creating the role models for future generations and breaking the avoidance cycle.

The key to being able to accomplish all of this lies in your comfort level with your own sexuality. The way you approach your child will be profoundly influenced by the inner feelings and understanding you have of your own sexuality. Many adults often leave these feelings unexplored. They do not want to take a closer look at their sexuality, their understanding of sexual issues, or the feelings they have surrounding them. Perhaps they fear they will become uncomfortable. Some say: "Let's leave well enough alone!" They simply go on with their daily living unaware of how their refusal to reflect on their sexuality impacts their daily lives, their choices and decisions, and colors their relationships with others.

The problem is that when your child begins to ask questions about sexuality, your discomfort with, or reaction to, those questions may not be coming from the questions themselves, but from deeper, unresolved issues in your own life. Your child, however, not knowing this, may interpret your discomfort as an indictment that there is something wrong with sex, something bad or dirty about it. S/he may even think your reaction means that there is something wrong with him/her for asking such a question or having such feelings.

Of course, this will not be intentional on your part. Most often, people are not even aware of the nonverbal cues that reflect their discomfort or uneasiness. Let's look at a possible scenario:

> Suppose Mom is baby-sitting a neighbor's six-month-old baby girl. She is changing the baby's diaper and her six-year-old daughter is watching. As she pauses to get some baby powder, the little baby begins to touch her vulva. Mom's daughter begins to giggle and Mom quickly grabs the baby's hand and pulls it away. Her daughter, surprised, asks "Mom, what's wrong?" "Never mind," Mom says tersely. "Go into the other room and play."

Mom has sent several messages to her child. It is quite possible her child will unconsciously absorb these and put her own meaning on them. Some of these messages could be:

- The baby was being bad
- I am bad for giggling

- Mom doesn't like babies
- Mom doesn't like changing diapers
- Mom doesn't like a baby touching herself
- There is something wrong with a baby touching herself
- There's something wrong with touching yourself
- Mom's in a bad mood
- I'm not supposed to see a naked baby
- There's something bad about a girl's body

The child may absorb some, all, or none of these thoughts. The question is why Mom was uncomfortable with a baby doing something that is very normal behavior for a six-month-old? Why did Mom avoid a perfect "teachable moment"? She could have used this opportunity to provide her daughter with sexual information that could have led to a comfortable discussion about the beauty and function of bodies; how boys' and girls' bodies are different; the importance of pleasure; the normal development of young children, and so on. What was really the cause of Mom's discomfort?

We could speculate and come up with many possible answers. Perhaps somewhere in her unconscious, Mom vaguely remembers being severely scolded for masturbating when she was a young girl; perhaps her own mother never permitted nakedness in the family; or perhaps she simply did not know how to handle the situation with her daughter. There are many possibilities. But the reality of such a situation is that we constantly deliver messages to our children about sexuality, and many times we are unaware of those messages. We do not take the time to ask ourselves why we are uncomfortable.

Ideally, Mom would take a minute out and ask herself why she reacted the way she did, both to her daughter and to the baby. When you can identify the source of your discomfort you can avoid or prepare for it in the future. Later she might be able to approach her daughter, apologize with a simple explanation, and provide the needed information such as:

> I'm sorry I was impatient with you before. It wasn't very kind of me. It was fun to have the baby over here today, wasn't it? Babies sure do like to touch themselves, don't they? Do you know why? [Listen and allow child to respond.] Well, they are trying to figure themselves out. You see they have this body and they aren't sure what it is for yet. So they put their toes and fingers in their mouth, and play with their ears; they are exploring! And since it feels good to touch their genitals, they like to do that too. You did all those things when you were little. Most babies do! By the way, what made you giggle?

Often there are deep-seated hurts and repressed memories that influence our responses to specific sexual situations. They may be serious or incidental, but we need to be aware of our motivation. These hurts or memories may have their roots in things that happened to us long ago or in something relatively recent. We need to examine these and deal with them so that they no longer control our responses and/or actions.

Have you ever said to yourself, "I'm not going to do what my parents did to me," and then turn around and find yourself imitating their exact behavior? Sometimes this is because we have not examined the issue enough to decide on an alternative behavior and so we simply do what is familiar to us. We need to know what motivates our behavior, especially in the sensitive area of sexuality. There is a saying that goes, "Sexuality is more caught than taught." This is certainly true in a family where behaviors are so easily repeated without examination.

A 1988 study conducted by Dr. Evonne Hedgepeth of The Evergreen State College in Washington shows a correlation between sexual attitude, sexual knowledge, and sexual comfort. Knowledge can make you more comfortable with sexuality, but a positive attitude is actually the more influential of the two variables. The more positive you are in your attitude towards sexuality, the more comfortable you are talking about it. The more negative your attitude, the more uncomfortable you are. This is particularly important when you are trying to instill values and lifelong attitudes in your children. If you are not comfortable with the topic yourself you are going to have a hard time talking about it and you will stand a good chance of passing along negative attitudes in the process.

To evaluate your comfort with sexuality you might wish to complete the inventory on the following page. This inventory, called *The Sexuality Comfort Inventory*, is the first part of the four-part instrument Dr. Hedgepeth designed for use with her research. I have used this with parents and educators all over the country with positive results.

The purpose in presenting this inventory is to encourage you to evaluate your present level of comfort with sexuality so that you might begin the work that will enable you to increase your comfort level and thus become more effective in talking with your child about sexuality and sexual issues. This is for your personal information only. Why not take a few minutes and see where you stand. You might be surprised with the results.

## Sexuality Comfort Inventory

PART 1: Please indicate the extent to which the following statements apply to you *in your personal life*.

*Section A:* For the following statements, please place a check under the response that most closely reflects your opinion:

| | Strongly Disagree | Disagree Somewhat | Neutral | Agree Somewhat | Strongly Agree |
|---|---|---|---|---|---|
| 1. I believe that sex, in general, is positive and adds zest to living. | | | | | |
| 2. I have a foundation of support for my values, knowledge, and beliefs about sexuality. | | | | | |
| 3. I am tolerant of sexual beliefs and lifestyles that are different from my own. | | | | | |
| 4. People have a right to diverse expressions of sexuality if they are non-exploitative. | | | | | |
| 5. It is OK for a person to choose not to explore his/her sexuality. | | | | | |
| 6. I consider sexuality to be an integral part of the total human personality. | | | | | |
| 7. In my opinion, sexuality is an acceptable topic for everyday conversations. | | | | | |
| 8. Sexuality is a topic worthy of academic study. | | | | | |
| 9. I view the topic of sexuality as an important part of the school curriculum. | | | | | |

*Section B:* For the following statements, please circle the number on the continuum that most closely reflects the way you feel about your own sexuality.

10. Basically, the way I feel about my sexuality is:

In turmoil.................................... At peace
1   2   3   4   5   6   7

11. The way I feel about my own sexual standards and behavior is:

Anxious..................................... Secure
1   2   3   4   5   6   7

12. When confronted with sexual values different from my own ideal:

Offended .................................... Tolerant
 1    2    3    4    5    6    7

13. In general, the way I feel when discussing sexual topics with others is:

Uncomfortable ...................... Comfortable
 1    2    3    4    5    6    7

*Section C:* For the following statements, please indicate how often you exhibit or experience the described behavior *in your personal life.*

|  | Almost Never | Seldom | Sometimes | Often | Almost Always |
|---|---|---|---|---|---|
| 14. I am open with others regarding my personal sexual experiences. |  |  |  |  |  |
| 15. I can discuss sexual topics with ease. |  |  |  |  |  |
| 16. I tend to avoid rather than explore sexual issues. |  |  |  |  |  |
| 17. I avail myself of opportunities to increase my knowledge of sexuality. |  |  |  |  |  |
| 18. I avail myself of opportunities to increase my comfort with sexuality. |  |  |  |  |  |

## Scoring the Sexuality Comfort Inventory

*Section A:* Moving from left to right, "strongly disagree" to "strongly agree," assign each column a number from "1 to 5." Then tally the number of checks you have in each column and multiply that number by the corresponding number you have assigned to that column. Then add together your final score from each column. (Note: missing responses should be counted as a neutral score of "3.")

*Section B:* Simply add up the total of the numbers you circled. (Note: Missing scores should be counted as a neutral score of "4.")

*Section C:* Follow the same procedure given for Section A, except for

no. 16. *For no. 16 only reverse* the assigned numbers "1 to 5" to score "5 to 1." (The reversal is due to the wording of the statement.)
Total all three sections for your composite score. The highest score possible is 93; the lowest is 18. High scores reflect high comfort with sexuality and low scores reflect low comfort with sexuality.

It would seem to follow that the lower your comfort level, the less comfortable you will be talking with your child and that the less comfortable you are the less effective you will be.

Now that you have a general idea of how comfortable you are with sexuality, you can begin to work on the areas where you are least comfortable. Your goal could be to get as close to a 93 as you can. In fact, you might want to save a copy of your score and take the instrument again at a later date to see if you have succeeded in increasing your comfort level.

There are many steps you can take to increase your comfort level. One we have already talked about is to examine your areas of discomfort and try to identify where/how these originated.

Other ways to increase your comfort level with sexuality are:

- seeking help from a professional sex therapist or counselor or talking with your doctor
- talking over problem areas with a trusted friend
- consulting with a member of the clergy or someone in pastoral care
- reading the professional books or journals, or viewing videos that explore sexual issues and provide correct and current information
- taking advantage of TV programs that offer accurate and current information on various topics surrounding sexuality
- reading any documents on sexuality published by your church
- attending workshops, classes, or seminars that may be offered by your local university, community college, area hospital, church group, or local organizations

There may even be a time when you might want to identify some area of your discomfort when in discussion with your child. For example, suppose your teen frequently makes jokes about you and your spouse divorcing. Even after polite requests from you to abandon such behavior, your child persists. You might decide to talk about this with your child. You could say something like:

*My parents divorced when I was young. They were very unhappy and fought a lot. I always felt like I was in the middle. So when I hear about someone divorcing, or someone makes jokes about divorce, it brings back some of those uncomfortable feelings I experienced as a child. When this happens I get very uncomfortable and have a hard time talking about it, much less laughing or answering questions about it. I hope you can understand that I am not trying to hide anything from you. You'll need to be patient with me, OK? Do you think you could hold off with the jokes for a while, too? I would really appreciate that.*

Approaching the matter this way, you are defusing the issue, for yourself and your child. By identifying your source of discomfort, you model maturity as well as relieve your child of having to interpret, or more likely, misinterpret your source of unease.

Learning about sexuality is a lifelong, and often complicated, process. By addressing issues when they arise, we can keep this process from becoming more complicated. By dealing with our own personal feelings regarding sexuality, we can provide ourselves and our children with the opportunity to experience the pleasure, the comfort, the healing, and the beauty of this special gift our Creator intended for us. Once you have become more comfortable with your own sexuality and sorted through some of your own sexual issues, you will be ready to prepare yourself to talk with your child.

# Chapter 3

· · · · · · · · · ·

∽

# Begin at the Beginning

One of the questions I am asked most often is, "When should I begin to talk to my child about sex?" My answer is always, "Whenever your child asks the first question." In order to facilitate lifelong communication with your child about sexuality, you need to encourage conversation from the first years on. You want to foster their trust and desire to seek information from you. Answering their very first questions and continuing as the questions become more complex and frequent will do much to subtly reinforce such bonding.

There is no "magic time" to talk with your child. Everyday, ongoing, casual conversations are best, with information given as your child asks for it. This style encourages frequent, comfortable communication and makes your child feel you are approachable. This method is preferred over the "tonight's the night we tell Cory about sex" method, and is much more effective!

In discussing sexuality with your children you are seeking not only to give specific information on a particular topic, but most importantly, to give your child the message that you are an *askable, available* parent. Encourage your children to come to you whenever they have questions or concerns. This means that from the earliest years on you need to set a pattern of communicating with them that makes it obvious you are willing to discuss any topic with them, and that you will make time to do so.

Listed below are some tips you may wish to follow that many have found effective in encouraging such discussions. Those listed pertain primarily to conversations about sex, but they may be helpful in discussing other topics as well.

*Begin gently.*

If you have not talked about sex with your child until now, some explanation may be in order. Explain to your child that you are concerned about the information they may be receiving from peers or other sources. You may wish to acknowledge that you are sorry you waited so long to talk about this. It is perfectly OK to acknowledge that embarrassment or personal discomfort has prevented you from doing so in the past. You may want to tell them that after careful consideration you have decided that you want information about sexuality to come from you, and that they should feel free to ask questions whenever they are concerned, curious, or confused.

It is preferable for you to talk with your children before they begin school. That is when they begin to get misinformation from rumors or from peers. If your child has not asked about sex before beginning school, it is a good idea for you to bring up the topic. For example you might say, *"Did you ever wonder how babies are born? Tell me how you think this happens."* This will give you plenty of opportunity to learn what they know and correct misconceptions. Hopefully it will also begin a pattern of their coming to you for information.

*Give permission for discussion.*

Your child needs to know that it is OK to talk about sexual issues at home; not only OK, but desirable. So it is up to mom or dad, preferably both, to give permission for such discussions to take place. A good way to do this is to begin a conversation about a sexual issue or topic. You might begin with a question such as: *"What do you know about the AIDS virus and how it is transmitted? Sometimes the technical talk on TV is confusing and I want to be sure you understand this because it is important,"* or, *"Have you ever heard that you can't get pregnant if you have intercourse when you are standing up? When I was growing up that was a major rumor. Do kids still pass that one around or are there some new ones by now?"*

By bringing up the topic of sexuality, you are subtly letting your child know that you are willing to discuss such topics in your home. By being specific, you invite your child into a discussion. By choosing a controversial topic, you give them the message that you are open to discussing even embarrassing subjects. If you are addressing a young adolescent, you may just want to take them out to lunch and spend some time with them, broaching the topic in this way: *"You know honey, there is so much confusion about sex today. I know there are a lot of rumors and stories about teens having sex, and I worry about your safety and your health. There's just so much danger involved. Do you ever feel that others are putting pressure on you to become sexually active? How do you (or would you) handle the pressure?"*

Or, you could simply invite your child to begin discussion in this way: *"I know you probably already know a lot about sex, honey, but indulge me. Pamper me and tell me what you know about sexually transmitted diseases. When I was growing up there were not so many to learn about and I am not sure I am up-to-date."* When you ask general questions like: *"Is there anything you want to ask me about sex?"* or *"Do you know how babies are made?"* you encourage a simple "yes" or "no" reply. Such answers do not lend themselves to discussion.

### Get comfortable.

One of the most important factors in effectively communicating positive information about sexuality is comfort level. If you are not comfortable with your own sexuality then you will have a more difficult time talking with your child about his/her sexuality. Your body language and nonverbal cues will quickly inform your child of your discomfort, even if your verbal cues are able to disguise your feelings. Unfortunately s/he may put a private interpretation on your discomfort and assume that you do not like sex or you think it is bad or evil. (See chapter 2.)

### Be honest.

It is OK to say that you do not want to discuss a certain topic due to personal reasons, or to acknowledge that you are uncomfortable discussing some things. For example, perhaps you were sexually abused as a child and you are uneasy talking about this with your child. You may want to admit your discomfort and, depending on the age of your child and circumstances of your discomfort, explain the reason for your uneasiness.

Or, you may wish to have someone else talk to your child about this topic, such as your spouse, family doctor, or perhaps a good friend. Just be sure this does not happen too often. Children often jump to conclusions and they may incorrectly misinterpret your reluctance to talk with them. They may conclude that sex is bad or that you don't like or understand sex. A better approach may be to give a partial explanation and tell them you will give them additional information at a more appropriate time. Just be sure you always give honest, truthful information. Attempting to motivate behavior using fear or ignorance is not a wise approach, and in the long run, may damage your creditability and your child's trust in you.

By the way, if there are such areas of discomfort that you haven't dealt with, I would strongly encourage you to do so. It is easy to inadvertently pass on unhealthy attitudes and discomfort to your children. Perhaps counseling would be helpful for you. Be the one to break the cycle.

### Allow for privacy.

When discussing matters of sexuality, try to find a few minutes of privacy when you will not be interrupted by your other children, neighbors, or phone calls. Try to keep a special time for you and your child when s/he can count on having your undivided attention. Set aside time after school, after dinner, before bedtime, or perhaps a "treat time" once a week when you will be alone with that child. Let them know that they are important enough for you to set aside a special time just to talk with them about what is going on in their lives.

### Be open.

Try to be open to your child's comments even when you do not agree with them or find them hard to listen to. You may wish to ask why they feel the way they do. At a later time you may ask them to consider another point of view and explain your feelings on that particular issue. Most importantly, tell them *why* you feel as you do. Try to be compassionate and understanding; realize that your child may not have thought about many of the issues surrounding sexuality on a serious level before. Remember they are coming at this from age 4, 12, 16, and have not had the experiences and opportunities for learning that you do at age 25, 30, 40. The advantage for them is that they also do not have the excess baggage you do. If you handle communications about sexuality properly, they may never have any!

### Don't be pushy.

If you disagree with your child, do so gently and drop the matter. If you come on too strong, your child may feel it is useless to continue discussions with you. The harder you push the more they may resist. Allow for differences of opinion. Given time, understanding, and experience, s/he may eventually agree with you, if you do not force or insist upon agreement at this time. Even if your child never agrees with you on certain issues, respect for his/her opinion is *always* in order.

### Be flexible.

Sometimes questions arise at inconvenient times. If a question arises on a busy day for you and you have errands to run, why not ask your son or daughter to come along and have your discussion in the car. If there simply isn't time for an adequate discussion, then save it for a day that's better. Just be sure you do get back to it, lest your absentmindedness be interpreted as avoidance, lack of interest, or lack of caring.

### Take your time.

Try not to rush discussions on sexuality. It takes time for young children, as well as teens, to understand what exactly is being discussed. They may need time to think about what you have said before they are able to respond, or clarify their thoughts enough to ask further questions. Besides, if you rush them, you run the risk of causing them to think you do not consider their questions or the time you are spending with them important.

### Team up.

If possible both parents should be involved in answering questions. Often, there is a subtle difference in the way moms and dads respond to the same question. Sometimes it is not so subtle, and that is OK, too. Different perspectives are often expressed, and both are of benefit to the child. Children need to hear what each parent has to say. If you are divorced, perhaps you could encourage your child to discuss some issues with your former spouse and provide that opportunity. If you are a single parent, and you do not have a friend, relative, clergyperson, or doctor with whom you feel your child would be comfortable, then just do it yourself, giving as much information as you can. Above all, don't worry. Just do the best you can.

### Try not to overreact.

There may be times in your discussions when your child says something that shocks you or catches you off guard. You may be surprised at some of the things your child's friends are doing. Overreacting to such comments or situations does not facilitate openness or learning. Try, in a calm manner, to explain your objection to your child and your concern for his/her welfare. Calm discussion, especially when objecting, is the best way to ensure that your son or daughter will continue to talk with you about sexuality.

Sometimes you are just being tested. Other times a child really is not sure how s/he feels. Remember most kids do not think beyond today; one of the goals of your discussions is to help your child develop a spiritual orientation toward sexuality, but that takes time. It is a developmental process. Often, forbidding a child to be with friends only makes those friends seem more desirable. If you remain calm yet firm in your convictions, your son or daughter may come to the same conclusion as yours on his/her own, but they need time to do so. If not, at least you will have modeled for them how to think things through carefully before coming to a conclusion. A valuable lesson indeed.

## Don't talk too long.

Avoid the "lecture" format. Long-winded explanations turn interest to boredom. Answer questions on a need-to-know basis. If your child asks a question, answer it with moderate but truthful information—brief and simple. If they want to know more, they will ask another question. Allow your child to dictate the pace. Given the opportunity, children will let you know what their needs and concerns are.

## Always clarify.

Make sure you understand what your child is asking *before* you give an answer. You can do this by saying, "Are you asking if . . . " or "Do you mean . . . " A teacher once related an incident to me about her twelve-year-old son. He was sitting at the kitchen table doing his homework when he suddenly asked her what an orgasm was. She was taken a bit back, but calmed herself inwardly and answered the question thoughtfully and carefully. Pleased with the way she had handled the situation, she turned to her son and asked if he understood. "Uh, yeah Mom, I guess so. But I think the word I meant was supposed to be *organism*. It would have spared them both some embarrassment had she clarified before answering!

### *Don't force an issue.*

Don't insist that your son or daughter talk about a circumstance or situation they do not want to. Give them some space, and allow them to try working some things out for themselves. Be sure you do not make the mistake of implying that you *know* the reason behind their silence. You could be way off base and alienate your child. If you feel the need to pursue your line of thought, you might say something like: "I wonder if this is happening because" or "I wonder if this is about." The best approach is simply to ask your child what is going on instead of interpreting it for yourself. If s/he does not wish to discuss it at that time, back off for a bit.

If you make it known that you are concerned, available, and willing to listen, they will bring it up in time. You can return to the matter at a later date. It is important that you respect their privacy and personal feelings. Of course this does *not* apply if you suspect a serious situation or sexual abuse of some kind. The use of a counselor may be helpful in circumstances where you have reason to fear for your child's safety and well-being.

### *It is OK to say, "I don't know."*

If you need help, try to find it from a doctor, member of the clergy, a competent counselor, or a friend you trust and respect. You might also try a church-sponsored agency or a hotline listing in the Yellow Pages. Your child needs to learn that understanding about sexuality is a lifelong process and no one has all the answers. Just be sure you do get back with the information requested so s/he knows you consider his/her question worthwhile. Professional sex counselors or sex educators may be of use. Professional sexuality organizations such as the American Association of Sex Educators, Counselors, and Therapists (AASECT) can give names of qualified professionals.

### *Never laugh or put down your child's questions.*

You may think the answer is obvious or simple enough, but it may have taken great courage for your child to ask the question. Children have a very delicate ego; often their self-esteem is very low, even without your knowing it. To have mom or dad laugh at them is the ultimate blow. I once had a fifth-grade boy tell me he was through asking his mom questions about sex because she always laughed and said "Oh Carlos, you know that—you're a big boy. You're just trying to tease me!" Sometimes she would even tell her friends, in his presence, about a question he had asked or a conversation they had had about sex. They would laugh and this was terribly embarrassing to him. No wonder. Remember: there are no dumb questions, only dumb answers!

### Be a good listener.

Don't do all the talking. Give your children a chance to express themselves and their concerns. You will make them feel important just by listening to them, and you may learn things about them you never knew. You do not always need to have an answer. Sometimes they just want someone to listen to them. As a friend of mine once said, "The best way to prevent teen pregnancy is to be a good listener!"

### Give concrete examples.

Always try to give examples that apply to the age and situation of your child. Children have difficulty understanding abstract concepts, especially when they are young. They are not developmentally able to do so. Preadolescents lack the ability to imagine goals too far in the future. It is better to stick with stories and examples that illustrate immediate or near consequences.

### Strive for balance.

If you are too conservative as you talk about sex with your child, you can unwittingly foster negative attitudes and feelings such as fear, shame, low self-esteem, awkwardness, and embarrassment. If you are too liberal, you may foster equally damaging attitudes and feelings such as lack of respect, promiscuity, irresponsibility, and disregard for commitment. But you can model a well-balanced approach, one that focuses on the beauty and gift of sexuality, enhances self-esteem, fosters spiritual development, enables maturity, and encourages the development of virtues such as respect, love, and commitment. In striving for balance you avoid the extremes at either end and your child becomes the beneficiary of your wisdom.

### Pray together.

There is an old slogan that says, "The family that prays together, stays together." Teaching your children to pray for help when making difficult decisions, when attempting to clarify thoughts, when asking for God's grace, when thanking God for gifts received, or when trying to carry through with moral decisions will help them establish a lifelong pattern of turning to God for aid. It will also create a loving bond within your family as you pray for your needs and the needs of your children.

# Chapter 4

. . . . . . . . .

~

# Self-Esteem:
# The Essential Ingredient

I suppose some of you may be saying, "Oh no, not that self-esteem stuff again!" I can understand your feeling that way; it is a topic that comes up frequently when educating about parenting. But yes, this is a chapter on self-esteem, and yes, self-esteem *is* an essential ingredient in raising a spiritually, sexually, and mentally healthy child.

Anyone who works with young people will tell you that self-esteem is critical to healthy emotional growth. Psychologists, addiction counselors, youth ministers, teachers, and clergy can all relate the important role a good self-image plays in the overall stability and development of young people. The fact is, self-esteem is the essential ingredient to successful personality integration at any age. We all need to feel good about ourselves when we look in the mirror in the morning, or nothing seems to go right.

You may ask, what has self-esteem got to do with sexuality? My answer is: everything! How can you grow into a loving and caring person if you can not love yourself? If you do not feel worthy of love, you may not know how to give love. You may not know how to receive love when it is given. Persons with high self-esteem are able to bring love and compassion to a relationship. They can see the importance of integrity and honesty in a loving relationship. They are able to bestow trust and exhibit confidence in their partner. They can display a willingness to assume responsibility for their actions and commitment to their loved one. Because they value their own talents, they are not threatened by the talents of others. Persons with high self-esteem are able to make decisions with confidence, so they encourage others to make decisions as well. They trust their own feelings, so they can respect the feelings of others.

All of the qualities listed above are qualities a good lover possesses. To become good lovers we must first love ourselves and understand the value of self-care. We must know what it means to be truly loved. When we are loved unconditionally, just for who we are, we learn what it means to be truly loved. High self-esteem emerges and flourishes from this kind of love.

When children have low self-esteem they have little reason to expect anyone to love them. They expect little from themselves or from anyone else. If they have not been given the chance to succeed at some kind of task at home, then they usually do not feel competent to face challenges elsewhere. If they have not been given the opportunity to make decisions about their own life, then they may not trust themselves to make good decisions. If they have not been given respect they often do not respect others. If they have not been given assurance that their feelings are natural and normal, and assured that it is good to have feelings, then they probably will not be able to identify their own feelings or respect the feelings of others. In fact, children with low self-esteem frequently develop feelings of distrust; they often show disrespect and ingratitude toward others. They tend to expect the worst, so they hide their feelings and isolate themselves emotionally from others. These are not qualities that make a good lover or a happy person.

Studies done on school-aged children indicate that as the child advances in school, self-esteem tends to drop. One such study evaluated the same students at the first, fifth, and eleventh grades. The self-esteem of the students was highest in first grade, with eighty-eight percent registering high self-esteem. By the fifth grade this dropped to twenty-five percent; and by the eleventh grade, only five percent of those *same* students measured high in self-esteem.

How can parents develop a healthy sense of self-worth in their children that will have staying power? Over the years I have picked up some tips from my experience as a parent and teacher, along with some wonderful suggestions from others, and I would like to share them with you.

Making your child feel lovable—and that is what we are talking about—is not a difficult task. But it is something you have to consciously and consistently work at on a day-to-day basis. If you begin when your child is in the womb—yes, in the womb—then you will be setting a pattern of loving communication that will become a part of your parenting style for the rest of your life. With consistency and luck, your child will begin to imitate your style and you will become the fortunate recipient of unconditional love. You will, in effect, be modeling for your child how to become a good lover.

Now for the tips: Because we know from science that babies have feelings and are receptive to some types of communication in the womb, pregnancy becomes the ideal place to begin:

Moms: Tell your baby frequently during the day that you love them and are happy s/he is going to be your child. Stroke your womb gently and tell your child you want him/her very much; that you are happy you are going to be their mother. Sing or hum your baby a song; make one up, a little song just for your child alone.

Dads: Snuggle close to the womb and gently place your hand on it, or stroke slowly across the womb. While you are doing this give your baby positive messages about how pleased you are to be blessed with her/him in your life. Tell your baby that you want him/her very much; that you are glad you are going to be his/her father. Tell your baby how much you love her/him. You might try a little lullaby too, Dad!

Perhaps you both may feel a little foolish the first time you do this, but please do not let that stop you. It will get easier and soon you will find yourself looking forward to this time alone with your baby. Before long, you will be having nice long conversations about how your day went and inquiring about their comfort as well. Give it a try. You've got nothing to lose and possibly much to gain.

- Once your baby is born, continue this practice of daily chats. Compliment your baby on his/her cute toes, lovely lashes, soft skin, and any other adorable features you choose. Have some fun, and do not be sexist in your comments!
- Learn to give gentle massages. Tender, loving strokes comfort and indicate your presence and care.
- Give lots and lots of hugs. Ask for them, too! The message you are giving your child is: "You are lovable."
- Continue the practice of complimenting your children. Each day find at least one thing they have done that you can praise them for. Always compliment your child on something genuine. False praise is noted and resented. Never fear that this will make them conceited. Conceit occurs when children have to praise themselves because they feel somehow inadequate. It is very important that children learn to recognize the things they do well at an early age. This will

make it easier for them to identify their strengths and gain self-confidence as they mature.

- As your children are able, give them little tasks to do that you know they can accomplish. It is important for them to experience success, so choose your tasks wisely, make them age-appropriate. To a two-year-old you might say: "Please put this magazine on the couch. Thank you, you are a big helper." A four-year-old could be kindly asked: "Please put these clothes in that drawer for me. Thanks, you really follow directions well!" This is particularly important for disabled children. Little tasks, easy to accomplish, give your children a sense of confidence and competence. You begin to instill important ideas: "Mom trusts me," "I can help my mom and dad," "Dad likes to have me around," "I know how to do many things," "I'm good at listening," "I can be a helper in my family," "I am good," "I am capable," "I am lovable."

- Encourage your child to make decisions as often as possible. The ability to make confident, thoughtful decisions is an acquired skill. Children need practice to learn how to do so. This helps them develop trust in their own abilities. If they make a poor decision, help them look on the bright side. Use the occasion to talk about what might have been a better choice and why. Assure them that everyone makes poor decisions and that the important thing is to learn from the experience.

Begin early. For example, as soon as they are old enough to understand how, allow them to place their own orders when dining out. Let them choose the color of a new shirt or blouse. Help them to learn how to make choices from a list of alternatives. Invite them to pick how they want to spend their birthday. You can control the expense and other practical details by giving them a list to choose from. It is good for children to get in touch with their likes and dislikes and have those respected. This is not to say they never have to do anything they don't want to. We are talking here about preferences when the option is theirs. Many adults do not know how they like to spend their time or how to relax because they were never given the opportunity to make those kinds of decisions when they were children.

- As soon as they learn to read or identify symbols, begin writing your children little love notes and putting them in their lunch box, purse or wallet, under their pillow, in their suitcase when they are off to camp, on the bathroom mirror, in schoolbooks or notebooks.

Be creative! Just a brief sentence lets them know that you love them enough to take the time to tell them so. As they grow older and begin to use computers, you can leave them messages there as well.

- Make their sandwiches in different shapes for different holidays (a cookie cutter is helpful). Let this be a surprise!
- Plan a dress-up party for little girls and boys where they can wear big people's clothes.
- Attend church together frequently.
- Make their favorite treat and surprise them with it.
- Have a holiday party and allow them to invite their special friends.
- Take time out for a one-on-one lunch so you can get to know each of your children better.
- Go see a movie or rent a video that *they* want to see.
- Ask your child to make a list of supplies needed in the kitchen.
- Take turns picking the radio station in the car.
- Show your child how to do repairs (age-appropriate) around the house, how to use tools and other household items. Let them watch as you work on things.
- Take a day off and go on a picnic.
- Teach them exercises to reduce stress: breathing techniques, yoga, music, mini-meditations/visualizations, taking walks, reading, *et cetera*.
- Make plans to have a breakfast where you can watch the sunrise, or a picnic supper where you can watch the sunset.
- Give them a small book with blank pages and show them how to keep a journal of their private thoughts. Respect their privacy!
- Sit down and read a book together.
- Allow them to daydream.
- Teach them to visualize.
- Go window shopping.
- Take a walk in the woods together.
- Pick up a little "Happy Day" gift. Something small—their favorite gum or candy bar, a book, a tape, something that says, "I know what you like, because you are important to me."
- Ask them to help plan a vacation. Let them make a list of places to visit or things they would like to do.
- Reinforce their strengths by saying things like: *"You know you're really good at writing." "You're very thoughtful." "You are good at calming your friends down." "You really know how to make grandma and grandpa feel comfortable."* Any special talent they have should be frequently acknowledged and encouraged.

- Tell them why you like their friends.
- Ask for *their* advice or opinion whenever you can.
- Invite them to plan a celebration in your home.
- Ask for their help even when you could work faster without it.
- Don't redo the chores you have asked them to do. It makes a child feel inadequate when you vacuum or dust over places they have worked on. A little dust will go unnoticed; a bruised ego will hurt for a long time. If they have been *deliberately* careless, then have *them* redo their chore.
- Alternate chores around the house, inside and out, so *everyone* learns to do *everything*. Resist gender categories!
- Allow children to decide among themselves what chore they will do for the day or week.
- Unexpectedly pick your children up from school and take them out for a snack.
- Give a hug instead of a lecture.
- Take the whole family roller skating.
- Plan a scavenger hunt for your children and let them "tent it" overnight in the backyard.
- Teach your sons and daughters how to make homemade fudge, popcorn balls, candy apples, or some other special treat on a school holiday.
- Bless your children with a short prayer before bedtime, like "My *dear child, I commend you to the Holy Spirit, to the powerful intercession of the Blessed Mother and I entrust you forever to their blessed care."* (This is one my mom said to me and I said to my children. I will always treasure it.)
- Never put your child to bed angry or with harsh words. Always make peace. Peaceful words help ensure peace-filled sleep.
- Go sledding with your children if you are lucky enough to live where it snows. Give them a "snow day."
- Turn the TV off one night and play Scrabble, Monopoly, Trivial Pursuit, or some other game the whole family can join in.
- Watch your child's favorite TV show with her/him.
- Take a family walk around the block.
- Go for a family bike ride. Make it a regular event if you can.
- Have family meetings where each person in the family takes a turn at conducting the meeting. These need not be long. Suit frequency to your family's needs, but keep them a regular event.
- Let your children takes turns leading the family in prayer before

meals. Encourage them to make up their own prayer from time to time. Allow every one at the table to add special intentions.

- Wash the family car together and give each family member a specific job. If the weather is right, wear swimsuits and have some fun.
- Take your child to work with you and let them see where you do your job. If this is not possible, at least show them the building or area you work in and describe your job to him/her.
- Show them the hospital they were born in.
- Do not overplay the importance of report cards. Don't overdramatize occasional poor grades.
- Sneak some bubble bath into your *teen's* bath water.
- Look through family albums and share memories.
- Tell them about the events that took place the day they were born.
- Acknowledge that we all have "down" days.
- Make up special traditions just for your family. Be sure to keep them. Example: Every Christmas Eve our family sings "Happy Birthday" to Jesus after one of the children puts baby Jesus in the crib. The "children" are now 27, 25, and 24. We still sing, even when there's company.
- Give your child a foot massage.
- Don't say anything when you could say "I told you so." Instead give a hug.
- Engage your child in pleasant and interesting conversation frequently. Stimulate their interest; be thought-provoking. Make sure you communicate about things *other than* rules and complaints.
- Institute a "family hug" and call for it frequently, especially when there has been little time to get together.
- Don't overreact when your child gives you bad news.
- If finances permit, treat your daughter or son to a manicure. If not, give it yourself.
- Remind your child frequently that s/he is made in God's image, and God doesn't make junk!
- Allow your child to be angry. Show ways to vent anger appropriately.
- Say "I love you" at least once a day to each member of your household.
- Display good papers, news articles, any and all possible accomplishments (even minimal ones) on the refrigerator or bulletin board for all to share joy and take pride in.
- Indicate honor and joy in womanhood by celebrating with a special dinner when your daughter begins to menstruate.

- Do not hide your own failures from your child. Model your acceptance of your own shortcomings for them. Teach them that no one succeeds at everything they do all of the time.
- Mail your older child greeting cards, or put cards in an unexpected place to be discovered.
- Take a child along with you shopping or running errands. It is a good time for an informal chat.
- Always make it clear that you love your child, that it is inappropriate *behavior* you disapprove of.
- Give your sixteen-year-old a surprise birthday party.
- Take a short trip with just one of your children. Alternate each year between mom and dad. Take turns taking one of your children at a time, someplace *they* would like to go, and do the things *they* choose. This is a wonderful way to show each of your children special attention and get to know each of them better. They get to know you better when they do not have to compete with everyone else.
- Plan an annual family picnic. Invite all your relatives.
- Celebrate your child's name day.
- Verbalize your feelings to your child. Allow them to see you as you are, owning your feelings and distinguishing feelings from behavior.
- Take time to tuck your teen into bed and find out how they are doing. Ask about their friends.
- Always take time to listen, even when you do not have it.
- Listen for what your child *is not* saying. Look for nonverbals.
- Tell your children you have experienced God's love through their actions.
- Buy your teenage son a pair of wild and crazy shorts, or silk ones, to wear at bedtime.
- Make or buy a plate that says, "You are special today," and use it to celebrate passing tests, getting a driver's license, dance recitals, winning games, and so on.
- Spend a night stargazing with the whole family. Lie on the grass, preferably in the country where you can see the stars clearly. Count shooting stars. Try to identify constellations!
- Hold a family talent show.
- Record your family history and stories on videotape.
- Write a family history book. Each member can contribute a chapter about themselves.
- Hold a family fashion show.
- Make a family quilt.

- Encourage your child to talk about his/her feelings.
- Treat your daughter or son to a backrub. Ask for one back occasionally!
- Design a family T-shirt to wear on outings and family events.
- Entrust a family treasure to your teenage child.
- Celebrate thirteenth birthdays in a special way.

I hope this gives you some ideas to try. All of these activities can be modified in any way to suit your family style and/or ages of your children. Many of them need not take up a lot of time; most of them do not cost any money. If you have more than one child, whenever you can, spend time with just one of them, even if only for a brief period. It is important to let children know that you see each of them as an individual with special and unique talents, needs, and concerns. It is your *effort* to show love, support, and encouragement to your child that is most important. This is a need none of us outgrow, but it is especially important if children are to acquire the self-esteem necessary to grow into happy, stable, and responsible adulthood.

Teach your children how to relax, how to relieve stress. One study conducted in the Kansas school system showed that forty-two percent of the third-graders were experiencing many of the same symptoms of stress that we find in adults. You are never too young to learn how to pause and take a deep breath, how to stop for a minute and calm down, or how to smile. Listening to relaxing music, taking a bubble bath, or learning how to take your mind on a brief vacation through meditation, are all stress-relieving methods young children can be taught and can love to learn! The earlier you teach your children stress-reducing skills, the more quickly they will become a part of their lifestyle. This may lessen the chance they will use drug and alcohol for stress relief. So get yourself a good book on stress-relieving activities and begin. Keep in mind that children remember more of what they see than what they hear. So if you want to encourage these behaviors in your children, you have to do them yourself.

As your children grow older, you may have to make more of an effort and be more creative with your methods to increase their self-esteem, but your love and encouragement are *extremely* important during the adolescent years. The teen years are a particularly hazardous time for your children's self-esteem, especially your daughters. Studies show that girls experience a notable drop in self-esteem, much more drastic than boys, during adolescence. One such study, conducted by the American Association of University Women (1991), found that girls tend to worry much more about their physical appearance than boys. Society gives them clear messages that they must be slim and attractive, must have figures and looks like those of models. Owing to this shift of interest, they begin to focus less on academics and more on physical appearance. Girls begin expecting less from life during adolescence. They begin to limit their expectations of themselves, feeling that they can not compete, especially in the male-dominated fields of math and science. Society repeatedly gives the message unconsciously, and sometimes consciously, that girls are expected only to look good and to be good mothers. Because of this distorted message, many do not even try to excel in other areas where they may be quite talented.

It is extremely important that brothers and especially fathers give their sisters and daughters the clear message that they are capable and lovable no matter what their physical attractiveness or stature. Studies show that if young girls are teased about their bodies at ages twelve or thirteen, they become ashamed of their bodies and are more prone to eating disorders. Boys are somewhat protected from this because they tend to gain their confidence from their talents and their abilities *to do* things. This serves to "soften the blow" when they experience changes in their physical appearance. However, society tells girls it's how you *look*, not what you *can do* that counts. This is true even in today's society where so many opportunities are open to women. Case in point: the TV weather forecaster who was hired on the condition that she *always* wear her hair the same way on camera.

So do not stop hugging your daughters and sons as they grow into womanhood and manhood, even though they may shrug you off! Touch and physical affection are important ways to build self-esteem. Do not withdraw these because you think your kids are "getting too old for that stuff." On the contrary, during the teen years more than ever, your children need appropriate displays of affection from you.

For a time I was involved in conducting counseling groups at an all-girl high school. One of the most frequent complaints from the girls was over their lack of contact with their fathers. They complained that their fathers did not pay any attention to them anymore. They would comment on how when they were little, their dads would take them on errands with them, let them sit on their laps, invest more interest and time in them and their friends. Now that they were teenagers, they felt that their dads had pulled away from them. They expressed hurt and confusion that their fathers no longer took time out to go "get a burger" with them. They said they missed being able to "play around" with their dads like they did when they were little. Some with little sisters and brothers felt left out because the little ones got dad's hugs, not them anymore. One girl lamented, "It's like he thinks since I'm sixteen I don't need his affection anymore!"

I think part of the problem comes when in early adolescence, say eleven to fifteen years of age, teens do not want to be seen with their parents. They go through a stage of needing to establish themselves as independent of their parents. This is a normal part of development. Some parents, in an effort to respect this desire for independence, gradually get out of the habit of showing affection for their teen. Others may have felt uncomfortable with their rapidly developing son or daughter, and have withdrawn affection out of an unconscious fear of sexual attraction. These sexual feelings are normal. Many mothers feel attracted to their teenage sons; many fathers feel attracted to their teenage daughters. Because we are parents, we may feel that there is something abnormal or bad about such attraction.

As I have said before, *feelings are normal*, all kinds of feelings, and *feelings are good*. What can be inappropriate or wrong is behavior. Feeling attracted to your physically maturing son or daughter is not bad; it is natural and quite normal to feel this way. Most parents do to some extent, whether consciously or unconsciously. Some, however, are not comfortable acknowledging these feelings. However, it is acting *inappropriately* toward your son or daughter that would be wrong. Fondling, prolonged kissing, or other sexual advances toward your child would not be normal or appropriate. Such behavior could cause serious emotional problems for both you and your child. It is not behavior of this kind I am encouraging.

What I am suggesting is that you always express *appropriate* affection toward your children, recognizing the importance of this affection, especially as they are developing into young women and men. I encourage you to do so verbally through compliments: "Your hair is so shiny!" "I'm so proud of you!" "You really look handsome tonight!" "You look absolutely lovely in that dress!" "You're developing some good-looking legs there, young man!" "I'm so lucky you're my daughter/son." "What a fabulous tie you picked out. Great taste!"

I encourage you to express your love through physical contact. Demonstrate your love for your children with gentle hugs, squeezes, pats on the back, stroking hair, backrubs, kisses appropriate for a parent, and other affectionate gestures. (By the way, excessive tickling is not affection; it is abusive.) Do not make the mistake of thinking your child has outgrown his/her need for such intimacies. If they do not receive hugs from you they may look for them elsewhere.

Keep telling them they are terrific kids and you are so glad they are yours! Take time out for them. Go to their games, their plays, their recitals, their swim meets, debates, whatever! Just be there for them. We have an ever-expanding life span, but we have our children to ourselves for such a very short time. Use that time to develop self-esteem through your care and support. Be good lovers. Begin a cycle in your family that follows this pattern: happy people make happy couples and happy couples make happy children and happy children make happy people and happy people . . .

# Chapter 5

. . . . . . . . .

∾

# Ages and Stages of
# Psychosexual Development

In order for us to be better parents, it is helpful for us to be familiar with the stages and behaviors that are considered a part of our child's normal development. This is an exhaustive topic and much has been written on it. There are well-known theories by Erikson, Piaget, Maslow, Kohlberg, and others. These are the foundation for this chapter. My intention is to focus here primarily on psychological development as it relates to sexuality. I plan to integrate various theories and present basic concepts. If you want more information or a more in-depth understanding, you may wish to consult the references at the back of the book.

As we begin to explore these stages, I would like to again remind you that each child is unique and will develop at his/her own pace. It should be understood that some children go through these stages earlier, or later, than others. No parent should try to *force* this development; it will occur in its own time. Likewise, the degree to which each child will manifest these behaviors will vary considerably. This is no cause for alarm. Let's begin!

## Birth to Age Two

We can see the development of sexuality in infancy. From birth the child is observing and sensing how adults respond to them. For this reason it is important that parents, from the very beginning of life in the womb, make their child feel welcome. A positive attitude toward your baby *can* be felt inside the womb. During this early period the baby is encouraged, both consciously and unconsciously, by family and by society at large, to develop a male or female identity and learn the expected behaviors for boys and girls.

*The first year is critical for the development of trust.*

Once a baby is born, touching, cuddling, holding, soft talk, and so on, are important ways of nourishing the child's concept of security and trust in the new world around them. If trust is not established by bonding with the parent, the child will experience difficulty in relating to others all of his/her life. Trust begins with the mother, father, or caregiver, and then gradually extends to other family members and relatives. As time goes by, it will broaden to include neighbors and those in the school environment.

*Infants and toddlers have a need to learn about their world, to feel, smell, taste, and touch things, to roam about and investigate.*

It is important that parents recognize the significance of allowing their child the freedom to explore and act on his/her own. Try not to hover over your child; watch from a distance. The parent's place is in the background, relaxed, not anxious, encouraging the child to find his/her own way out of simple, safe dilemmas. Do not jump up and rescue him/her each time s/he gets stuck. Let her/him try out a few solutions first. These early situations present the parent with opportunities to help the child feel a sense of accomplishment and self-mastery. This is the beginning of healthy self-esteem.

*Infants explore their bodies.*

Beginning in the womb, every ninety minutes boys experience an erection and girls experience vaginal lubrication. This *normal* sexual phenomenon continues until toilet training. From then on, this is experienced by all of us only during sleep. It is quite normal for infants to touch and play with their bodies. It is crucial that parents permit this natural exploration. This lays the foundation for learning and believing that the body is good and thus begins the development of a positive attitude toward sexuality.

### Infants need affection.

And lots of it! Studies have shown that infants deprived of touch and other forms of human contact frequently develop the symptoms of a malnourished child and can die.[1] Those who work in rehabilitation in prisons report that the people they are least likely to rehabilitate are those who have been denied love, abandoned, or abused in the first year of life. Those are the prisoners who do not know how to love because they have not experienced love; they have never bonded with anyone. Beginning in infancy, and continuing throughout their development into adulthood, children need to be held, cuddled, touched, kissed, stroked, massaged, and talked to. This cannot be overstated! Talk to your infant, even if you are just walking through their room. Pat them as you pass by their crib. Pick them up frequently. Do not make the mistake of thinking you will spoil them. This is not the age at which that phrase has any meaning. As mentioned above, this continual contact is necessary for bonding to take place.

## Ages Two to Five

*During these preschool years, the young child begins to realize what it means to be a boy or a girl.*

Current research suggests that by age two sexual identity is formed and irreversibly set in place. Experimentation, fantasizing, playing, sex role reversal, and role playing help to reinforce their ideas of who they are. The way parents treat "their *tiny, little* girl," or, "their *big, strong* boy" sends definite messages to the child, who at this age operates like a sponge and soaks up all presented to his/her senses. The young child is unable to differentiate reasonable from unreasonable. If little girls are protected and pampered while little boys are allowed more freedom to investigate and get dirty, a pattern for a double standard has been set. Clear messages are sent to the child as to what boys can do and what girls can do. This is also the time when young children identify with parents of the same sex, and play "copy cat," imitating adult behaviors to see what they feel like. This may mean they copy adult curse words. They also begin the "family romance" ("When I grow up, I'm going to marry mommy" or "When I grow up I'm going to marry daddy"). This is normal and natural and should be responded to with understanding.

*Toddlers learn that boys and girls have different anatomy.*

It is necessary that children learn the correct names for all of their body parts and those of the opposite sex. Nicknames should not be used! Young children need to know that boys have a "penis" and girls have a "vulva." Neither is missing anything, nor will boys lose their penis if they are bad. This is the time to tell them, in simple terms, how their body functions.

Curiosity about the bodies of others also is common during this time; exploration (playing doctor) is quite natural. (See chapter 6.) Questions about babies and where they come from begin about this time. They also need to be told that bodies of boys and bodies of girls are equally valuable even though they look different and have some different parts. They can be taught that one sex is not better than the other and that both sexes are capable of many and varied responsibilities and challenges. Parents convey such messages both verbally and nonverbally.

Because of toilet training during this time, children become very conscious of their genitals. The best approach to this on the part of the parents is low key; it will pass. Many times parents find this fascination difficult to ignore due to the reactions of others.

A friend shared this story: She had taught her son the correct names of all the parts of the body and had used them in casual conversation with him. One day, when he was five, grandma came to visit. The little boy went out to play and came in minutes later crying and pulling down his pants. "Mom," he cried, "take a look at my penis, I hurt it real bad!" Mom stopped what she was doing and came over to have a look. She calmly asked questions about how her son came to fall off his bike, and reassured him with a hug and kiss that both he and his penis were going to be just fine. Grandma in the meantime observed all this with an open mouth! My friend did not know what to expect. When she was able to speak, grandma commented about what had taken place. "I wish I could have been that comfortable with my children and their bodies when I was raising them. That was so natural." Yes, natural, and handled beautifully!

*Motor development takes place.*

And how! This is the time children learn to walk, run, and jump. They learn to talk in sentences and ask questions. Children become increasingly proud of the many things they learn and are able to do during this time. Parents can build self-esteem by recognizing these new-found skills with encouragement, support, and praise. If parents are overly restrictive the child may become secretive. So give young children room to experiment. Since they have acquired these new skills, they have a need to use and develop them.

### Young children begin to develop a conscience.

The young child, eager for love and acceptance, looks to his parents to approve or disapprove of his or her actions. S/he learns what "no" means, which means s/he has to learn to give things up. During this time, s/he will also learn to respect the property of others, that not everything is hers/his. Not an easy lesson! This is the time to allow your child to begin making choices. Parents can now begin to teach about alternatives and help children learn that some choices can hurt and others can help. Parents should begin to set reasonable limits and provide information about consequences of behavior.

### Young children have a need to socialize with others of their same age.

Learning how to get along with others is an important task during these ages. Respect, sharing, responsibility, control, honesty, all of these are values, as well as skills, to be learned in the context of how to get along with others, both inside and outside your family. Learning that all people are different and that differences must be respected in any type of situation is a great value in socialization.

### Young children learn to take initiative for their own behavior.

It is necessary and important that they do this. This gives them feelings of accomplishment and self-worth. Much of this can occur during toilet training if properly handled. Before this age, children are not capable of training because developmentally they are not able to exercise muscle control over their bodies. Parents should begin training only after consulting with their doctor as to the proper time. Toilet training is important because, among other things, it teaches the young child inner controls. On the other hand, it can lead to excessive inner control, which may in turn lead to obsessive behavior later on. Parents should avoid approaches that focus on punishment and guilt, and stay away from using phrases such as "you're a dirty girl," "you're so messy," or "you've been a bad boy."

### Children begin to experience feelings of guilt.

Often these feelings revolve around toilet training. The parent should take special care not to make the child feel they have been "bad" or "failed" when they do not respond quickly to training. A system of reward is recommended by most professionals. Verbal rewards can take the form: "It's very good to tell me when you need to use the bathroom," or "I'm so proud of you for coming to tell me you needed to go to the bathroom!" Nonverbal rewards could be a new crayon or permission to play outside. Use of food, however, is not recommended. Because of a lack of ability to understand clearly right from wrong, guilt at this age should be downplayed. Parents, always distinguish the *act* from the *child.*

### Children are filled with curiosity.

This is the time to answer questions about pregnancy, birth, breast feeding, and such, with brief but honest answers that you will build on as time goes by. Suppose your child asks, "How did the baby get in you?" An appropriate response would be: "Well, you know that God made all of us, and you know he made boys and girls differently. God made daddy's body to fit into mine. Sometimes when daddy and I want to love each other in a special way, daddy puts his penis into my vagina and together we help God make a new baby. We call this 'making love,' and that's how YOU got here!" Use correct terms. *Womb* or *uterus*— not *tummy.*

Presenting sexuality in a positive, joy-filled manner paves the way for genuine respect and awe of sexuality. Five-year-olds will hear words on TV such as *AIDS, rape,* and *abuse.* It is important for parents to explain in a basic way what these words mean. Now is the time to explain sexual abuse, avoiding strangers, inappropriate touching, and so forth. Honesty at every stage is essential. By allowing our young children to ask these questions, we lay the foundation for future discussions about sexuality. When you listen and agree to answer, you are giving your children permission to discuss sex, permission you will be glad you gave as they grow into their teen years. They should know they can always come to you with their questions. This is the only way you can be sure they are getting correct information and a Christian point of view.

*Young children can begin to understand and respect privacy.*

Now is the time for parents to teach a child that a closed door requires a knock. Parents need to respect the privacy of the child as well. Knock if your child's door is closed. Children should be taught to respect the property of others, and be instructed not to go through others' drawers, purses, or wallets. This is a good time to talk about courtesy and telephone manners, too. Be sure to caution against saying, "No one is home but me."

*Young children need constant reassurance that they are wanted and loved.*

At every stage of development this is the critical factor. Hugs, kisses, touches, and verbal *I love you's*, all help satisfy the need for security and affection that children have as they grow up. They must know that no matter what else happens you will always love them. They also need to see parents holding and touching one another, expressing affection and love. This interaction between parents, siblings, and grandparents contributes to their sense of comfort and feelings of "being safe." It is only in this kind of atmosphere that they will continue to grow and thrive, emotionally and physically.

## Ages Six to Eight

The development we have seen thus far has been rapid and quite noticeable. From ages six to eight, there is still ample development going on, but it is more internal than external, not as visible. By now the child's basic sexual orientation is set in place.

Years ago, due to a misinterpretation of Freud's theories, this "latency" period (ages six to twelve), as it is often called, was thought to be a time of little or no sexual development or interest. Some felt it would be harmful to talk about sexual issues with this age group. However, for the last twenty years, noted psychologists who have carefully studied Freud's work and further monitored the development of this age group have rejected both of these ideas as misreadings of Freud. Rather, latency is now understood as a time when sexual interest and physical development is not as *observable* as it is in earlier and later years.

We have learned from listening to their language and watching their behavior that children this age are still very inquisitive and interested in sex and are continually developing in their understanding of sexuality. There is never a time when we are without sexual interest or curiosity. There are times, however, when this interest takes a backseat for awhile.

Charles Sarnoff, author of *Psychotherapeutic Strategies in the Latency Years*, is the most prominent authority on latency today. He and other noted authorities postulate that when Freud spoke of latency, he was referring to the fact that at this particular time in their development, the child's body has no power over them. That is to say, prior to this time, and again later during puberty, the child is driven by bodily impulses and urges created by hormonal changes and growth taking place in the system. But during this latent period, those hormones are more at rest. Also, the "family romance" between child and parent, begun during an earlier stage of development, has been put on hold, so the child can focus more of the sexual energy on school. This "romance" emerges again during puberty, presumably as a preparation or practice for the intimacy of marriage.

Freud himself supported the idea of sexual information and education for school-aged children. He advocated and approved of a "gradual and progressive course of sexual matters . . . at no period interrupted, in which the school takes the initiative."[2]

Because the child is now entering the world of the school, the focus of their attention is on the *concrete:* what they can see, feel, touch, and taste. They do not have the reasoning power to understand the abstract concepts of sexuality or other abstract ideas such as death at this stage. They understand only what is concrete, what they can see and observe.

Many experts in the field observe that for the child who has not had sexuality education, this is the best time to begin it. There is no interference with great fluxes of emotion due to hormonal imbalance such as teens experience in puberty. The child is able to concentrate and focus on *observable* sexuality issues such as: learning that all biological children have a mother and father; learning that there are many types of families; learning that all people are different; learning that no one has the right to abuse another; learning that babies grow inside their mothers, and so one. These are all concrete aspects of sexuality that the child of this age can understand and come to respect. This is the age at which the foundations for more complex issues is laid. This is just the same as with any other topic the young child studies. For example, in math we begin with concepts a child at this level can observe and understand: 2 + 2 = 4. This is the foundation for more abstract learning that will take place in later grades. Other developmental issues at this stage are:

*Children experience relationships outside of their families.*

As young children begin school, one of the most fascinating things they experience is meeting new people and making new friends. Parents should be ready to listen to all their stories about this new-found world of school and all its excitement and mystery. Mothers and fathers need to take care not to be jealous of the new attachment of their child to the teacher. This is an important and necessary attachment, one on which future attachments will depend. If this one goes smoothly—the parents understand and enjoy the child's praise and idolizing of the newest "role model"—then the child will feel it is OK to care about others. Some parents may, however, react with jealousy and displeasure: "All we ever hear about is Miss Cohen," or "I'm getting sick of hearing you talk about your teacher, don't you love me anymore?" When you react in this way, your child quickly receives the message that it is not OK to form attachments and friendships with others. This is a harmful attitude. It teaches a child to hold back feelings and avoid talking to parents about topics that they sense make parents uneasy or upset.

*Children learn new skills.*

During this time of formal learning, the young school child will be testing out many new skills. It is important that parents react to these with praise and enthusiasm! The success or failure they experience at this stage of development will set the tone for all future school learning and learning of new skills. It is important for the child to succeed at this stage; if they do they will become excited about learning and anxious to face the challenges of education. If they do not succeed at this stage, they may likely view school as a place where they cannot succeed, a place where they feel shamed and humiliated, a place to be feared and hated. Feelings of inferiority need to be dealt with at once by parents. Support and encouragement, coupled with close communication with the school, can help ensure success at some level of accomplishment.

*Children learn to communicate.*

Communication skills are the basis for all relationships. Good communication skills increase chances for successful relationships with others.

Children at this age begin to learn how to respect the feelings of others. They learn to share, to listen, to compete, to forgive, to receive, to suffer loss, to support, to comfort, and to be open to differences. Because of all this, many new friendships are formed, mostly with friends of the same sex. Parents will find themselves negotiating disagreements and broken hearts as they try to teach their child tolerance and understanding, what it means to be in relationship with others. There is a tendency at this stage to name-call and tease.

### Children are challenged to accept differences.

Because most children at this age have not had a lot of experience with children from other cultures, backgrounds, and races, they will be learning how to accept differences and be open to other possibilities in family life and family practices. They will come into contact with children who are "different" from them, children with disabilities, different socioeconomic backgrounds, or religious backgrounds. This is challenging for the child. Prior to this time, they have found comfort in sameness and so they sometimes have difficulty learning to accept diversity in other children. Parents who are aware of this can help by modeling: "Let's invite all your classmates to your birthday party," or "Why not ask all the girls on the team to come for a treat," or "Why not send all your classmates a valentine." Of course many times you can not entertain everyone. It is important then to make sure that your child is not just excluding one or two children. Boys and girls should be seen and treated as equals. Limitations because of sex differences should be avoided.

### Children learn the basic facts of life.

By this age children should understand that a baby is born through the love and physical union of a mother and father. Basic concepts can be understood: babies are born through their mother's vagina, some mothers nurse their babies from their breast, babies grow from cells—egg from mom, sperm from dad—babies grow in the womb and develop month by month. Menstruation should be explained to both boys and girls; more physically mature girls should be given more in-depth information. The average age of first menses is twelve in this country, but many girls begin menstruating as early as nine, so you want them to be adequately prepared and look forward to this event. Fear, shock, and a negative attitude can contribute to difficult periods, traumatic and painful experiences for those unprepared.

Sexual abuse should be gently but honestly discussed. What to do should this occur should be carefully explained. The parent needs to take care so that the child does not confuse abuse with normal, healthy affection between family members and friends. Overreacting can cause unnecessary fear and constant suspicion. Once again, the parent is reminded to use correct terms for the anatomy. You need not worry that you will harm your child with too much information. When information is given by parents in a loving manner, children will digest the information they need to know and disregard the rest. Teen pregnancy is usually the result of too little information, not too much!

### Children continue to explore what it means to be female and male.

Exploring what it means to be a girl or a boy will continue throughout this time. Children should be taught to value themselves as male and female. Children will ask many questions of parents and others regarding jobs and who can do what. Parents need to take care that they encourage both their sons and daughters *equally* in their understanding of challenges and job opportunities. Children will continue to look to their parents as role models. Their playtime activities will reflect this exploration of roles. Children may develop a special relationship with the parent of their same sex. This is a necessary developmental learning task and should not provoke jealousy. This special relationship can be encouraged by small outings and activities just for the two of you—just do not overdo it. In single-parent families, rely on a relative or special friend to help out. Grandparents can be great for this role modeling.

### Children begin to exercise independence.

Because they are now being exposed to other authorities at school and at their friends' homes, children this age may begin to subtly reject parental authority. They may not eat the sandwich you fix them for lunch. They may stuff their hat in their coat pocket at recess instead of wearing it on the playground. They may not want to wear the shirt you picked out for them. And so on. They are learning to make decisions based upon what *they* want. They will begin to solve some of their own problems and take some responsibility for their own actions. This is a good time for parents to discuss household and family chores, and invite the child to pick the ones they would like to be responsible for. As you set patterns for the future, parents may wish to begin watching some TV shows with their child and talking about certain programs in light of religious beliefs.

## Ages Nine to Eleven

This stage of development is called the preadolescent stage. This is a time of transition for the young child—not quite a teen, no longer a little child. During this time the child may become more modest and begin to express the need for privacy. The curiosity of sexuality at this age still stems from *external* needs, from what they see going on around them, or from what they hear others say or view on TV. Most, as yet, have no internal needs that prompt this curiosity. They are curious about sex but remain somewhat detached in their interest. It's all about someone else and what they are doing—not about me. In other words, they don't get hung up on sex like teens do. However, they are coming very close to the time when they will begin to experience rapid bodily changes. They are capable of masturbating to orgasm. They need to be prepared for what to expect in terms of their own sexual development, and because they will begin to experiment to varying degrees with their sexuality.

*Preadolescents will experience different rates of maturation.*

Because the rate of maturation is an individual one, preadolescents need to be continually reassured that they are normal. They will worry if they are not growing or developing as fast as their friends. "Early bloomers," both girls and boys, need to be prepared for attention from older children and other consequences of early development. "Late bloomers" need understanding and reassurance that they will eventually develop, although they may not follow the growth patterns of their peers. Boys and girls need to be prepared for how to deal with taunts and teasing from their peers. They may begin to feel emotional ups and downs. Those of smaller stature should not be given false hope that they will become giants. Girls generally will develop about two years ahead of the boys. This should be explained to both boys and girls. Parents should teach young people that they are worthwhile and lovable, regardless of their size. By the way, now is a good time to stop calling them *children* or *kids*.

*Preadolescents need to be provided with detailed*
*information regarding puberty, menstruation, pregnancy,*
*childbirth, sexual intercourse, and male and female*
*anatomy.*

Such information should be given, using correct and complete terminology, in an atmosphere that is relaxed and comfortable. The preadolescent now needs clear, positive, and thorough explanations and understandings of the body and all its functions. More in-depth explanations should be given regarding prenatal growth and development; male and female sexual responses, the purposes and causes of vaginal lubrication, male erections, and wet dreams; how a child is conceived; what circumcision is and why it is performed; what encompasses proper menstrual hygiene; and various types of feminine products. All of the physical changes as well as the emotional mood swings of puberty should be carefully discussed. Because the preadolescent may begin to initiate sexual intercourse as early as age twelve, all questions should be answered thoroughly as your young teen asks for information. The preadolescent needs to be taught that learning about sexuality is a lifelong process, and that sexual development and maturity take place over time. The body and all aspects of sexual functioning should be presented in a positive way and appreciated as beautiful and good, gifts from God to be respected and cherished.

## Preadolescents are capable of increased spiritual understanding.

Sexuality and religious values should be discussed within the context of spirituality. Your child at this stage is beginning to form his/her own personal value system. Observations and experiences are continually incorporated into that system. It is important that parents begin helping their preadolescent to understand sexuality as it is properly viewed by people of faith: as a wonderful gift from our Creator that carries with it certain rights and responsibilities. Parents will want to teach the unitive and procreative dimensions of sexual intercourse. The preadolescent can begin to understand that intercourse is only *one way* of expressing love, and that there are many others. Sexual attraction should be presented as good, offering opportunity for personal growth. Young people can begin to understand that God *loves us unconditionally*, when we succeed in adhering to religious principles, as well as when we fail. Parents should model this forgiveness.

## The preadolescent is capable of greater responsibilities.

Because of new skills and greater physical and intellectual abilities, the preadolescent should be given greater responsibility within the home and family. Her/his efforts at attaining greater independence should be respected. The young person's ability to make decisions and choices should be met with more frequent opportunities to do so. Do not be surprised if you find your authority being challenged. This goes with the territory! These are the years many will begin to make decisions about nicotine, alcohol, and drug use as well as sexual activity.

*Preadolescents need opportunities to relate to the opposite sex.*

Many parents have trouble with this one! Preadolescents are growing into a time of their lives when social interaction becomes all consuming. Romantic crushes are common. They will begin to experiment with boy-girl friendships and social relationships. The stress and strain of male/female relationships during the teen years often bring about confusions, tension, and embarrassment. Because of this, the young person needs to practice being around members of the opposite sex in relaxed, nonthreatening situations. There is no better place for this than in their own home. Informal group gatherings are the best. Encourage your child to invite others to your home *when you are there.* In this way, *you* will see the kinds of friends your child is making *and* you will be giving them the opportunity to meet one another in a safe place. Yes, it will be inconvenient at times, and noisy! However, you will be setting a pattern that your children will follow throughout their teen years, and as years go by, you will be grateful you did so.

Sports teams, hobby clubs, church groups, and community clubs or organizations all provide healthy atmospheres and opportunities for young people to get to know one another. Just be sure you check out the leaders, their proposed activities, their attitude toward competition, and their regulations before you agree to allow your young teen to participate. This is also the stage to reteach the equality of the sexes and the appreciation of differences in male/female attitudes.

*Preadolescents begin to develop the process of critical thinking.*

The preadolescent is beginning to learn about subtleties and differences in ways of thinking about things. This is the ideal time to point out to them the demeaning and disrespectful way advertising and the media often treat sexuality. Teach them to discern and evaluate as they watch

TV, view movies, observe commercials, and the like. Challenge their thinking gently and be careful not to "run it in the ground."

## Preadolescents need friendships.

If you already have children this age or a little older, you are already well aware of this point! Friendships with peers will become the center of the adolescent's life for several years. The peer group begins to have a strong influence during these years. The mature parent understands this and is not threatened by the teens' attempt to pull away from the family, as they increasingly spend more and more time with their friends. This is a good time to help them learn about the qualities that make a good friend. Many squabbles and upsets will occur at they attempt to discover who their "real" friends really are. Guide them in an appreciation of trust, equality, honesty, loyalty, patience, understanding, kindness, and responsibility. Help them discover that to have good friends you must be one!

## Ages Twelve to Fourteen

Psychologists and counselors often refer to a client as someone who is following their own or someone else's *script*. What this means is that often we are told by others how something *should* be or we tell ourselves over and over how something *should* be for us. Examples of this are: "That boy will never amount to anything!" or "I'll never be able to get through this, I just can't handle it!" Once we internalize these messages, we tend to live them out, right or wrong, good or bad. Unless, of course, we take the time to question or rewrite these scripts.

I bring this up because many people have written a script that says, "The teen years are hell for parents!" "They say" that teenagers are horrible and unbearable, and that raising teens is a disaster. Some say we should go from childhood to adulthood and skip the teen years altogether. A terrible idea!

I disagree with that script. In fact, I *strongly* disagree. Don't let anyone else write your family script. Write your own, and make it positive. Raising teens is challenging for everyone, but so is falling in love. Raising teens can be great fun if you allow it to be. Teenagers love to laugh; they have a great sense of humor. They are generally honest and open, ready to tell you what they think and feel. Teens have lots of enthusiasm. They are bubbling over most of the time. Teenagers are fun, loving, and kind. They can be thoughtful and caring. It is up to *you* to determine what raising a teen will mean in your family. It is up to you to see that you give your family permission to enjoy one another. It is up to you to enjoy watching and guiding as your young children grow and mature into young women and men. I suggest you celebrate with the entire family as your children enter their teen years: a family party, a special dinner, your teen's favorite dessert, or even a toast will do! Hispanics have a wonderful tradition to celebrate womanhood for their fifteen-year-old girls called the "Quincenera." We would all do well to follow a custom that helps both our boys and girls celebrate who they are becoming. Perhaps if we did, instead of constantly complaining about teens and criticizing their lifestyles (which incidentally they copy from adults), our teens could live up to a "new script."

And so it is with this in mind that we come to the critical stage of puberty. Critical because it is at this early age that young teens are making major lifestyle decisions. From now till about age nineteen, the teen will be trying on various identities to see which one fits best. Up to this point the child's interest in sexuality has been, as I mentioned earlier, external. Beginning with puberty this focus changes. The interest in sexuality and surrounding issues now results from the internal needs experienced by the young teen. Now they want to understand the technicalities involved in sexuality and bodily functions; they want to know everything because *they* are experiencing new sensations and feelings! This intense desire and need for information becomes immediate and all consuming, because they have a *personal* interest at stake.

Beginning with this stage, the teen attempts to integrate what s/he knows with what s/he does. This is the time when values learned begin to be values lived. Teens develop a clearer understanding of what a Christian attitude toward sexuality is all about, and how these attitudes differ from those that do not follow Christian principles. During this stage of development the teen needs constant reassurance that s/he is normal, that it is OK to become independent, that exploring new feelings and taking risks is quite normal and a healthy part of growing up when pursued with careful thought. The desire to compete and excel is strong. Struggles to become independent and challenges to established authority continue to be major issues as teens try to prove themselves. It is likely that young teens will begin to withdraw from their parents and look more to their teacher for information.

Peer pressure becomes a big issue. The importance of consequences needs to be stressed. A wise parent will allow teens to experience the consequences of their actions. Young teens, however, are not good at predicting the consequences of their actions. Boundaries are still needed, although parents should accept more input from the teen regarding these. Hormonal imbalances and rapidly developing bodies will be accompanied by clumsiness as young people attempt to adjust to their new bodies. Patience and understanding are required by parents and siblings as they resist the temptation to make fun of this awkward, and often embarrassing, stage. It is reassuring and helpful if parents relate stories of their own confused feelings and difficult episodes during puberty.

## Teens are able to understand that the physical and the psychological go hand in hand.

It is important for parents to explain to their teens that actions never happen in isolation. For example, as they begin to experience intense sexual feelings they need to have an understanding of how these feelings are related to, and prepare them for, sexual intercourse. How drugs and alcohol affect and interconnect with sexual behavior should be thoroughly discussed. "Just Say No" is not enough of an explanation! Parents can present at this stage how menstruation, nocturnal emissions, marriage, intercourse, and pregnancy all interrelate.

## Teens experience frequent feelings of insecurity and inadequacy.

It is at this stage of development that peers become the all-important source of affirmation and acceptance. Because of changing bodies, mood swings, and feelings of insecurity and inadequacy, teens need constant reassurance that they "fit in," that they are normal and will be accepted by others their own age. Cliques and gangs are formed in efforts to provide this support. Dressing a certain way, wearing the hair in a particular style, and listening to music adults tend to dislike all provide ways for the "youth culture" to stick together and assure one another that they are important human beings, different than the rest of society. Parents can help by providing continual support and understanding about seemingly trivial issues such as looks, size, skin condition, and the like. Parents can intensify their efforts to build self-esteem in their teen. This is the time to give *lots* of hugs and *verbalize* your love for your teens; they need to know you will not abandon them for any reason. Parents, however, must realize that young teens are going to look primarily to their peers for the assurance that they are OK. Strange hairstyles and clothing are best handled lightly. It is not unusual for teens to go through several phases of "being unique" before they find a look they feel really fits their personality.

### Teens want order and discipline.

I know this seems a questionable statement to make, but it is nevertheless true. I know what you are thinking: "She's nuts! She doesn't know my kid!" Mind you, I did not say teens will *ask* for this order and discipline, nor did I say they will accept it *quietly* when it is suggested or administered, but they do want it and need it. They want to know what their boundaries are, who and what they can count on, who can be trusted. Teens are beginning to devise and implement strategies for coping with their sexual urges and drives. They need help with this, especially from parents. Setting reasonable boundaries on curfews, sleepovers, or parties is an important way to give your teen a sense of balance. It's easy for them to get out of control. Parents can help bring them back to reality. It is also important that parents respect the limits that other parents have imposed. Even when you don't agree, you should never ridicule or make fun of the rules of other families.

### Teens experience emotional instability.

Because of the hormonal imbalance that occurs during the teen years, it is normal for teens to experience emotional outbursts and occasional mood swings. The young teen struggles with many difficult issues, many that have lifelong consequences and effects. We all may remember some of the pressures we faced as teens: pressure to get good grades, pressure to be involved in many extracurricular activities at school, pressure to make new friends, pressure to adjust to changing bodies, pressure to be accepted, pressure to be "good," pressure to be part of a group, pressure to have a girl/boyfriend. I am sure you could add a few. All of these pressures add up to stress, and emotions are strongly influenced by stress. Parents need to be aware of the sources of stress in the life of their teen, to talk about these openly and honestly, to offer coping mechanisms or counseling support when needed. Openness and acceptance on the part of the parent will do much to aid the young teen in stabilizing emotions and learning to cope with these new physical and psychological influences.

### Teens are searching for their sexual identity.

One of the major tasks of the teen years is to identify and come to accept one's sexual identity. Given the confusion added by developing bodies, hormonal imbalances, the prejudices within families and of society at large, not to mention religious sanctions, it is no wonder this is one of the most difficult of the developmental tasks. Teenagers need to be given complete and accurate information about what it means to be a heterosexual or homosexual person. We know that gender identity is fixed by this age. There is little anyone can do at this point to change it. The statistics on reversibility are extremely low.

When giving information about marriage and childbearing, it is important that parents recognize the possibility that one of their children may be gay or lesbian. Parents should show love and acceptance for all of their children; all should be treated equally. By facing the possibility of having a gay or lesbian child, the parent can be ready to give the love and support that will be necessary for their child to survive in our culture as a homosexual person. Homosexuality should be talked about openly and honestly as the parent aids the teen in the understanding of sexual identity and sexual orientation. The research indicates that true homosexual persons have no choice as to their sexual orientation. The matter of choice comes in when we talk about behavior and sexual activity.

Your teens, homosexual and heterosexual alike, should know that there are many good and wonderful homosexual people in our society who have contributed much to our world. There should be no tolerance in your home for jokes about sexual orientation. Likewise, parents should not avoid talk about marriage and children in front of their gay or lesbian child, to the expense of their heterosexual child. Once again, the situation calls for balance and equality. Information should be readily available for *all* of your children to help them choose the way they will live out their sexuality.

It is particularly important for parents to reassure their teen that same-sex friendships are *not* the same as homosexual relationships, nor does having a homosexual experience make you gay or lesbian. It is also perfectly normal for teens to have "crushes" on teachers and others they admire of the same sex. Teens worry about this and need to discuss it to resolve their fears.

## Teens explore, experiment, and take risks.

It is a part of normal development for teens to experiment to some degree as they explore their sexuality and what it means in their lives. They do so in many other areas of their lives. The degree to which they experiment will vary. For example, long before they get their driver's license, they have a try at putting the key into the ignition, starting the car, or maybe even backing it out of the garage. They may be permitted to drive on an abandoned country road. They may have their own key made. They may take the car for a little ride without you knowing about it. Long before they begin to drive we start warning them about things to be careful of. "If you ever have your tire blow out, take your foot off the gas at once, only gradually put it on the brake!" We create imaginary problem situations for them and tell them how they should handle these.

Before they begin high school, we take them to the school and show them around. They may even spend a day. We spend a lot of time talking about what life will be like in high school, how it will be different than elementary school. We tell our children what they might expect to happen in various situations in this new environment. On their own they may talk to others who go to the school to find out what it is like; they may read brochures on the school. They may go to the school on their own time and just look around. All these behaviors are perfectly natural and normal whenever we enter a new situation or begin a new phase in our lives. We need to be prepared for what we might experience. We like to check things out and see what lies in store for us.

Because teens take risks and experiment in all areas of their lives, parents should be sure they have discussed all possible issues surrounding sexual behavior, *well in advance* of their teen's dating years. Teens should be given *explicit* information on dating etiquette, sexual intercourse, contraception, masturbation, pornography, teen pregnancy, date rape, sexually transmitted diseases, AIDS, and drug and alcohol abuse and their effects on pregnancy. This information comes best from parents comfortable with their own sexuality.

Parents should be especially sure they have discussed any sexual behaviors that could be harmful or dangerous. Only when you discuss these issues *yourself* can you be sure your teens have the information and sources of help you want them to have. Parents can be the ones to present postponing sexual intercourse until marriage as both positive and possible.

Above all, frank and honest discussions about sex are an absolute necessity! By having such conversations ahead of time with your child and answering their questions about the mysteries of sex, you just may defuse some of the urge to experiment. Research supports that children who are able to talk with their parents comfortably about sex and have a solid knowledge of their bodies and how they function, postpone intercourse for a longer time than youth who do not. Anyway, you have nothing to lose but your embarrassment!

## Teens are loyal.

One of the most endearing characteristics of teens is their fierce sense of loyalty. They are most generous with this loyalty, sometimes to the point of using poor judgment. However loyal they are at this stage of development, parents do well to take advantage of this tendency to reinforce and remind their teens of Christian teachings and values. Present positive reminders that God has entrusted them with the precious gift of sexuality and has given them the responsibility to respect and care for this gift. The ability to reproduce should not be taken lightly. This is a good age at which to appeal to their sense of reason, stressing the logic of good behavior. It is unfortunate that because teens are so trusting, they are often naive in their dealings with others. Because they lack experience they are vulnerable and therefore frequently exploited by others. Parents can help protect their teen by explaining topics such as date rape, sexual abuse, and sexual deviations. These should be discussed candidly. The chances that your teen may encounter these is great. They need to be prepared to handle situations as they may arise.

## Teens are self-centered.

Whether we like it or not, this is the stage when young teens feel the world revolves around them. They are so focused on their own feelings, insecurities, looks, faults, and perceived defects that they often forget to ask about your feelings. This self-centeredness occurs as they try to understand themselves and their developing body, with the flood of feelings and confusion that accompanies this age. Parents can help by acknowledging these feelings while encouraging their teen to look to broader issues that may be involved. For example: "I know you and your friends have planned this party for some time now, but you knew from the beginning it was going to be on Grandma's birthday. How about a compromise? Spend an hour with Grandma and then go on to your party." Parents can also provide occasional opportunities for their teens to participate in some adult activities with them, so they can learn from your behavior and the behavior of other responsible adults: bowling with friends; a backyard barbeque; dining at a nice restaurant, letting the teen order for the parents, and the like.

## Ages Fifteen to Eighteen

The major quest of the older teens is to find their role in life. This challenging task may take up much of their energy and involve their emotions and thoughts for several years. Because it is a task of major importance and consequence, it deserves this kind of effort. Deciding what they will do with their life is part of that task. Choosing a career in today's multifaceted world is no easy task. Parents need to recognize this and allow time and understanding as their older teen goes through this process. When I was growing up, the careers open to women were nursing or teaching, or being an airline hostess, secretary, hairdresser, or religious sister. If you were not interested in any of those choices, you got married. Today, there are literally thousands of careers open to women.

Opportunities for men have also increased immensely as new technology has created new jobs and obliterated many old ones. So, try to give your young adult some space and time. It's a different world than the one you and I grew up in. Maybe by the time you were twenty-one you had your life course charted out and were already steering your course. This is not the case for many young people today and that doesn't mean they lack intelligence, motivation, or creativity. There are different rules and processes today, and mom and dad need to acknowledge this.

In terms of sexual development, the older teen will be building on all that has gone before. Information given in the past will need to be repeated as the older teen comes face to face with situations discussed but not encountered before. Repetition facilitates learning, so please don't say, "We've been all over this before. Didn't you ever pay attention?" Although they may have paid perfect attention, circumstances may now demand more detail and/or additional information. Maybe they didn't listen before, but if they are asking now, parents are wise to take the time to go over things, one more time. Frequent conversations at this stage of development are extremely important.

Parents need to continually express their love and concern for their teen. One way to do this is to inquire about their child's concerns, friends, school life, or feelings. More freedom is called for in setting curfews and personal decision making as teens mature and enter the work world. Older teens are capable of assuming their own responsibility for church attendance and other faith-related responsibilities. Reminders from parents are best when they don't take the form of nagging.

*Older teens need a broad base of information.*

Because teens are struggling with the issue of independence and have a great desire to make their own decisions, they need to be provided with available resources in the community that may be of help to them.

Older teens should be seeing the doctor on their own and assured that confidentiality between patient and doctor will be respected. Mothers should help their daughters choose a gynecologist. They should begin having private yearly checkups. If there are any Natural Family Planning Clinics in your area, you may wish to suggest that you and your daughter attend these sessions together. Young women need to learn all they can about their bodies and its cycles, whether or not they choose to use NFP.

Information along these lines should also be discussed with your son. Family planning is definitely a couples issue. This is a *mutual* responsibility and your sons should know as much about a woman's body as possible to facilitate carrying out this responsibility. Teens should be made aware of church groups that offer various types of support as well as medical clinics, in case they desire these types of services or simply want information.

Teens should be given information on contraceptives as well. Denying information is risky. If they are to make appropriate choices, they need *all* available information. All options and alternatives should be explained. We have no way of knowing if and when our children may need access to this information. An honest discussion is essential. Carefully explain your beliefs and feelings. Listen to your child's response. Interact, do not dictate. I like the way James and Mary Kenny talk about this in their book *Making the Family Matter.* They remind us:

> God gives us a wide variety of choices. God neither forces us to make "correct" choices nor hides information about "immoral" ones. All information is readily presented to us in creation. The parent who is open and honest about the possible options and the means to these options is more likely to have teens who will bring home the hard problems.[3]

*Older teens need a more complete understanding of the physical dimensions of sexuality.*

The teen in this new and advanced stage of development is ready to take in and appreciate information from a new perspective. Good books, based on Christian perspectives, about love and marriage, dating relationships, homosexuality, coping, or how to handle stress, plus a good medical source that deals with sexuality and topics such as contraception and pregnancy, will give your teenagers a more complete base of information. These provide them with references and also allow them to reflect and think things through for themselves, thus respecting their independence. It is very necessary that teenagers have *all* the information available at their disposal. It is wrong for us to keep information we may disagree with from them. We are preparing them to live life on their own, to be independent and mature, to make good and wise decisions and choices. To do this, it is essential that they are presented with both sides of every story. Only then can they make a choice that will reflect *their* acceptance of, and commitment to, the Christian way of life. To do any less would be to deceive them. To do any less would be to place their life in danger as they enter the world in which AIDS and other serious sexual diseases and abuses are prevalent.

### Older teens desire frequent dating opportunities.

At this stage dating will become a very frequent and important activity for many, as older teens struggle to learn and understand relationships better. Many are not as afraid of their sexuality as they were a few years ago, and they are beginning to learn what it means to exercise self-control in dating situations. While younger teens begin with group dates, many teens at this stage will want to double or single date. (Just a reminder here that all children develop at their own pace. Don't be worried if your child takes more time to date. Do give your teen the opportunity to discuss with you concerns and worries they may have about dating. Remember though, *not everyone* grows up and gets married!) Church-related youth groups, as well as school activities, can provide positive and wholesome dating opportunities where teens mix with others of similar values.

During the dating years, parents have a right to know where their teen is going, with whom, and an approximate arrival time home. However, parents must be aware that it is quite natural and normal for teens to change their plans on the spur of the moment. Dates that have been arranged weeks in advance may be subject to the whim of the moment! Because teens travel in groups, plans often change when some of the group have a better idea, or when someone can't get the car as planned. This happens a lot in the teen years. Parents need to be aware that their teens may have given them correct information when they left the house, but that by the time everyone got together, something else may have been decided. Your teens may not always have control over this, especially if they are not the drivers.

Be flexible and patient. Request a phone call when plans are changed, but be understanding if now and then you don't get it. Sometimes it really is impossible for a teen to get to a phone! Don't assume your son or daughter is deliberately being deceitful or hiding something! Listen to explanations before you make judgments. If forgetting to phone becomes a pattern, however, then have a serious talk with your teens. If this doesn't get results, decide upon a measure that will help them with their "memory" problem. I suggest you try housework, yardwork, car washing, and such. Grounding is not particularly effective and should be used sparingly if it is to show results. When teens are grounded week after week, other, more serious problems tend to arise. So be careful with that one! The keys to surviving teen years are flexibility, patience, and prayer!

### Older teens do fall in love.

I'm always distressed when I hear parents say things like: "What does he know about love, he's just a kid!" or "You just think you're in love, you don't know what real love is!" Remarks like this completely invalidate teens. Such remarks are disrespectful of their feelings and are best left unsaid. Many teenagers do fall in love. Many do know what love means. It is more effective to explain that there are many different kinds of love and many of these do not involve marriage. In fact, you may love someone very much and yet realize that marriage to this person would not be the best thing for either of you. This approach doesn't invalidate the love that may exist! If a parent is concerned about a relationship, it would be better if they just said so: "I am concerned about this relationship you're involved in, and this is why . . ." Try to avoid statements that put down your teen or his/her friend; don't deny or belittle feelings they may have for each other.

### Older teens are capable of greater reasoning powers.

At this stage of development, the teen is becoming more and more capable of critical thinking. And think they do! Causes and ideals take on a new significance as these young adults begin to save the whales and the world. They begin the quest for that which can be meaningful to them. As they approach the later years of this stage, they may begin to question their church and resist family practices of faith. This is a *normal* part of development. The young person has newly acquired powers of reasoning and thinking. They are anxious to try these out and see how others respond to their ideas.

Parents can expect lots of questions and some resistance to previously followed traditions or family rituals. In many instances older teens must reject what has been spoon-fed to them so that they can take it apart, examine it, and (quite often, with some revisions) claim it anew as their own. Asking significant questions as your teens question the world around them is a good way to challenge their reasoning powers. This is a much better approach than flying into a rage and accusing your teen of losing his/her soul, especially if you want them to talk with you again. Like Peter Pan, parents need to have a lot of "hope, trust, and a little bit of pixie dust!"

*Older teens are capable of a deeper understanding of the spiritual, emotional, and social dimensions of sexuality.*

As teens learn more and more about themselves and, therefore, others, they are able to better understand how their sexuality colors and influences many areas of their lives. This is the time to reinforce the idea that sexuality involves their total personhood: spiritual, psychological, social, and intellectual, in addition to the physical. The way they talk and dress, the manner in which they relate to others, the places they choose to go, the people they socialize with—these are but a few ways in which they express their own personal sexuality. Older teens are capable of understanding that sexual intercourse is only one way to express their sexuality. They are able to better comprehend the difference between love and sex.

They can be invited to appreciate the wisdom in saving intercourse for marriage. Parents can explain why their church encourages them to do so. Older teens can appreciate the diversity of behaviors of Christians and others without a faith tradition. They can plan definite, concrete strategies for dealing with their sexual drives, urges, and impulses in dating relationships. They can appreciate how appropriate sexual behaviors show respect and love for others. They are more tuned into listening to their bodies and identifying the signals of the human sexual response. In addition, they can be aware of the role of emotions in sexual behavior.

Older teens can understand what it means to choose alternatives to intercourse as they learn to practice self-control and self-discipline. They begin to appreciate the fact that they do have some control over their behavior in response to sexual urges. The older teen can understand and value the role of the family. Because of this our young people need to be encouraged to reflect on the importance of the family, to show respect for the institution of marriage and the part it plays in establishing committed, respectful relationships into which children can be born, raised, loved, and then relinquished into society, making our world a better place in which to live.

## Ages Nineteen to Thirty

In years past, young adults of this age were most often married and living on their own. Owing to increasing financial and educational pressures, however, it is not uncommon for adults to remain at home during most of these years. This has resulted in many complex issues for parents and their adult children to deal with, especially in the area of sexuality.

Psychologists tell us that at this stage of development (remember we are in development all of our lives), the main task facing the young adult is to establish intimacy. This means we learn how to share our feelings with others (no small task!). To accomplish this we generally search for one person in whom we can confide with comfort, confidence, and trust. This significant other is not always easy to find; for some the search takes longer than for others. When we do find this person we generally enter into a permanent relationship. For most Christians this means the sacrament of marriage and the commitment that goes with it.

Sex is often confused with intimacy. To be sure, sexual intercourse can certainly be an act of sharing intimacy, but it is not *always* so. Young people look for someone to trust, to share thoughts and feelings with. Many of our young adults today are from homes that have been split apart due to divorce. Still others are living with a single parent who chose not to marry the mother or father of the child. Many of these young adults have never experienced intimacy in their family of origin. Many are lonely and have no place to go with their thoughts and feelings. Many do not know *how* to establish intimacy.

So it is not surprising that they may confuse sex with intimacy. Sometimes they think that if they can sleep with a partner successfully, they can spend the rest of their lives loving them too. The two do not always go hand in hand. Good sex does not necessarily mean good relationship. But society has laid the groundwork for accepting this type of reasoning. Because of this, it is not really surprising that the number of young people engaging in sexual intercourse is so high.

National studies indicate that by age twenty, eight out of ten males and seven out of ten females have engaged in sexual intercourse.[4] Following the trend of more sexual involvement, the number of sexual partners on college campuses has also risen considerably in recent years. One study done in 1988 in a conservative region of the country reported twenty-two percent of college women having had seven or more partners. A rise from seven percent in 1981.[5] Researchers from various regions of the country all report similar findings. The reality is that college students are engaging in sexual activity frequently and many of them with multiple partners. Even with the threat of AIDS winding its way across the country, being more careful about sexual activity does not seem to mean *total abstinence* or *limiting partners* to many college students. While there are many reasons for this casual, and in many cases careless, attitude toward sexual intercourse, my purpose is to confine my discussion to what this means to the parent who is trying to cope with this situation as it may exist with their college-aged child.

We are in a bind! Our sons and daughters may go off to war to perhaps give up their lives at age eighteen. Also by age eighteen, our young adult children are determining the fate of our country as they cast their votes in elections. In past years, many were married by age eighteen.

Thirty years ago the average age for starting puberty was sixteen. Given that most were married by age twenty, the law-abiding Christian was looking at about four years of dating and sexual abstinence. Today the average girls starts puberty at age twelve. Never before have our young people stayed in school for such a long period of time. Although a short time ago a college education was thought to prepare you for a life of luxury, today a master's degree is needed to get a job that will perhaps pay your rent and maybe with a second income take care of your family. Owing to these and other social and economic factors, young men and women are postponing marriage until the mid to late twenties and early thirties. Assuming they still begin dating at age sixteen (many begin earlier), our Christian adults today are looking at eight to eighteen years of dating and sexual abstinence.

Many Christian parents find themselves faced with situations that the majority of parents in past generations did not have to deal with. We have no role models to follow here. Instead, many of us have young adult children who are unmarried and sexually active. "Living together," for many young adults, has become a step in the marriage process. This is not really a "recent custom." It was part of the Jewish marriage process during the time of Mary and Joseph for betrothed couples to live together before exchanging marriage vows. In April 1994 the Rabbinical Assembly's Commission on Human Sexuality presented a report to the Committee on Jewish Law and Standards. The report says, "Committed, loving relationships between mature people who strive to conduct their sexual lives according to the concepts and values described above can embody a measure of holiness, even if not the full portion available in marriage." The report continues to maintain the absolute standard of sex only within marriage but recognizes that not every person will live up to those standards. This report is an attempt on the part of the Conservative rabbis to imbue premarital relationships with Jewish values and make those relationships more holy. They encourage fidelity and commitment to the partner and offer guidance for sex outside of marriage. The report condemns casual and promiscuous sex. While it takes no definite stand on homosexuality, the report suggests that the traditional teaching against same-sex relations be reexamined in light of Judaism's commitment to civil rights for homosexuals. In recognition of changing sexual practices, this pastoral letter is the first modern attempt to come up with a sexual ethic by any branch of Judaism.

The Evangelical Lutheran Church has also debated passage of a social statement of sexuality that likewise is an attempt to bring a sense of religious values to today's permissive secular attitude of promoting casual sex. Many other churches are beginning to see the need to offer guidance in the area of sexuality. (I have already mentioned the Catholic document on sexuality released in 1991.)

Traditionally, the theology of sexuality was based on the theology of marriage. Today there seems to be a growing awareness of the need for a theology of sexuality independent of marriage. This is seen as necessary due to the vast changes that have taken place in our society and our church over the last century, and because of new information from the physical and social sciences. In past centuries our understanding of sexuality focused on procreative needs.

When we were a culture of agrarians, we needed large families to help maintain farms. In 1860, due to poor nutrition, inaccessible medical care, and farming accidents, it was necessary for a couple to have 6.5 babies in order to ensure that 2 of those babies would reach adulthood and begin families of their own. By 1970 that number had dropped to 2.4 babies.

In 1860, the average length of marriage before one partner died was twelve years; in 1970 the average length of marriage before one partner died was forty-two years. With approximately thirty years of post-child-bearing years in a marriage, the focus in this century has shifted from the procreative to the unitive dimension of marriage. The emphasis is on relationships and how couples can live and grow together in loving, caring, and intimate relationships, long after child-rearing ends.[6]

When people remark, "It's a different world today," they are quite right. Our society looks very different than it did a century ago, even fifty years ago! With medical advances, longer life expectancy, new medicines, availability of contraceptives, an industrial-based society (rapidly becoming an electronic society), societal and social changes, and ecological considerations, just to name a few, couples no longer depend on a large family to maintain economic stability.

In fact, the reverse is true today. A large family, once the mainstay of society, has become a potential economic liability. Children reach puberty earlier and remain single for a longer period of time than ever before, due to economic and educational reasons.

These factors and others have contributed to a different understanding of sexuality and thus the need for a theology of sexuality in addition to the existing theology of marriage. We are all sexual beings from the cradle to the grave, but not all of us marry. Guidelines for living out our sexuality, independent of marriage, would seem most helpful and necessary.

I bring this up here because it is important to the discussion of morality and our adult children. They are living in this society of ours with its exploratory and divided approach toward sexuality. They are influenced by the confusion and tension being felt among individuals within churches. Young adults know there exists indecision about which way our society as a whole views sexuality. They have experienced the extremes and are looking to find their own way, hopefully a way of balance. They have access to much more historical as well as current information than we had at their age. This generation has grown up watching Operation Desert Storm as it was happening. They have seen the minister or priest denounced for sexually molesting their classmates. They do not view the world in the black-and-white manner that was so much easier to do in generations past. Young people today have a more "global perspective." They are more aware of world events and multicultural traditions. Immediate access to a broad base of information has made them question and challenge traditional beliefs and values. As they view the historical perspective on which the churches base some of their teachings, the younger generation poses, "There's another way to look at this. Don't you see?"

I think this whole situation leaves many adults uncomfortable and somewhat confused. We love our children, we think they are good, spiritual, and religious people. But their understanding of sexuality may be different from ours. Their understanding of commitment and responsibility may be different as well. How then do we reconcile this with their choice of lifestyle? I would suggest to you that we don't have to!

It is my understanding of my Christian faith that God will do the judging at the appropriate time. It is also my understanding of my faith that I have the responsibility as a parent to raise, educate, and love my children *unconditionally*. The four sources of Christian ethics commonly held by most Christian theologians are as follows: 1) the Bible, 2) the tradition of faith, theology, and practice, 3) philosophical accounts of essential or ideal humanity, and 4) descriptions of what actually is and has been the case in human lives and societies. Many young adults today feel they are making solid moral decisions using such criteria, or similar models for moral decision making.

I do not propose that all young adults today in their sexual experimentation are doing the right thing. Nor am I suggesting that all couples should live together before they marry. What I am saying is: parents cannot dictate the morals their adult children live. We should follow the morals that our own conscience dictates ourselves, and leave our adult children free to decide for themselves what is moral or immoral in their lives.

You as a parent must live out your faith as you understand it, as it has been revealed to you. Therefore, your adult children should respect your right and responsibility to do so, just as you respect their right and responsibility to live out their faith as they understand it, as it has been revealed to them. All of us need to remember that each of us has had access to different information and lived in a different kind of church (though it may be the same denomination), sometimes with teachings that may have broadened or changed because of increased information and understanding. We are all responsible for the truth as we know and experience it. Respect for diversity is key to our getting along.

On a practical level, your home belongs to you. When your adult son or daughter brings home a friend from college, or from out of town, you should decide who sleeps where. Your child should respect your decision or find a motel, relative, or friend who is comfortable with the alternative. If your adult child announces to you that s/he is planning to move in with a loved one, my advice is as follows: If you are uncomfortable with this decision and feel it is not according to the dictates of your faith as you understand them, tell your child so. However, I would urge you not to sever relations with them.

Jesus taught us to love and to love *unconditionally*. That means loving someone when you don't agree with them. Loving someone when they do things you don't like or understand. As parents we are called to this kind of love. Parents have a responsibility to model Christian love to their children. It is this very modeling of love that has brought more than one "prodigal" back home. (Adult children know very well the difference between tolerance and approval.) If you cut off your relationship with your children, you will not have the opportunity to continue teaching them of God's love and forgiveness. As long as you remain accessible to them you have the opportunity to model Christian behavior and invite them to follow your lead. Once you shut the door, they see nothing but rejection and hatred, certainly not the model we have been given in the New Testament.

## Conclusion

Just a few suggestions as we come to a close with this chapter. At all stages of development, enjoy your children. Be open to questions. Be honest in your answers. Give concrete examples. Lavish children with hugs, praise, support, and encouragement. Invite choices and decisions. Share feelings. Listen well and often. Always make time to talk. Model love and trust. Pray a lot!

# Chapter 6

. . . . . . . . . .

✿

# Inviting Morality

We live in a society today where there is much brokenness. The majority of our children today under age eighteen are living in single-parent households. In the average American household today, a child spends only seven minutes a week of uninterrupted time talking with a significant other. This *excludes* time spent criticizing behavior or lecturing on rules.

- It is estimated that one of every three girls and one of every five boys has been sexually abused by the time they reach age eighteen. For females, this abuse is most likely to occur within the family. The most common age for this abuse is eight to twelve. Men abuse about ninety-five percent of female victims and about eighty percent of male victims.[1]

- Eighty-five percent or more of those molested will be abused by a relative, close friend, or neighbor.[2]

- The American Humane Association reported in 1981 that 750,000 children were physically abused or neglected. Injuries occur most frequently to young children less than three years old, and in young teens twelve to sixteen years of age.[3]

- At the college level, one in four women will be sexually assaulted during her four years at college. Seventy percent to eighty percent of those women will know their perpetrator. Nationally, the incidence of date rape is highest among women in their first year of college. One man in fifteen will attempt to force sexual activity upon an acquaintance or date sometime during his four years at college. (Date rape is rape committed by someone the victim knows.)[4]

• We are a culture of rampant addictions and compulsions. John Bradshaw's research on the family tells us that over sixty million people today are seriously affected by alcohol use. Sixty percent of American women, and fifty percent of American men have eating disorders. Research is just beginning in the area of sexual addictions, but it is estimated that this equals the number of chemical addicts.[5]

• In February of 1989, the *American Psychologist* reported that fifty-seven percent of high school seniors have tried an illicit drug, ninety-two percent of seniors have had some experience with alcohol and sixty-six percent reported very recent use; thirty-seven percent report at least one occasion of heavy drinking. One fifth of the seniors were daily cigarette smokers.

• We cannot look to change the behavior of our youth until we adequately address the behavior of our adults. Children learn what they live. The family is the most significant molder of behavior in children. Parents have much more influence on their child's behavior than they are willing to admit.[6]

• Studies show that teens who have poor communication with their parents are more likely to engage in sexual activity at a younger age than children who have good communication and close relationships with their parents. They are also less likely to begin smoking and drinking early.[7]

• Daughters and sons who have good communication with their mother are more likely to postpone intercourse longer than those who do not.[8] On the other hand, father-son communication about sexuality is linked with earlier sexual involvement. It seems fathers may condone sexual activity in their sons, linking this with society's attitude of expected male potency.[9] Parents of both sexes are more apt to discuss morality with their daughters and biology with their sons. The double standard still prevails, inadvertently fostered by mother and father alike.[10]

• Parental supervision is associated with later onset of intercourse.[11]

- Early dating is associated with early intercourse. Teens who do poorly in school and have lower educational expectations are more likely to engage in sex during adolescence than those who do better in school.[12]

- The average age for first intercourse is 16.2 for females and 15.7 for males.[13] In the inner city studies show this as low as 12.6 for females and 12.3 for males.

- Family experiences during adolescence are crucial in determining personality traits and predispositions for adolescent pregnancy. If the teens experience a marriage where their parents live out frequent hostility and display a distance from each other, the teens are more likely to become promiscuous and less likely to use contraceptives responsibly. Teen mothers frequently describe poor relations with a mother who was neither affectionate nor respected.[14]

- Forty-two percent of 8,000 youth, enrolled in grades five through nine, in religious-affiliated schools, claimed their parents *never* discussed religious topics. Forty percent of these young people said they wanted more opportunity to discuss sexuality with their parents. In this same study

  12% of all 5th graders
  16% of all 6th graders
  15% of all 7th graders
  17% of all 8th graders
  20% of all 9th graders

said they had engaged in sexual intercourse.[15]

- Higher levels of moral judgment are found in a domestic environment marked by the expression of opinions between parent and adolescent.[16]

- Suicide rates for adolescents, 15–19 years of age, have quadrupled from 2.7 per 100,000 in 1950, to 11.3 in 1988.[17]

- Over half of high school seniors have used illicit drugs.[18]

- One survey estimated that as many as 700,000 young men may have at least ten sex partners a year, putting them at considerable risk of sexually transmitted diseases including AIDS.[19]

• Every year, an estimated *minimum* of 3.3 million children witness domestic violence.[20]

## Accept the Challenge

As is evidenced by the statistics noted above, our children are growing up in a world filled with much dysfunction and confusion in the areas of sexual behavior. I believe we are living in a transitional time, a time when many of us, as parents, have no role models to follow. There are new and complicated issues surrounding sexual behavior coming to light. There are theories surrounding human sexual behavior continually unfolding before us, theories that are often reported at the same time to us and our children through the media. This gives parents little time to assimilate this new information for themselves before they discuss and/or answer questions about it with their children. As parents, many of us cannot look to how our parents handled such situations as an effective example. For a great majority of us, sexuality was not discussed comfortably or effectively in our homes.

Could it be that a great many of the dysfunctional and unhealthy choices reflected in the studies listed above are in part a result of past societal and familial inability to deal with the topic of sexuality and sexual morality in an honest, well-balanced, and open manner? I believe that is so. Parents today have available to them a new understanding and considerable new information in the areas of sexuality and sexual morality. They have the ability to bring this understanding and learning to their children and thus provide their children with healthy, balanced role models to follow when they grow up and have their own families. Today's parent has the opportunity to break the destructive cycle that has caused major problems and maladjustments too numerous to mention, and begin a new cycle of communication and responsibility that will benefit generations to come.

One of the greatest challenges we face as parents comes as we try to encourage and develop a sense of morality in our children. It is the responsibility of the parent to help the child develop a conscience. The correctly formed conscience will enable the child to make careful moral decisions. This ability to discern or make correct moral decisions is an *acquired* skill that parents can teach their child. Over the years, as the child matures into adulthood, this skill is learned, developed, and fine-tuned. Learning about morality and how to make moral decisions is a process. For parents to invite and teach this skill, they need to have a clear understanding of what morality means to them.

I would like to acquaint you with a model of morality that I feel is useful when trying to help our children understand the complex topic of sexual morality. Charles M. Shelton, S.J., has developed an understanding of morality that is based on our ability to identify with and respond to the feelings of others. This empathy, he feels, is the basis of all relationships, and empathy is the key to moral behavior. Our hearts help us to know what is moral.

In his books *Adolescent Spirituality* and *Morality of the Heart*, Shelton defines a moral person as one who makes moral decisions based on "other-centered" values. Such a person possesses a natural sense of empathy, a sense of care and compassion that has been worked out through one's conscience. We make our moral decisions using our conscience, and our conscience is influenced in its formation by our life experiences.

It is true that our conscience is also formed by the rules and regulations we learn. However, we need to create a balance between knowledge and feelings; both are important in moral decision making. Balance is advised. Shelton rightly reminds us that although moral principles help guide emotions, emotions energize moral principles. Both dimensions are necessary, and either dimension alone would be inadequate.

To help our children learn how to develop and maintain this balance, we need to ask significant questions. These questions will challenge them to examine their own thoughts and feelings, and relate them to the knowledge they gain. Their final answers will be their own code of morality, a code that will enable them to take responsibility for their actions and behaviors both now and in the future.

Shelton believes that sometimes this process involves admitting and owning guilt. Appropriate guilt is healthy and crucial for the development of one's moral life. We all need to accept responsibility for our actions. Again, the key is balance. We need to help our children develop an *appropriate* sense of guilt without dwelling on it or allowing guilt to consume them. When our children are faced with difficult moral decisions, we can help by asking them significant questions and by showing compassion and listening as they reflect on our questions.

Essentially, we begin to face the challenge of helping our child develop a conscience the moment we become parents. Christian tradition teaches that a person has an obligation to have a well-informed conscience. The Roman Catholic tradition instructs that a Christian in good conscience follow four key steps when making any moral decision or when considering a decision contrary to a particular church teaching:

1) Be aware that this decision is a serious matter.
2) Know and understand fully the church's teaching on that matter.
3) Read and discuss with someone knowledgeable in church teaching the gravity of such a decision.
4) Pray and give serious consideration to the consequences of your decision.

We are led to many of the important decisions of our lives by our faith experience, our life experiences, our knowledge, emotions, and vocational situations. When a Christian makes a moral decision s/he ought to have followed a process which includes *all* of the above considerations. Such a process is called *discernment* and is described clearly and concisely in *Human Sexuality: A Catholic Perspective for Education and Lifelong Learning.*

> *Discernment* [is] that process by which a person uses one's own reasoning ability, the sources of divine revelation (Scripture and tradition), the Church's teaching and guidance, the wise counsel of others, and one's own individual and communal experiences of grace in a sincere effort to choose wisely and well. . . .

> Moral decision making is a particular type of discernment process. In order to decide the right course of action, particularly about matters that may be complex or controversial, Catholics must be open to the wisdom of God manifest in all those sources cited earlier in this chapter—one's family, the Church, the Word of God, the sacraments, communal and private prayer, the stories of the saints. At the same time data from the physical sciences, information from the social sciences, and the insights of human reason can all contribute to one's discovering moral truth. . . .

> In the end, whether choosing one's vocation or making a moral decision that relates to or affects one's vocation, each person is bound to live with and to stand by his or her own discernment or perception of God's will.[21]

These kinds of decisions in the matter of conscience are a serious issue. They involve looking at both *objective* and *subjective* morality (see chapter 7). The implications of such decisions, and such a process, cannot be understood fully by a young child or teenager. We do, however, have a responsibility as parents to explain and encourage this process according to the age, emotional and intellectual level of development of our child. Therefore, part of our responsibility as Christians is to give our children a basic understanding of the teachings of our church so that they can grow into this deeper level of Christian maturity.

> We must teach with courage and fidelity the Church's doctrines concerning sexuality and sexual morality. . . . At the same time we must offer compassion and understanding to those who fail to discern or to live out God's loving will. . . . [We] must take time to listen to questions, concerns, and insights from the learners [our children]; to respect their integrity and sincerity; and to facilitate their ongoing search for knowledge and a deeper understanding of truth about the mystery of human sexuality.[22]

If we do not live up to this responsibility, which we took on at their baptism, then we are doing them a grave injustice. First and foremost, let us remember that they are beginners, young learners in their faith, and it is our obligation to see to it that they learn church doctrine as it stands today. If we do this, then we are giving them a chance at maturing in their faith with a solid foundation to guide them. The attitude with which we develop conscience is crucial because it will determine the method we will use to do so. Our attitude, and thus our method used, will depend to a great extent on how we view ourselves in our role as parents.

I would like to take a look at three very different methods or styles of parenting. As you read, think about which of these methods are closest to the way you raise your family. Which do you think you would prefer as a family member? Which is closest to the way *you* were raised?

The first approach comes from the parent who disciplines the children with an authoritarian style. This parent presents them with a list of rules to be followed and responsibilities to be carried out and determines who will do what. This parent sets rigid limits, insists upon inflexible boundaries, inflicts punishments routinely, commands set behaviors, makes all decisions of consequence without input from family members, dictates how family members will carry out commitments to their faith, and *demands and determines morality.*

The second approach comes from the permissive parent who fails to discipline at all. This parent ignores the behavior of the children, looks the other way when standards should be set, avoids making value judgments, makes few demands, leaves the children on their own to regulate their own activities, sets no boundaries, enforces few rules, leaves decision making to the whim or mood of the moment, seldom communicates or dialogues with the children, is indifferent to or *ignores morality*.

The third approach comes from the parent who disciplines the children using an authoritative or interactive style. This parent presents the children with a list of responsibilities that need to be fulfilled and encourages input from members as to who will carry out various responsibilities, negotiates reasonable limits and appropriate boundaries, clearly explains guidelines for and consequences of behavior, suggests participation of the entire family in the decision-making process whenever possible, uses punishment sparingly focusing instead on realistic consequences or alternatives, fosters an understanding of faith commitments and encourages participation, *invites morality*.

Of course there are always exceptions to everything, but generally speaking, the authoritarian and permissive parenting styles are ones that breed discontent and incite various levels of rebellion within families. These are divisive and in the long run do not produce emotionally stable or well-adjusted adults. Children from both these styles of parenting lack the ability to be assertive; they tend to be dependent. Through different means, each style has shielded the child from stress and thus has inhibited the development of the ability to tolerate frustration.

Studies show that moral development is impaired when the father uses power and assertiveness inappropriately. The same is true when the mother uses her love to control behavior. For example, the mother withdraws love excessively when the child does not do what the mother wishes, and bestows love only when the child acts according to her dictates.

The authoritative, interactive style, by contrast, encourages independent thinkers and mature adults who accept responsibility for their actions. The child's individuality is encouraged and respected and s/he has the opportunity to try out new skills. Children of authoritative parents tend to be independent and socially responsible. Likewise this interactive style is a positive factor in moral development.

Because *morality is a way of knowing*, intellectually and emotionally, *what I ought to do*, it requires acceptance and internalization on the part of the child, not merely obedience. Consciously and unconsciously, parents influence moral decision making. I would encourage you to be interactive. Pay attention to your child. Listen to what your child has to say. Try to understand the child's point of view, even if you don't agree with it. Engage in calm and open discussion. This process enhances acceptance and internalization. *Invite morality.* As time goes by, you'll find yourself following this pattern of communicating without even thinking about it. It will have become part of your parenting style.

God does not dictate morality, nor did Jesus. Neither are we programmed to behave morally. We are created with a free will. We have the ability to make moral or immoral choices and are given endless opportunities throughout our lives to do so. A friend of mine, Charles Bouchard, O.P., explains it this way:

> Although we are not programmed for morality, there is a way in which we are "created for happiness," that is, we are not created completely blank slates, but have a "seed" of divinity and true happiness in us. Morality is really a process of discovering, through example, experience, memory, repetition, what really makes us "happy" or fulfilled, in the long run. We do have a free choice, but I believe that God created us with a slight bias toward the morally good.[23]

To this end, our loving Creator has provided us with a powerful role model in Jesus, who in turn presented to us an ideal for responsible moral decision making. It is up to us, however, to choose moral behavior. As human beings we are in control of our behavior. We are invited to choose responsibly. I would suggest that God is authoritative and not authoritarian or permissive. It is this same opportunity that we ought to offer our children, the opportunity to make their own choices whenever possible, increasing this opportunity as they grow into their teen and young adult years. If we do so, we will be preparing them for their future.

As your child grows and develops in his/her understanding of morality, you will be faced with numerous situations in which you will have to choose a method of response. You will begin to develop your style of communicating and parenting. My hope would be that your style would be authoritative and interactive, and your response would follow the example modeled by Christ—inviting your child to morality.

What follows are some general suggestions psychologists, theologians, educators, and other professionals who work with children and young people advocate. These should be practiced from infancy to adulthood, adjusting according to age level. Although touching on moral behavior in general, I will focus mainly on sexual morality.

You may notice that in what follows we will spend quite a bit of time on masturbation. This is because masturbation is seen by many parents as a matter of concern, and because at different stages of development, this behavior tends to resurface and demands different types of responses on the part of the parent. However, it is certainly not the only behavior we should consider when teaching our children morality, nor should we overemphasize or dwell on it. There are many moral issues. We have space here to treat only a few, so I have tried to use as examples the ones I am most often questioned about.

## Present Sexuality as Good

We are sexual beings from the womb to the tomb. Our sexuality is an important dimension of our personality. Once again I encourage you to think of sexuality as involving our spiritual, psychological, social, and intellectual, as well as physical selves. We were made sexual beings on purpose. The human sexual response is no accident of nature. Nor is it an accident that the Bible begins with the story of creation and reproduction. I believe this indicates the importance of sexuality in God's divine plan.

Our sexuality draws us into relationships with others. It is designed to do so. Current findings by developmental psychologists show that beginning in the third trimester of pregnancy, baby boys begin to experience penile erections. Baby girls begin to experience vaginal secretions during this same period. After birth these psychosexual responses continue every ninety minutes, day and night, until about age three when, during toilet training, we learn to inhibit these natural, normal responses. However, from this time on, this normal response still continues during our sleep.

Noted author and psychologist Fran Ferder has done much work in the area of psychosexual development. As pointed out in a book she coauthored with John Heagle, *Your Sexual Self,* this normal sexual response is designed to draw us into relationship with others. We are so created as to seek out others with whom to relate and connect. The ultimate goal of psychosexual behavior is love.

Sexuality, then, is an awesome gift. It is not some part of ourselves to be dreaded or feared. Sexuality is not something to be hidden or denied. We have no reason to be ashamed of our sexual or erotic feelings. Sexuality is a beautiful God-given gift and a tremendous responsibility. Be positive in your attitude and present sexuality in a positive manner to your children.

We have a body whose actions are primarily under our control. We have a choice as to how we react to human bodily responses. We control our behavior. We have nothing to fear from our feelings, unless we have not adequately prepared ourselves for living out our sexuality, keeping within the norms of a spiritual framework. Such preparation comes from learning as much as we can about our bodies, understanding how our bodies respond to sexual stimulation, setting personal limits on our behavior, knowing what our strengths and weaknesses are, and acknowledging the behavior we are called to by our God, by our faith dimension.

Through everyday occurrences and events we should communicate to our children that sexuality is good. We begin this during infancy. One of the ways we communicate this is the way we respond to infant masturbation. It is quite normal for infants to touch their genitals. They are exploring and getting to know their own bodies. They are beginning to identify feelings, including those of pleasure and pain. Psychologists today affirm work done in 1905 by noted psychologist Alfred Adler regarding infant sexuality. The understanding is that the infant exploring his/her own body is beginning to develop skills that relate to survival and interpersonal security. Not only is this exploration harmless but important and necessary.

The wise parent allows this exploration and development to take place, thus giving the message, "Your body is good. Pleasurable feelings are good. It's OK to explore your surroundings. It's good to know how your body works."

As the child grows and toilet training begins, the parent is again faced with the opportunity to give positive messages to the child about sexuality and bodily functions. The mature, knowing parent faces this challenge with positive methods and rewards based on desired behavior. The message given to your child should be, "Your body is good. Learning control of bodily functions is both good and necessary. I will help you learn how to do this. Together, we will accomplish this task. Sometimes you will fail and that is OK. I love you whether you succeed or fail."

When parents react to toilet training with disgust, impatience, and insensitivity, the child gets messages like the following: "My body is bad. I must be bad. Mom and dad don't like me unless I am perfect. I must always be in control. It's never OK to fail." The psychosexual harm that comes from the rigid, punishment-based approach may be lifelong, and may cause many complications in behavior and relationships, sexual and otherwise. Because control becomes the issue, the sense of the goodness and naturalness of the body and its functions suffers irreparable harm. The self-esteem of the child is greatly diminished as well. The wholeness of God's gift becomes fragmented and broken.

We are presented with yet another opportunity to respond in a positive way to sexuality when our child begins to play "doctor." Sometime prior to beginning school it is likely your child will, in some way, explore the bodies of others. Children at this age are curious. "Does everybody look like me?" "Does mom or dad look like me?" "Do boys and girls look the same?"

This behavior is very normal and is to be expected during early childhood. It is important for the parent not to overreact to this situation when it arises. Should you find your child "playing doctor," simply suggest that s/he do something else. Distract him/her. Ask him/her to come and help you with a chore, or make an offer of cookies and milk. Gently remove her/him from the situation and calmly explain that it is not a good idea to expose oneself to others or to ask others to expose themselves.

Tell him/her you understand that s/he is curious about bodies and offer to get a book that shows how boys and girls, men and women are different. Then drop it! Punishment is not appropriate here, nor is a long lecture. Overreaction will simply create additional curiosity or the reverse: fear of knowledge about the body or of sexual feelings. Overreaction may cause your child to stifle natural feelings of curiosity, to see these as bad. Unfortunately, control once more surfaces as the main issue, and your child's positive sense of self and sexuality suffers because of this.

In the young child, masturbatory behavior is likely to emerge once again. This normal conduct should be treated in much the same way as playing doctor. Children at this age are not capable of sin. Sin should not even be mentioned at this age. If your child is playing with him/herself in the privacy of their room, it need not be mentioned. If this occurs in a public place, then calmly tell your child that it is best not to touch yourself in front of others. You may tell them that such behavior in public is not appropriate and that other people do not like it; such things should be done in private.

In this way you are not demeaning the child or the goodness of the body. Nor are you indicating that there is something wrong with feeling pleasure. You are, however, teaching your children to begin learning how to control their desires and actions. You are also teaching appropriate public behavior. At the same time, you are reminding children to show respect for themselves and the feelings and opinions of others.

## Invite, Don't Dictate

In the course of my travels around the United States and Canada giving lectures and training teachers, I am constantly confronted by confused, unhappy, and sexually dysfunctional adults. I work mostly with professional educators and parents. I also work with religious, clergy, and students of all ages. There are frequently those individuals who seek me out after a lecture or training session to ask a question or ask for advice. Although each story is unique, most people have one thing in common: they grew up in a home where sexuality was ignored, repressed, or abused.

Most of these adults report having had little or no conversation with their parents about sex. If there had been conversations, these were negative, punitive, dictatorial, and/or overplayed, thereby discouraging future talks. This all-too-typical response to sexual issues causes destruction that adult men and women spend years trying to identify and deal with. Some never come to terms with themselves as sexual persons and many are unable to understand or change the pattern of their sexual dysfunction.

Let me give you an example: A few years ago, I was doing teacher training for a large diocese. I conducted sessions with the teachers that went on for several days. At the end of the final session, a somewhat shy, very pregnant young woman in her early thirties came up to me and asked if we could talk privately. As we spoke she told me that she had been married four years to a man she loved very much. But, she said, she was frigid; she could not enjoy intercourse nor achieve orgasm. She explained that when she was a young girl, her mother had walked into her bedroom unexpectedly and found her lying on her bed masturbating. She said her mother was furious and began yelling at her saying spiteful and hurtful things. She accused her daughter of being a "slut." She told her that only dirty women with bad reputations did such things, and that if she truly loved God, she would never do something like this again. Days later she was still bringing up the incident, shaming her daughter over and over.

The young woman related to me how, as a young girl, she had tried rigorously to avoid and stifle sexual arousal, including *any* erotic feelings she might experience. She carefully avoided anything that might be sexual in nature, to the point of changing the TV channel when a couple was kissing. So fearful was she that her arousal might "take control over her" and cause her to become a "slut."

We're talking about *healthy, normal arousal* from watching a romantic scene in a movie, talking with a boy she found attractive, or holding hands and cuddling with a boyfriend. Her understanding from her mother's overreaction was that if masturbating was so terrible, any feelings that might sexually arouse or stimulate her must be terrible too.

She was so afraid of that happening again that she simply turned off and repressed her human sexual response system. Twenty years later, married and pregnant, she had never been able to allow herself to receive the love her husband had been trying so patiently to share with her. He, too, was having self-esteem problems due to his assumption that he must not be a very good lover if he could not even help the woman he loved to enjoy sexual intercourse and orgasm.

This woman's concern was not so much for herself as it was for her husband and her future child, not to mention her students. She was afraid her husband would get tired of her inability to enjoy intercourse and avoid her altogether. She was also worried that she would unwittingly pass on this miserable cycle of misunderstanding sexuality as sin. She was rightly concerned that her nonverbal behavior would negatively influence her students' attitude toward sexuality. After worrying about everyone else, she was finally able to admit that she herself wanted to be able to experience the joy of healthy sexuality and enjoy a normal sex life with her husband.

Where could she go to talk about and get help with this problem? She certainly couldn't go to her mother. Because of her distorted view of sexuality, even talking to her doctor was awkward and embarrassing. She was ashamed. She blamed herself for being unable to get over "her problem." Even though intellectually she had reasoned things out and worked some of them through, she still had been unable to turn around years of denial and repression. "What is normal, healthy sexuality?" she asked me. "Why can't I enjoy my marriage?" "Am I really a slut if I enjoy sex too?" "What if I find out I'm really a passionate woman?" "What's wrong with me?" Questions I hear all too often from people who due to experience or circumstance have a distorted view of what it means to be sexual and spiritual.

I'm happy to say that in this case there was a happy ending. I was able to refer the woman to a counselor who over time was able to help her work through some of her issues surrounding sexuality and religion. It took a few years of hard work for her and her husband, but they were commited to each other and to their marriage. Both were determined that this was an issue worth their time and effort.

Sad to say, this is not an unusual story; I could write pages of them. Young teachers, old teachers. Young parents, old parents. Clergy, students, religious. I have heard so many tragic stories. Many of the stories don't have a happy ending. Some husbands are not patient or willing to do their part to help rectify a situation. Some wives don't care enough about themselves to go through the hard work of getting in touch with their sexuality. So many people reject and deny the importance of sexuality in their lives. So many lives are affected from misunderstanding God's wonderful gift!

There are many people suffering today because of a parent's overreaction to masturbation, dating, kissing, what constitutes appropriate dress, magazines, and other sexually related issues and situations. Even though many parents were well-intentioned, the damage was done. Whether an overreaction or a legitimate concern, these issues must always be handled gently by parents. There are so many messages about self and body contained in admonitions of the kind I have just described. Parents need to be aware of the power they wield.

When a young person is given neither an opportunity to respond nor an opportunity for calm discussion, choice, or explanation, the results can be confusing and disastrous. This is what often happens when parents try to *dictate* morality. What ends up being communicated, unfortunately, is *inappropriate guilt* for having normal sexual feelings, a disgust for the body and its functions, and/or a fear and shame of natural and healthy sexual response.

How might her mother have responded? Developmentally, we understand that masturbation is normal behavior in the young child. We also know it is typical for this behavior to surface several times during development, one of these times being puberty. We know that modern medical opinion is clear that there is no physical harm in masturbating. Keeping this in mind, the loving parent will respond with gentle, understanding communication. The parent will respect the young teen's right to privacy. Only if the behavior becomes obsessive or abusive should the parent express concern to the adolescent.

Masturbation is not an issue in many religions. Many modern theologians, reevaluating past religious interpretations based on current scriptural and medical information, encourage that the issue be downplayed. Theologian James Nelson in his book *Embodiment* writes:

> The Bible does not at any point address the subject of masturbation directly. A text sometimes associated with this issue is the story of Onan (Gen. 38:6–10), though the application is a misinterpretation of that biblical episode. . . . Certain biblical emphases have conditioned the historic Christian negativity toward masturbation, particularly when it is done by males. Equally important has been the historic combination of sexist dualism with biological misinformation. If the male seed was the only active element in the transmission of new life (the woman providing only the ground for planting), then masturbation was tantamount to the deliberate destruction of

human life—there were, after all, "pre-formed people" present in the semen. A strict Orthodox Jewish view at times even held that the death penalty could be administered to a male masturbator.[24]

The Roman Catholic tradition opposes masturbation based on its teaching "that sexual orgasm ought to be linked to marital intercourse, which, by definition, serves both lovemaking and life-giving purposes."[25] Because masturbation is not seen as unitive nor procreative, it is viewed as morally unacceptable.

However, in the Catholic Church as well as in some of the mainline Protestant religions that still oppose masturbation, there appears to be a growing tendency to downplay isolated acts, particularly in adolescents, and focus on the *overall* behavior of the individual:

> Pedagogical efforts and pastoral care should be focused on the development of the whole person, seeing these actions in context, seeking their underlying causes more than seeking to repress the actions in isolation.[26]

This pastoral approach suggested by many churches today seems to be the most advisable for those seeking a spiritual balance:

> Little benefit appears to be gained from focusing directly on the masturbatory behavior. Highlighting the malice of each act of masturbation only serves to compound the problem and drive the person further into self. For this reason, directing the counselee to activities that are other-centered appears to be the most effective remedy for treating adolescent masturbation. . . . Professional psychological consultation should be recommended only in those instances in which it is clear that the masturbatory behavior stems from serious psychological maladjustment and the counselee could benefit from such professional therapy.[27]

There are many reasons young teens masturbate, some of which have nothing to do with sex or sexual pleasure. Often it's about comfort and security. There may often be underlying unconscious issues or problems the adolescent is seeking relief from. If there is a pattern of excessive masturbatory behavior, this possibility should be explored. In such a case counseling might help. For example, if stress is the cause, a counselor could present more appropriate methods for handling stress and/or assist the adolescent in determining the possible underlying cause of the stress. The counselor, as one emotionally uninvolved, might also help ensure a more balanced approach to the topic.

Inviting sexual morality in such a situation as this, the parent of the adolescent could explain the potential harm in becoming isolated from one's friends and activities. Thoughtful, balanced discussion with your adolescent could include an explanation of the relationship between psychological health and spiritual health. The parent would explain how a *preoccupation* with fantasy and self-pleasuring in some cases could lead to habitual or possibly compulsive behavior. Though not common, such compulsivity could lead to an inability to relate to one's partner in a mutually intimate, love-sharing relationship in the future.

It is important that the parent not *overreact* to the situation or use language that would cause undue guilt or shame. The parent should make it clear that s/he is not opposed to the idea of sexual pleasure, rather the concern is the possible abuse of pleasure. Encourage your child to ask questions regarding your explanation to be sure s/he is not drawing incorrect conclusions or becoming overly fearful about his/her normality.

In *all* situations, it is better for the child when the parent responds with thoughtfulness and openness, showing respect for the child by discussing all matters in a calm, honest, and gentle manner. Sexual dysfunctions are rampant in society today, and these dysfunctions take many forms. One contributing cause for these dysfunctions appears to be overreaction by the parent to a sexual behavior or situation as the child was growing up.

## Take a Developmental Approach

The next recommendation suggests that as parents raising children, we take a developmental approach when attempting to instill sexual mores and values in our children. What this means is that parents need to become familiar with the ages and stages of psychosexual development. In other words, *what* to expect from your child as s/he grows up, and when you can expect it to occur. It may also be helpful to be guided by a model of what a sexually healthy Christian adolescent is like (see list, p. 88)

As parents teach sexual morality to their children, it is advisable for them to take these developmental stages into consideration. It is important that parents be aware of what is considered normal behavior at various ages, so they can more capably address moral development. There is no gain in presenting a moral concept at an age when a child

## Sexually Healthy Christian Adolescents

- Recognize sexuality as one of God's special gifts
- Respect and appreciate their own bodies
- Decide what is personally "right" and act in accordance with these values
- Express love and intimacy in appropriate ways
- Avoid exploitative relationships
- Know and claim their values
- Communicate effectively with family and friends
- Know and understand church teaching regarding sexuality and respect such teaching when making decisions and choices involving sexual behavior
- Take responsibility for their own behavior
- Ask questions of parents and other adults regarding sexual issues
- Enjoy sexual feelings without necessarily acting upon them
- Assertively communicate and negotiate sexual limits
- Understand the consequences of sexual activity
- Communicate desires not to engage in sexual activity and accept refusals respectfully
- Demonstrate tolerance for people with different values
- Talk with a partner about sexual activity before it occurs, including limits, contraceptive and condom use, and meaning in the relationship
- While the Christian ideal is abstinence before marriage, if sexually active assume responsibility for pregnancy and disease prevention
- Make decisions regarding moral behavior using an informed conscience and follow the process for making moral decisions
- Are aware of and understand the impact of media messages on thoughts, feelings, values, and behaviors related to sexuality
- Practice health-promoting behaviors, such as regular check-ups, breast or testicular self-exams
- Interact with both genders in appropriate and respectful ways
- Seek further information about sexuality as needed

Source documents: *Human Sexuality: A Catholic Perspective on Education and Lifelong Learning,* 1991, and *National Guidelines for Comprehensive Sexuality Education,* 1991.

is unable to understand that concept, or when lack of emotional, intellectual, or physical development interferes with the child's ability to follow through with moral principles.

The stages of development can be helpful to parents in determining when to make a child responsible for certain behaviors. For example, it is quite permissible for a female toddler to be permitted to play in the yard or at the beach on a hot day, dressed only in a diaper or panties, without clothing covering the upper part of her body.

However, in American society, by the time the child has reached school age, we would expect that she appear in clothing, covering her upper and lower body, appropriately. From the developmental standpoint, a toddler would not have yet developed the moral or mental capacity to understand the reasoning behind proper clothing. While still limited in full reasoning ability, the five or six-year-old would nonetheless understand a basic concept of modesty, that of being appropriately dressed in public. So the parent would not hold the toddler to the same standard of responsibility that would be expected of a school-aged child. By the time the girl had reached her teen years, unless she were mentally challenged, we would expect her to know and understand not only the moral reasoning behind modest clothing but also expect that she know and respect the civil law in this matter.

We approach the child at his or her level of physical and intellectual reasoning. Moral development likewise corresponds to the intellectual levels of development. The six-year-old, while perhaps understanding to a degree the social responsibility to dress appropriately, would have little understanding of the moral responsibility to do so. A child this age cannot understand abstract concepts. With the six-year-old we might say, *"When you go out in public, you have to be fully dressed because in our country you are supposed to be. People expect you to. It is considered the appropriate thing to do."*

With the teenage girl, we would appeal to, and invite a higher level of moral reasoning: *"You know, your body is good and beautiful. All of our bodies were designed by God to give pleasure to the eyes and the heart, to awaken sexual desire. By creating our bodies to stimulate a desire for physical intimacy, God ensures that males and females will have the desire to bond with one another and create new life. This is one way our Creator sees to it that our world continues. Because of this, you have a responsibility to be aware of the powerful effect you have on others. Yes you! So when you choose clothing to wear out in public, you need to keep in mind the response, both physical and emotional, that you may stimulate in others. Then you have to decide if you are comfortable with that response, if that is the response you want to inspire. You must decide if what you are wearing is appropriate or not. I don't want you to hide or be ashamed of your body. I want you to be proud of it. It is your God-given gift and there is nothing in any way wrong or bad about you looking attractive. I want you to be happy with your body and respect it. I also want you to respect others. You need to decide if what you are wearing does that.*" (Sons need this little chat as well. Modesty is not simply a female issue. Always strive to overcome the double standard!)

Even for the teenager there will be gaps in development that will affect her ability to completely understand what you are suggesting. The college student would have a greater capacity for understanding, due to age, development, and experience, and would thus be held more fully responsible.

I would like to add a word of caution here. We need to be careful lest we imply that males and females do not have control over their bodies. In other words, provocative clothing or inappropriate dress is no excuse for inappropriate or immoral behavior on the part of the beholder! No one can blame his/her behavior on the way someone else is dressed. (Rape, for example.) Most of us have the power to control our actions and behaviors. Therefore, we should not imply to our sons or daughters that dress *alone* is capable of causing immoral actions on the part of another. This would be untrue. Responsibility lies within each of us for our behavior, regardless of the behavior of others. I am speaking here of behavior freely chosen.

This, like most other sexual issues, is a delicate area. If we are too conservative in the way we treat sexuality with our children, we run the risk of making them ashamed and embarrassed of their bodies. They may be afraid of their own sexuality or feel guilty over normal, healthy feelings of sexual arousal. If we are too liberal in our treatment of sexuality, if we set no boundaries or standards, then our children may treat sex in a casual and promiscuous manner. They may show a lack of respect for themselves or others. It's important that we strive for balance and employ common sense.

You might be wondering who says who develops when? Who sets up these developmental levels? Scientific knowledge, large studies conducted over long periods of time in various cultural settings, theological studies, reports from all types of professionals who work with children and young people, previous findings in the field of psychology and medicine, all of these have contributed to the formation of norms for developmental stages. These stages of development tell us what is normal, expected behavior as children grow and develop intellectual, physical, and emotional skills and abilities.

It is important that parents understand that all children are individuals. Not every child will go through every stage at the indicated time. But *all* children should go through *each stage* at some time, to some degree, to become physically and emotionally mature. Time variations are normal. Parents should not become concerned about this unless there seems serious reason to do so. You will find more specific information about the stages of psychosexual development in chapter 5.

## *Know What You're Talking About*

We live in a world where continual advances in technology, social science, medicine, and psychology give us constant and rapidly changing information. Sometimes the information does not change, but rather our ability to understand and interpret the information increases as discoveries are made and philosophies are developed more fully.

This is also true in the area of certain religious traditions and church teachings. We have access to more information than ever before. When the advances in the sciences and the uncovering of past civilizations by archaeologists using modern techniques combine with our most recent understanding of human behavior through medicine and psychology, we are brought to new understandings of what it means to live out our lives as spiritual beings.

Sometimes we are stretched. More often we are challenged by these new understandings. As new knowledge becomes evident we face many decisions in the area of ethics and practical application. Through these difficult times we rely on prayer and the assuredness of God's goodness. We trust that we will be guided by our Creator in our efforts toward a deeper understanding and appropriate application of such knowledge to our faith.

Because we live in a society where skills, information, and values become obsolete so quickly, we can no longer leave education for children alone. We parents must be learning too! It is very important that adults be continually educating themselves in the area of faith and morals, so that they may accurately pass new and correct learning on to their children. Most of us go to great lengths to see that our children receive the best education we can afford. Because of this our children often learn about new developments before we do!

Parents need to keep up. We have to realize that our children are not being taught the same things we were taught. Material is not presented to them in the same way it was presented to us. In short, they are growing up in a different world than we did, just as we grew up in a world strange to our parents, and were exposed to methods of education far different from those of our grandparents. Do you remember your parents ever commenting: "This world is going to the dogs!" "Things just aren't the same as they used to be!" "I don't know what this world is coming to!"?

As the saying goes, time marches on, and it's difficult for many to accept change. It is especially difficult in the areas of faith and morals. It would be much easier for us if things could stay the way they always were, but they don't. Change is not bad; it can even be good. One thing is for sure, it's sometimes difficult to adjust to.

Change means life and growth. When you consider how many changes you have witnessed in your lifetime, you cannot expect your church to continue using outdated methods and theories to teach your children. It might be easier to do so. Then we adults could just continue the faith we experienced as children. We wouldn't be challenged to grow into a more mature faith.

But we are no longer children, as St. Paul reminds us. We must make ongoing efforts to educate ourselves in our faith and try to understand reasons surrounding current church teachings. This takes time and effort. It means we have to read and, yes, study! Please don't misunderstand. You don't have to be an expert, but you should try to be in touch with what is current in the area of sexuality if you are to dialogue with your child effectively. If you wish to grow in your understanding of your faith you might consider such time well spent. You will have a hard time talking with your child about sexual morality if you are not up to date as to what constitutes sexual morality in your church.

Let me give you an example. When my mother dated as a young woman of eighteen, she was never allowed to go on dates alone. Her older brother had to ride in the back of the buggy! (Her brothers, however, did not have to be chaperoned unless the girl's parents provided for this! By the way, Mom's ninety-one now.) Mom tells of young men coming to her parents' home when she was in her twenties, and having to sit in the parlor or on the porch to talk, always with someone else present. This was considered proper behavior. A "good girl" wouldn't have it any other way! She never phoned a boy in her life, and certainly never paid for a date. Her swimsuit as a young woman included bloomers. Her ankles barely showed. In fact, showing her ankles as a teenager was considered quite provocative! (Very much like my dad's reaction to my two-piece suit, some fifty years later.)

When I began dating at age sixteen, I never once had to have my brother go along to chaperone. My first single date was at age seventeen. When a boyfriend came over to the house, we could go just about anywhere in the house and be left alone to talk or watch TV, except of course for my bedroom. That was off-limits! My dates always drove and paid for everything. The exception was when I asked a date to my prom, because it was an all-girls' school; he still drove, but I paid for the date. That was also one of the very few times I ever called a boy on the phone. "Good girls" didn't do that sort of thing; the boys would think you were "fast"!

I was not allowed to sit in a car with a boy in my driveway or on the street. We had to come in the house if we wanted to sit and talk. (What would the neighbors say if they saw us parking?) I was not permitted to wear red slacks. I could wear the same identical pair if they were black. It was the color that was the problem. My father felt that only prostitutes and loose women wore red slacks. Once, when I attempted to wear a pair of red slacks to a college picnic, I was sent back to my room to change. When I was almost twenty-two, I finally bought a two-piece swimsuit—not a bikini—for my honeymoon. My father *still* thought it was disgraceful attire for his daughter under any circumstance!

In the seventy-plus years since my mom was a teen many things have changed. My daughter "group dated" at age fourteen, and began "single dating" at age sixteen. She could go just about anywhere in the house to entertain. Once my daughter began to date, she often drove the boy and paid for the date. Many a night she sat out in the car, or in the yard, with her date talking for hours. It was not at all uncommon for her to call a boyfriend or take responsibility for making all the arrangements for a date.

Today, my daughter is twenty-seven, lives in her own home, wears a bikini, and looks great in it. She wears red slacks and even boxer shorts! "Good girls" today consider all of the above quite ordinary and very moral behavior.

The point is obvious—times do change. Could you imagine any family today having two kids in the same place at the same time so that one could chaperone the other? Could you imagine telling your daughter she had to be chaperoned, but not her brother? (I am aware that in some cultures this is sometimes still done, but from talking to many parents all over the country, I know it is becoming obsolete and very hard to enforce.) It would have been a disservice to my children had I tried to hold them to all my father's standards of what was morally correct and appropriate. My father and mother were influenced by their upbringing and the cultural and moral values of their time.

We view different things as socially and morally acceptable today. A bikini in mother's teen years would have been cause for arrest and definitely an issue for church discipline. Today, we tend to see morality arising more from who people are and how they lead their lives rather than from what they wear. Our emphasis is on *how* they behave with a date rather than on who accompanies them. This is not to say that there are no limits. There will always be limits; there *should* always be limits. But those limits will always be influenced by the society and culture in which people live. Societies and cultures change.

In decades past, Christian morality was largely negative in approach. Up until the last thirty years, morality focused on the "concupiscence of the flesh." For readers under forty who did not grow up with these words, let me explain that *concupiscence* means "lust." As I was growing up, we were frequently reminded that we were to avoid sexual thoughts, desires, and/or activities. These were viewed as temptations that might lead to "concupiscence." It seemed as though *it* (sexuality) was always there in the shadows, lurking, waiting to ensnare you. It's very hard to see sexuality as a *gift from God* under this interpretation.

Stemming from the fifth-century influence of St. Augustine, sexuality was seen as a *problem* to be solved. Intercourse was viewed as an act to be *redeemed* only by giving birth to children. Morality was measured in acts and by degrees from a checklist of sins. Most moral discussions centered mainly around *sexual* behavior. The life of the Christian centered around achieving perfection. Morality itself was rendered from a *legalistic* (law-centered) outlook. Sin and obedience were emphasized.

In recent years church attitudes toward morality have become more positive and pastoral. The emphasis has shifted from the act toward the person. We have grown in our understanding of what it means to be a Christian, of what comprises Christian behavior. Sexuality is now identified as being a good and special *gift* from God. Intercourse is recognized as being *equally* unitive and procreative and *not* in need of redemption. Morality is evaluated more in terms of intent and capability on the part of the person. It is also being viewed "holistically," that is, less in terms of individual, isolated acts and more in terms of the whole moral lifestyle of the person. That is not to say that individual acts are unimportant, rather that they are only one of several indicators of morality.

Finally, our understanding of morality has broadened to emphasize *all behavior*, not just the sexual. We are taught the life of the Christian centers around service, to loving and caring for our neighbor, to pursuing justice for all. Church judgment has become more *pastoral* (person-centered) in view. Today, forgiveness and personal responsibility and growth are emphasized.

In times past, the patriarchal church approved of wifebeating as long as the instrument used was no larger than the thumb; intercourse was seen as the wifely duty and could only take place, morally, in the "missionary" position. Pleasure, always suspect, was not even a consideration. Today, the church recognizes that indeed rape can take place within marriage, decries domestic violence, and tries to help and understand *all* persons involved in injustices. Men and women are seen as *equal partners* in marriage; giving and receiving pleasure has been recognized as legitimate, good, and even a potential source of grace.

Unfortunately, many Christians today still experience some confusion about what their church does teach. Some do not have an appreciation of the manner in which our understanding of certain teachings have been expanded, or of how, in some instances, the *focus* has changed, but not the teaching itself. Many fail to understand *why*, historically, a teaching existed in the first place.

This confusion has several causes, but I believe there are two major factors that have resulted in the biggest problems. The first one is that as the hierarchy's understanding of church teaching in relation to current knowledge of the human person began to unfold, there was not enough time and energy devoted to passing along these explanations to the laity. Many good practices (and Christians too!) got lost in the shuffle simply because the reasons for including or excluding these practices were not sufficiently explained to the laity.

The second reason for continuing confusion and lack of understanding, in my opinion, is quite simply that many people, when presented with opportunities for learning about their faith, choose to ignore the opportunities and do not participate in adult education. The attitude of many adult Christians is one of "I went to school already, I don't need to go again!" So any attempt for updating and educating adult Christians in their faith, any challenge offered to learn and grow as the churches learn and grow, is met with complacency and sometimes even contempt. No wonder the clergy and religious educators get discouraged!

Because faith is a mystery, pieces of the mystery are continually being uncovered as Christians live and contribute to their time and place in history. We do not have all the answers. We never will on this earth. We are on a journey of faith; we learn as we go. Faith requires that we trust past experiences and build on these with new learning. Morality will always be subject to its time and place in history. As people of faith, we are given the responsibility of knowing how our lives today fit into that historical perspective. It is within the context of this understanding we endeavor to invite, encourage, teach, and model morality for our children.

## Begin Early

As I mentioned in a previous chapter, parents should begin sex education as soon as their child asks the first question. So too, from an early age, we need to give children standards to live up to. We cannot wait until a child is sixteen and then begin to talk about morality. By that time, it's too late. We instill morality gradually; we develop conscience over time. So, it is best to begin early discussing values such as respect, trust, modesty, and honesty with your children.

We do not, for example, take candy or gum from the store; we do not take money from our brother's bank; we do not walk around outside our home naked; we do not keep a friend's toy; we do not copy from others in school; we do not lie to our teachers, and so on. At an early age we may need to insist that the candy or money be returned. We may need to accompany our child to return a toy or face a teacher.

When a child is young, s/he should be taught to use the correct names for all parts of the body. Using correct names from the very start encourages respect for and acceptance of the body and, therefore, themselves. Nicknames often demean and lessen respect. If a child can say "elbow" s/he can say "vulva" or "penis." When these words are presented as normal and natural, the child responds accordingly.

When nicknames are given only for the sexual parts of the body, we can give the message that it's OK to joke about these. We send signals that there is something "different" about these parts, perhaps something to be embarrassed about, perhaps parts of our body of which we should be ashamed. We do not send these messages consciously. Seemingly insignificant messages, repeated in various forms over time, are in reality responsible for the ways we and our society as a whole view women, men, the body, the sex act, and sexuality itself.

Parents need to take care not to tell jokes, use slang, or make comments that demean sexuality or relegate it to an act alone. Likewise, jokes that demean women, men, gay people, races, or ethnic cultures are inappropriate and contribute to negative attitudes toward the sexes and sexuality itself.

"What does she know? She's just a broad." "Now there's a hunk I'd like to sample!" "Who cares if she can't cook, look at those jugs!" "Take a look at his bod, I bet he's a good lay!" "My, my, I'll bet he's sweet!" "I've heard black men have more staying power!" Comments like these treat people as objects and show disrespect for them. When our children repeatedly hear us talk like this or when we allow them to continually talk like this, we are contributing to and helping form negative attitudes about sexuality. We are modeling a lack of respect for others.

Over time, *attitudes are internalized,* accepted as fact. If these are never thought through or reexamined, they can be responsible for disrespectful, unfair, stereotypical treatment of the same and opposite sex, and for a significant lack of understanding of the beauty and wonder that sex and sexuality can bring to a relationship. Such attitudes can keep a relationship tied to the bounds of the physical, never recognizing opportunities for growth into truly intimate relationships that include emotional and spiritual dimensions. If you've never been exposed to or experienced these dimensions, you don't know they are possible. You don't know how to attain them.

Please understand, I'm not suggesting that your household become the land of "Mary Poppins"! Reality prevents our attaining perfection. Balance is what I am asking for here. Occasional jokes or comments may be unavoidable and can be treated good naturedly without lectures. What I am concerned about is an *atmosphere* where continual lack of respect and negative attitudes are fostered and allowed to exist unchallenged.

Another issue that demands we talk to our children at a young age is early maturation. As you may know, the average age for young girls to begin menstruation is now age twelve; some begin before this, some later. The average age in the fifties was sixteen. The point is our young girls are maturing earlier than ever before. We should not put off discussions about sexuality, thinking our child is not ready for that yet. Better too soon than too late!

You will not harm your children by giving them too much information. They will simply do what they always do when they are not interested in, or ready for, what you are saying: tune you out! However, if your talks with them have been ongoing, when such information becomes of more interest to them, they will feel comfortable approaching you with questions.

It is typical for parents to underestimate their child's need for information. Educators tell us a five-year gap exists between when children *actually need* information and the age at which parents *think* their children need information. Remember this is not the world in which you grew up. You cannot apply communication practices of the past with today's children. Ample information is readily available to them in today's world; they are bombarded with it. That's why it is important that parents talk with their children and present the Christian viewpoint before the child has internalized the ways of the secular world.

The Woman's Division of the American Medical Association conducted a study several years ago that found that the fifth grade is the ideal time to work with children in school in regard to personal-choice issues such as smoking, drug abuse, and use of alcohol, as well as personal responsibility for lifestyle decisions and choices. This was found to be the optimum time to address lifestyle issues. This is why the antismoking and drug abuse campaigns begin in first grade. By the time children are in fifth grade they have the necessary information with which to make decisions about smoking and drugs.

Professionals recommend that one of the best and most important qualities of a good parent is consistency in approach to discipline. This should begin in early childhood. Parenting styles work best when both parents agree on the approach to be used. Discuss how you will handle a particular situation together in private, then present a united front to your child.

As you strive together to set standards of morality within your home, you may need to reprimand, to set boundaries. These boundaries should be age-appropriate. Boundaries should not be carved in stone. They should change and become more flexible as your children age.

Likewise, as children grow older, parents should invite morality by allowing the child's input in establishing the boundaries. For example, when your child is ten you may set the time s/he has to be home in the evenings. As your child grows older and begins dating, you may wish to sit down together and discuss curfew time, arriving at a mutually agreeable time together. Let's say that as your high school teen begins dating, you may feel 11:00 or 12:00 P.M. is a reasonable curfew. However, by the time your teen is a junior or senior, insisting s/he be home by 12:00 P.M. may be unreasonable due to distance, providing others with rides, interference from the later curfew of others, or times of dances. There may be times when cleaning up after a dance, crowds at a restaurant, involvement in a group game, or giving a stranded friend a ride home inhibit a teen from following his/her set curfew. An effective parent allows the older teen, who knows the particulars, to set the time. If this privilege is abused, renegotiation is necessary.

Young people must learn to understand that privilege carries responsibility. A phone call when a late arrival is anticipated should be insisted upon. However, punishment when a teen is fifteen or twenty minutes late is not advisable. Teens need to feel their judgment is respected and honored. When you respect your teen and accept their explanation you instill in them confidence and trust. This usually encourages them to try even harder to respect and abide by your rules.

In other words, we need to give our children the opportunity to grow in self-control, rather than imposing control from without. So begin early, be consistent, make sure your limits are age-appropriate, be reasonable and flexible, and allow for input from your children.

## Model Desired Behavior

Several years ago, my family and I went out for a stir-fry dinner, a family favorite. At the end of our meal we were all served our fortune cookie. It's a tradition of ours always to read these aloud and comment as to whether we believe the right person received the right fortune. I opened my cookie and discovered a beautiful Chinese proverb that read, "Children have more need of models than of critics." I took the paper home and taped it on my desk in my office; it's still there. To me it is a reminder of the very essence of parenting.

When I was growing up, the youngest of six, my father had a favorite saying that he chanted whenever one of us kids caught him doing something he had specifically told us not to do. It went: "Don't do as I do, do as I say do!" I love my dad dearly. He's eighty-six now, and sometimes he still says this to his great-grandchildren. However, I hate that phrase! True enough, Dad often used it in jest, but it's a cop-out. In reality it means, "I can do whatever I want, but you must do what I tell you to do." In other words, this behavior I want from you is not really that important or significant, because I don't even do it myself.

This is not a phrase I use with my children. Most of us have spent tons of money educating our children, and it's a credit to them that they are wise to this faulty thinking. We must *be* what we want them to become. There is no other way, no easy way, no short cut.

Once a mother came to me distraught over her daughter's promiscuous behavior. She was worried because her daughter was developing physically at a young age, and was attracting the attention of older boys. She wanted me to talk to her and encourage her to slow down. The girl was in eighth grade at the time.

A few days later I made it a point to ask the daughter to stay after school and help me. This gave us an opportunity to talk casually. I brought up the subject of her early development and asked her if she was comfortable with her body, did she know how to handle attention from older boys, and what some of the dangers of early involvement were. As we continued talking, it became clear that the mother, recently divorced, spent little time at home. Some nights, the daughter related, her mom's current boyfriend spent the night. She knew this because she got up to go to the bathroom and realized that he was sleeping there, even though by the time she rose for school, he was gone. She said her mom was having a tough time with the divorce and sometimes came home drunk. She was confused by the contradiction of her mom's lectures to her and her mom's behavior. She felt that her mom was a good woman, and she was obviously involved with men. Why then was her mom so uptight about her involvement with boys?

I contacted the mother and told her of my conversation with her daughter. The mother's response indicated to me that there was little I could do to help the girl. "Well, what am I supposed to do," she responded, "quit living till my daughter is out of high school? It's not fair for her to compare herself with me!"

If parents are unwilling or unable to admit and address their own dysfunctional behaviors, the children will not address theirs either. Counselors, schools, and friends alone cannot fix what is broken in the adolescent child. There needs to be a network of support coming from the home. The child needs to *see* appropriate behavior modeled. Parents must live out what they say they believe. Inviting morality will only work when the parents themselves have accepted the invitation.

## Give Your Child Some Space

Kids need space. We have to be on guard that we do not smother our child's attempt to become independent. After all, the main goal of parenting is to raise children so that they become spiritual, moral, and independent thinkers who will follow their conscience and not the crowd. We should not be the ones making their decisions the rest of their lives.

Yet so often I see parents who want to be involved in every decision their child makes. Others never let their child have any experience at making decisions; those parents make all their decisions for them. I think this is often because the parents are afraid their child will make an immoral or unwise choice. Refusing to allow them to choose is not going to help. Our children need to be free to make mistakes while there is still a safety net of love around them. They will experiment and try out behaviors. This is part of growing up.

This is especially true in the teen and young-adult years. I speak of inviting morality; it was a lesson I, too, had to learn. One lesson was taught me by my youngest son. Once when he was nineteen, attending college, and still living at home, he helped me learn an important lesson in giving space.

My husband and I had spent the night in a nearby town with friends one Saturday. On returning home late Sunday morning, I found him sound asleep. Assuming he had missed Sunday Mass, I became irritated with him before he ever opened his eyes. By the time he finally got up and meandered into the kitchen, I was on my way to angry. "Hey Mom, what's up? Did you have a good time yesterday?" "Yes," I replied rather curtly. "You must have had a good time last night too. Slept in did you?" "Yea, I was dead," he replied. "I'm out of here now, I've got a soccer game at 1:30. Love ya!" I could not hold back any longer, "What about church, or have you forgotten it's Sunday?"

Grinning from ear to ear, he shook his head and rolled his eyes as he strolled back into the kitchen. He gently put his arm around my shoulder and squeezed me, "Patty, Patty, Patty. It's so hard to let go of the kids, isn't it?" he chided. "I thought you said it was up to me to practice my faith, and that my relationship with God was on *my* shoulders now." "You're right, I did say that," I replied, somewhat embarrassed. "Still, I know you slept in this morning, and now you've got enough energy for a soccer game, so. . . ."

"Mom, you're doing it again, it's supposed to be my responsibility, remember?" Then he kissed my forehead as only a 5'10", seemingly seven-foot-tall, son can do to his mother; he waved as he again walked out of the kitchen. He called from the front door, "Hey Mom, chill out! Steve's picking me up at 4:30 this afternoon for 5:00 Mass at St. Monica's." He then winked as his head appeared around the corner one more time, "Had you worried, didn't I, oh ye of little faith!"

He *had* thought about his responsibility to God; he had made plans to carry that out. I did not give him the credit he deserved. I crowded his space and I should not have. I was not honoring an agreement we made. I was trying to dictate. I was wrong. Even if he had *not gone* to church that day the decision was *his* to make, not mine.

Jeff was right, it *is* hard to let go. He was nineteen and capable of weighing the consequences of his decision. We worry that our kids won't do the *right* things, the things *we* want them to do. We try to control their behavior to fit *our* own standards.

But I would never have experienced the joy I did had I insisted he go to church because *I* thought it was right for him. No, the warm glow I felt inside and the quick "Thank you, Lord!" I whispered were because my son had accepted an invitation on his own. He was going to church because *he* thought it was important!

In examining stress in families, researchers John Conger and Ann Peterson drew the following conclusion after working with many families:

> Adolescents need rules and norms as guidelines; but, they cannot be expected to mature into responsible adults if they never have the opportunities to express their opinions, to think through the possible consequences of their actions, and they must have the safety of being able to question authority without fear of reprisals and punishment.[28]

I couldn't agree more. I believe that's the way Jesus wants it too. That's the behavior he modeled for us. Remember the story in the Bible where the young man comes to Jesus and asks what he should do to be saved? Jesus responds with several examples and the young man indicates that he has done most of these. When Jesus challenges him further, the young man declines.

But Jesus doesn't berate or shame the young man. He accepts his decision. Jesus did not *insist* that the young man give away all he had and come with him. Instead, he *invited* the young man and then allowed the young man to make his own decision. Another point worth noting is that Jesus accepted the young man unconditionally and didn't withhold his love when the young man didn't choose what he was offered.

Even though it may be difficult, we need give our adult children the freedom to make their own decisions based on their understanding of the issues. Our part in this process is to give them *all* the information at our disposal. It is wrong to hide information from our children just because we are afraid certain information might lead them to make a choice we disapprove of.

We must trust in truth. We can offer alternative suggestions. We can listen as they struggle with their choices. We can challenge them to take the high road. But ultimately, we need to respect their right to make their own decisions and we must, to follow the manner of Christ, love them regardless of their choices.

## Inviting Morality

- Accept the challenge
- Present sexuality as good
- Invite morality—don't dictate it
- Take a developmental approach
- Keep current; know what's going on
- Begin early
- Model desired behavior
- Give your child space
- Love your child unconditionally

# Chapter 7

. . . . . . . . . .

~

# Loving Your
# Gay or Lesbian Child

"If a man does not keep pace with his companions, perhaps it is
because he hears a different drummer. Let him step to the music
which he hears, however measured or far away."

*Henry David Thoreau*

### Befriending a Gay or Lesbian Child

I wonder when Thoreau wrote these words if he had any idea how
often, and in how many varied contexts, his words would be quoted.
As I put together my thoughts for this chapter, these were the words
that kept coming back to me, over and over again. They simply felt like
the right words with which to begin.

Let's be honest. One family in four has a homosexual member. Life
as a gay man or lesbian woman in our American society today is filled
with pain and hardship. We do not live in a society where homosexuality
is accepted as normal development. Because of this, the gay or lesbian
person is often ridiculed with open hatred, treated with disgust, despised
and feared by many, often forced to live in isolation, deceit, and secrecy,
and as a consequence may lead a very lonely existence.

I do not think this type of life is what any parent would choose for
their child. How then does one prepare a homosexual child to survive,
let alone be happy, in such an environment? That is what I propose to
discuss in this chapter.

My first conscious encounter with a gay teen came about twenty years
ago when I was teaching a high school religion course for my parish

youth program. My husband and I had junior and senior students. Our focus was marriage.

We held weekly meetings in our home and had about sixteen teenagers in regular attendance. We had been meeting with our group for about five months when one night after the meeting, one of the boys asked if he could stick around and talk to me alone. I said this would be fine. It was not unusual for this to happen. From time to time a teen was faced with something s/he did not want the rest of the group to know about. Still I had no idea how that evening would impact the rest of my life.

The young man—"Ben" we will call him—was a cool guy. He was seventeen, good-looking in a *GQ* sort of way, and intelligent. He was active in school and in every club and group you could name—an officer or leader in most. Ben was articulate, dynamic, a real "go-getter." He dated a lot, always managing to find attractive and energetic girls. Ben was an active Catholic. His faith meant a lot to him and he was not afraid to let others know that.

A very open young man, every week he would come bouncing in, and everyone would quiz him on what he had done in the past week—whom he had dated, what new project he was involved in at school, and so forth. The boys wished they knew how to get the girls as interested in them as they were in Ben! The girls took every opportunity to talk with him and sit next to him in hopes that he might ask them out. In short, nothing I knew about him had prepared me for what Ben had to say to me that night.

After everyone was gone, he and I sat down in the privacy of my living room to talk.

"I don't know how to begin, Mrs. Miller," he said in a shaky voice, one I had never heard before. I told him to relax and get comfortable. "Just start anywhere," I remember saying. "Well, I'm really scared. I'm *really* scared. Something's wrong. I'm so mixed up. I just had to talk to someone, and my parents wouldn't be of help right now." He stopped and began to softly cry. With tears quietly running down his cheeks, he whispered, "I thought you'd understand, you'd know what I should do."

Ben then told me he was worried about his sexual orientation. It seems he and one of his closest friends, a friend he had double-dated with many times, had an uncomfortable situation arise in the last few weeks. His friend, Sam, had lost his father suddenly to a heart attack. Naturally, the young man was in the state of shock. Ben tried to help and give support. He had gone to his friend's house as soon as he heard the news and had tried to comfort his friend.

Ben was an affectionate person. It was typical of him to hug me and everyone else in the group each week when he arrived and left. It happened that he was sitting with his arm around his friend, talking, when he suddenly realized that his feelings for his friend were unlike those he had felt for any of the girls he had dated. He withdrew his arm, suddenly embarrassed and scared.

His friend picked up on his sudden change in attitude, and as Ben explained what he was feeling, his friend admitted that he, too, had felt there was something "different" about their friendship than anything he had experienced with others. So, they talked about the situation. Being mature and sensible, they both realized that their emotions were on edge due to the death of Sam's father. They decided it would be best if they did not see each other for a couple of days, then meet again and talk.

They did just that, but when they finally got together the next week, they found they were not able to keep their friendship as it had been before. Something had definitely changed. A realization had taken place, one that scared and confused them both. They were too frightened and ashamed to go to their parents. "They'll be so disappointed in me," Ben had sobbed. The young man had decided to ask my advice and take it from there.

Me! Not yet out of my twenties, I had no experience or training for this kind of situation. What was I going to say to him? I kept looking at his face, his eyes filled with pain and fear. He wanted to be a "normal" guy; he wanted everyone to like him. He wanted his parents to be proud of him and they were, at least until now. Now, he stood to lose everything he had worked so hard for. He was a model child, a model student, and a model boyfriend. How could he possibly be gay? That is what he wanted me to tell him.

"How could this happen to me? I don't want to be a homo! Everyone will hate me! Oh, my God, what will my parents do? You can't tell them, Mrs. Miller. You must promise me you won't tell them! You wouldn't do that to me would you?"

All I could see and hear was his pain. He was so confused. He was terrified. This was not the way his life was supposed to go. He had made so many plans. What would he tell his girlfriend? How could he get through school if he confided in her and she told someone? His reputation as one of the most popular and respected boys in school would be shot. His life would not be worth living.

He sobbed; he was shaking all over. I put my arm around him and held him. As he cried, I prayed that God would give me the right words to say. I knew nothing about homosexuality. I suddenly realized I knew so little about life! Here was this young boy in so much pain, more pain than I had ever known. What was I to do for him? How could I help?

To be honest, this was not the way I had pictured gays. I thought they would be weird, you know, strange. I had thought, "If I ever meet a homosexual, I'll know it right away for sure!" Yet, here in my arms was this hurting young man, almost a child. He was a young man I admired and respected. I'd often thought to myself that I hoped my sons would be like him. Here he was, shattered and shaken in my arms, and he was telling me he was gay *and* that he didn't *want* to be gay.

How could this be? Why can't he just *not* be gay? Why can't he go back to dating girls the way he used to, and just forget about this incident? Why did he keep saying, he *didn't want* to feel this way? Could he not just stop it? He didn't have to see Sam anymore, did he? Probably when he went to college he would forget all about this mess.

Together Ben and I worked out a plan of action. At the beginning, we talked about the fact that having a good friend of the same sex did not mean either was gay. Even having one or two homosexual encounters does not indicate a person is gay. He said he understood all of that, but still felt this situation was different than "friendship." "It just doesn't feel like anything else I've experienced before," he said.

After suggesting he give it some time, and keep some distance from Sam so he could think clearly, we decided a visit to a counselor might give us a place to start. I assured him that I would do nothing without his consent and would wait awhile before talking to his parents. He felt that when he spoke to his folks he wanted to have some answers for them, a way to talk about things.

Next, I put him in touch with a good psychiatrist I had been told about and he arranged for a visit. What a disaster! The doctor, apparently quite homophobic, did little more than add to Ben's list of problems by telling him he would end up hustling on the street! Just the understanding Ben needed.

Fortunately, by now, Ben and I were a team. Together we survived that setback. We were going to keep at it until we had some answers and some plan for the future. In the meantime I heard about a psychologist who worked with clergy and religious sisters in our area and decided to give him a try. You can well imagine what I went through trying to convince Ben to give it "just one more chance." He was still scared and hurting. He dreaded telling his story again and again. Finally, he agreed to give the new doctor a try.

This doctor did not condemn Ben to life on the street. He listened to his story and asked thoughtful questions. He gave Ben some ideas and literature to think over and they made another appointment. Ben was working and paying for these visits on his own. He still was not ready to talk to his parents. I encouraged him repeatedly to do so. From what he had told me I really felt they would stand by him. But he wanted to wait, so we did. Since he was eighteen now, and legally an adult, I felt I had to respect his decision.

With the doctor's help, Ben was able gradually to calm himself, and while he was still uncertain and afraid, he felt more able to deal with his situation. In the meantime, he graduated from high school and went away to college. After he had been away about four months, his mother called me and asked if she could come by and talk to me. Again I prayed for guidance. I called Ben and asked him how he wanted me to handle this. He said it was OK. He felt it was time to talk with his parents and explain what was going on. I was so glad. I really felt this was the best thing. Although I know many parents are unable to deal with their children's problems, I really felt Ben's parents would stick with him.

His parents came to see me several days later. As I suspected, they knew their son was troubled, but didn't know what the problem was. "He won't tell us what's bothering him, but I know something's wrong," his mom said.

Praying once more for the right words, I told Ben's parents that he felt he might be gay. Their immediate reaction was one of concern for their son, followed by questions of how they could best help him. They wondered if somehow they were responsible for their son's homosexuality, if somehow they had "caused" it. There was no condemnation or rejection of their son, only sadness and feelings of helplessness that their son was hurting so much. They were afraid for their son, for how others would treat him. Would he get beaten up? Rejected by family and friends? Lose his apartment? Would anyone hire him if they found out he was gay? Ben was a lucky young man! I have since seen parents disown their child upon hearing such news.

We talked for a long time that night; we all cried; we even laughed a little. By the time we parted, I knew that no matter what the future held for Ben, his parents would always be there to support him. We discussed causes from the perspective of what was known at that time. We talked about Ben's childhood. We talked about his relationship with his father, his mother, and siblings. I told his parents what we had done so far, and why. They understood his reluctance to tell them. Still, they were hurt to think he doubted their love and support. They were re-lieved that he had found someone to talk to and thanked me for "being there" for him. They were confused and uncertain about what they could do for their son.

Most of all they were proud of him. They were proud that he had sought help, proud that he had taken on the responsibility of paying for the doctor. They wanted to do whatever they could to help him. We parted with many hugs and some tears.

Later that night Ben called his parents and told them he would be coming home that weekend from school so they could talk. My role was now to take a back seat and let the parents and their son work things through. It has been many years, but I will never forget the many lessons I learned throughout that experience.

I still see Ben from time to time. He is now a medical doctor with a good practice, well respected and well liked by his patients. He eventually worked through his questions and tensions. He tried many different roles before he finally concluded that he was, indeed, a homosexual man. For a long time he denied it. He continued dating girls and tried to make these relationships turn into the experiences they are for heterosexual men. It did not work.

For a period, he became involved with drugs and alcohol. He couldn't stand the thought of never being a father, never having a family. He saw what his friends did to gays at college who "came out." He heard the constant jokes and ridicule, and he didn't think he could take it. He even considered suicide. Through all this time he kept going to church. He kept talking with his parents. He kept trying to make some sense of it. But it didn't make sense.

"Everyone thinks they have it all figured out," he once told me. "They think if you are blond-haired, blue-eyed, and thin, you are gay, and if you've got dark hair, dark eyes, and are solidly built, you are straight for sure. It's just not that way at all. I get so sick of listening to these people who think they know everything. Oh, Pat, why did this happen to me? Why am I like this? Why am I gay?"

I was so naive! But I did have two redeeming qualities—I gave good hugs, and I knew how to listen. I guess that's why he came to me, or so he thought. The reality was that I needed to hear his story. I needed to be challenged to grow. At that time, I was a volunteer religion teacher, and a young wife and mother. I had taught third and fourth grades previously. I had no idea I was going to end up a sexuality educator; I would have laughed had you even suggested it.

But God does have His/Her way with us. I know now that Ben came to me that night so I could write this chapter today. Because Ben changed my life for the better. By watching Ben over the next few years,

I learned about courage. I learned about faith. I learned about love. Ben gave me the courage to share with you what I have learned.

My experience with Ben was just the beginning. I have since met and come to know many gay men and women, most of them Christians, all of them wonderful people. Ben inspired and challenged me! I was determined to learn all I could about homosexuality. It has been a long and sometimes difficult journey. There is so much we don't know about how people become gay or straight. There are several theories, but no one definitive answer—not yet at any rate. Hopefully, research will continue in this area and someday soon we will have a better understanding of how it is we come to be heterosexual and homosexual people.

We still don't have the answer to Ben's question as to why he is gay. After a time, Ben quit asking. Instead, he decided his life *was* worth living, and he was going to face and accept his homosexuality. He went to medical school and focused all his energy on his studies. He graduated with honors and has done very well for himself. There are few who know he is gay. Gay doctors, he says, don't get patients, at least not those doctors who are known to be gay.

To be sure, there are many gay men and lesbian women in the medical field, and in most other careers, who have not made themselves known for fear it will ruin their career. They have worked hard and some have spent thousands of dollars to become respected professionals. Some have married and raised children, just so others will not guess they are homosexual. Most are respected in their field and in their communities. The respect they received as individuals in their work and in their community would be destroyed if people knew they were homosexual. In all probability most would lose their jobs and their homes; many families would suffer unbearably—as if being known as gay or lesbian had somehow changed their personality and professional capabilities.

None of us knows what goes on in the homes of our neighbors. We judge most people by their public lives. We have no idea how they live their private lives. And yet, we will not tolerate "public performance" alone when we judge homosexual people. We are *certain* they are *all* sexually active, *all* practicing *deviant* sexual acts, *all* encroaching upon "decent" people's territory. We tell them they have no business being teachers, doctors, or health care workers. We tell them they have no business sharing housing. We do not want them in our government, in our churches, or in our schools. They suffer incredibly at the hands of many so-called Christians.

Why am I telling you all this? Because you must know it, and believe it, if you are to stand beside and support gay and lesbian children. You certainly won't need to know it in order to love. You will love because s/he is lovable, because s/he is your child. But you will only be able to stand beside and offer support if you know what will be encountered in our uneducated and prejudiced society.

People decry racial prejudice, and rightly so. However, many of these same people refuse to hire someone who does not fit their criteria of a "real" man or woman. Many decry the thousands of Jews killed in the Holocaust. Many of these same people say AIDS is God's way of punishing the gay community (by the way, AIDS is currently over sixty percent heterosexual in the worldwide population). I'm always eager to ask, "Do you think syphilis is God's punishment on the *straight* community for having sex?" After all, before penicillin, syphilis resulted in death too.

You will need a lot of strength and courage to be a good mother or father to your gay son or lesbian daughter. Your heart will be torn in two as you listen while others thoughtlessly make a game out of gay/lesbian bashing. You will cry inside every time someone remarks: "Well, isn't he *sweet!*" or "Now she's a *dyke* if I ever saw one!" Many a night you will be silent while others laugh about their gay waiter or refuse to go to a restaurant because it's "usually full of gays." You will want to cry aloud when someone wiggles their hips and remarks, "Oh, you know I'm not that way."

You will be worried about physical harm to your child as s/he enters the homosexual community, worried because you know that some gay and lesbian people engage in sexual activities that are demeaning, disrespectful, and harmful. (It should be noted that such activity is not limited to the homosexual population. There is plenty of evidence of deviant activity among heterosexuals as well.) You will worry that your gay or lesbian child will not be able to maintain celibacy. You will worry about AIDS, as do the parents of heterosexual children. You will worry about state amendments that leave your son or daughter unprotected from discrimination in the job and housing markets as well as other areas.

One way for a Christian to get through all this is prayer. Prayer will help ease your pain and sorrow as you grieve for the suffering your child has to go through. Prayer will help you to be strong when you meet your child's "new friend," and wonder what the relationship will be like. Prayer will give you the strength to seek out education and support in this area. Prayer will model to your son or daughter the trust and hope that comes with belief in God.

I do not mean to paint a dismal picture. I do mean to be realistic and to prepare you for what you may encounter. On the other hand you may well be one of the more fortunate ones whose child finds him/herself supported by generous and caring friends. S/he may be fortunate to find clergy who minister with compassion to the gay and lesbian community. Your child may find work in a place where an atmosphere of support and acceptance facilitates a productive and successful career, where people are judged by their work and not by their sexual orientation.

At this point there is no way of telling what lies ahead for you or your child. You can only proceed together with hope and love. As you do, here are some points of information about homosexuality that may in some way help or at least facilitate your understanding:

## Facts about Homosexuality

People have many intense and varied *feelings* about homosexuality. Listed below are some of the *facts* that have been determined by scientific biological research and studies conducted in the behavioral sciences. Some of these are presented by various authors in the book, *A Challenge to Love.*[1]

- People do not choose to be homosexual. They discover that they are.
- Approximately thirteen percent of males are homosexual. Approximately seven percent of females are lesbian.
- There is no evidence that homosexual teachers attempt to seduce their students any more than do heterosexual teachers.
- Not all homosexuals are sexually active.
- In 1973 the American Psychological Association removed homosexuality from its list of mental and emotional disorders.
- In the original language of the Bible the terms *homosexual* and *homosexuality* are never used. Those terms did not exist until 1890; neither did the term *heterosexual.*
- Suicide rates among homosexuals are three times that of the heterosexual population.
- Many homosexuals live in committed, monogamous relationships.
- Homosexual persons have made many important and significant contributions to our society and world.
- Homosexuals look like everyone else. You cannot tell if someone is heterosexual or homosexual by looking at them.
- According to a 1986 survey conducted in Seattle, Washington, forty percent of homeless youth identified themselves as gay, lesbian, or bisexual.

- Half of the lesbian and gay youth report that their parents reject them due to their sexual orientation.[2]
- A common misconception is that gay and lesbian persons are child-molesters. In reality, ninety-five percent of all child sexual abuse is committed by heterosexual men.[3]
- Homosexual adolescents are two to three times more likely to attempt suicide than male heterosexual adolescents. Up to thirty percent of youth suicides each year are committed by lesbian and gay youth.[4]
- A 1989 military study concluded that gay men and lesbian women demonstrated "preservice suitability-related adjustment that is as good as or better than the average heterosexual."[5]
- The military dismisses approximately 1,500 members each year because they are homosexual.[6]
- A Gallup survey of a cross section of the American population of adults aged eighteen and over showed that fifty-seven percent of those interviewed felt homosexuals should be allowed to serve in the military.[7]
- In 1992, Colorado voters approved a constitutional amendment prohibiting civil rights protection on the basis of sexual orientation. This measure invalidates the laws in several Colorado cities that did extend equal rights to lesbian and gay citizens. Currently thirteen other states are considering passing this law.[8]
- Lesbians and gay men are the most frequent victims of hate crimes and are at least seven times more likely to be crime victims than heterosexual people.[9]

### How can I tell if my child is gay?

At this time, we are unable to trace the cause of homosexuality to any one identifiable source. Current evidence strongly suggests that during development in the womb, at a critical period, there is set in place a predisposition to be homosexual or heterosexual. After the child is born but by the age of two, environmental factors combine with this predisposition to determine the child's sexual orientation. Parents will not know for *certain* they have a gay or lesbian child until s/he *tells* them so.

Many people mistakenly equate "being effeminate" in males with "being gay." This is simply not the case. There are actually *few* gay men who fit the "effeminate" category. It is only because this behavior is so easily observable that many assume every man presenting himself in this manner must be gay. The same is true of excessive masculine behavior in females. This is not evidence that such a woman is lesbian. These are stereotyped behaviors. While they are behaviors manifested by a *few* gay and lesbian people, they do not represent *all* the thousands of gay men and women in our country. It is also true that there are heterosexual men and women who exhibit this exact same behavior. As a matter of fact, most gay men and women who do not wish their homosexuality to be discovered carefully avoid any such behaviors or actions that would identify them as being homosexual.

You definitely will not be able to tell orientation by looking at your child. Homosexual people come in all shapes and sizes, races and cultures, and cross all socioeconomic boundaries. While you may question some of your child's behavior as being "atypical" for a boy or a girl, you will not *know* his/her orientation until s/he shares it with you.

Certainly, the years prior to adolescence provide few definite indicators of one's sexual orientation.

It is usually during the adolescent years that boys and girls may begin to question their sexual orientation. Many gay men and lesbians say that by the time they were in junior high school they felt they were somehow "different." Some maintain they always felt they were "trapped" in someone else's body. Still others say it was not till their late high school years that they began to suspect they might be gay or lesbian. A few have not discovered their homosexuality until midlife.

The point is that during some period in one's psychosexual development a person *discovers* s/he is lesbian or gay. They do not choose to be homosexual; they just find out they are. For most people this discovery leads to confusion and trauma. The best approach parents can take is to keep the lines of communication open between themselves and their children. Assure children by word and attitude that they are always free to discuss any situation that may concern them.

Let it be known that all of your children are important to you and that you would never abandon or disown any of them for any reason. You can speak up when others tell "homo" jokes or *any* jokes that ridicule others. Let your child know you do not approve of prejudice or bigotry in any form. This openness on your part may give them the confidence and trust in you, which will enable them to talk with you about feelings that make them feel uneasy or uncertain.

There are many parents who never suspect their child is gay or lesbian, and are shocked upon learning so. Other parents report that although they did not suspect their child was homosexual, they were conscious that something seemed to be wrong with, or troubling, their child. For some parents, having their child tell them that s/he is homosexual is simply confirmation of what was suspected for some time. Some parents have more than one homosexual child.

The point is that there is no pattern. Each person, each situation is different. The following behaviors are reported by some parents of gay and lesbian children as being the ones that concerned them and/or drew attention to the question of their child's sexual orientation.[10] I offer them for your consideration:

• During the teen years it is normal for young males to show some interest in pornographic magazines. It is also typical for them to hide them from parents, especially mom, for fear of disapproval. *Some* homosexual teens *may* show an unusual interest in same-sex pornography or so-called "muscle" magazines.

• There is cause for concern on the part of any parent if their teen begins to withdraw from activities, avoid school functions, and/or isolate him/herself from friends. Sometimes parents notice a change of friends or a change in groups of friends on the part of their child for no apparent reason or explanation from their child. Often this change is out of necessity; it is forced, not desired. For example, one mother, when discussing past situations with her now known lesbian child, reported this incident. Her daughter played soccer with the same group of girls for years. They were friends on and off the field. It seems that while she was in her latter years of high school, the coach called her in one day and told her it would be best if she quit the team. When she asked why, the coach replied that some of the girls no longer wanted to shower with her, since they heard she was lesbian. Her daughter, forced to quit a team and a sport she loved, had to seek out a new group of friends. She remained silent about the cause for dropping from the team and about the new friendships rather than tell her parents the real reason for the change. They did not learn until years later the real story behind the situation.

• Parents should monitor *unusually* close relationships between their son/daughter and an adult of the same sex. However, it is important to remember that it is a normal part of development for teens to have close friends of the same sex. It is also normal for them to have crushes on adult members of the same sex. Parents should be very careful not to confuse this normal stage of development with a homosexual orientation. Overreaction on your part will do a great deal of harm. One good indicator of a healthy relationship might be the openness with which your child discusses and engages in this relationship. If your child is unduly secretive and hesitates to tell you where s/he is going or with whom, you may wish to talk with him/her about this. Please do not assume the relationship is a homosexual one.

• Gay and lesbian children often "come out," that is, identify themselves as being homosexual, to friends and schoolmates long before they tell their parents. This is frequently due to fear of being rejected or abandoned by the parent. Referring back to the normal stages of development as discussed in chapter 5, we recall that determining one's sexual identity is an important task for the adolescent. A healthy approach to one's sexuality is to ask questions about sexual orientation, sexual behaviors, and other sexual issues.

Most boys and girls go through a period when they will question their sexual identity and wonder if they are heterosexual or homosexual. It is good for them to do so because if they are courageous enough to ask the question of themselves, they will be able to work through the answer and put the matter to rest. This will enable them to approach their own sexual orientation with comfort, confidence, and satisfaction. This can also enhance their ability to enjoy a mature, healthy, sexual relationship. Secure in their own sexuality, they will feel no need to ridicule, scorn, or feel threatened by the orientation of others.

Those adolescents who ignore the question, or avoid thinking about the answer, may remain uneasy and uncertain about their sexuality the rest of their lives. This is evidenced by the fact that in our American society so many people are "homophobic." That is, they have an unnecessary and unnatural fear of, or prejudice against, homosexual persons.

Research has been able to identify people who are most likely to be homophobic. Findings show that these people tend to be rigid in thinking, more authoritarian, intolerant of uncertainties, and status conscious. Their attitudes are more dogmatic than others. They feel more guilt about their own sexual impulses and they are more sexually rigid than others. Such persons also tend to believe in the traditional family power structure that consists of a dominant father, a submissive mother, and obedient children. Homophobic persons tend to view homosexuals as sick, dangerous, and perverted.[11]

Such attitudes are destructive to personal self-esteem and feelings of comfort with one's sexuality. They can inhibit a person from achieving a positive attitude toward sexuality and prevent that individual from enjoying a healthy, enriching sexual relationship with a significant other in their lives.

## What Causes Homosexuality?

The definite cause of homosexuality is unknown at this time. There are several theories put forth by professionals and currently under study. These theories presently seem to center around the following issues:

1) Sex hormone imbalance (during prenatal and early neonatal development, when hormones influence the sexualization of the brain). This is thought to set a predisposition for homosexual orientation.
2) Influence of one's environment (social and psychological influences prior to the age of four can irreversibly determine sexual identity).

It would be impossible for me to adequately explain these theories in this chapter; volumes have been written on them. The theories and the research surrounding them are definitely not as simple as they may appear.

Suffice it to say that most researchers feel it is an *interaction* of the biological and the environmental at a *critical* phase of development that determines the outcome of one's sexual orientation. In this regard I would like to quote from John Money's book *Gay, Straight, and In-Between*. Money, one of the most respected researchers on the subject of sexuality, writes:

> The basic principle is developmental determinism, which pertains to the developmental history of when the brain becomes homosexualized (or correspondingly heterosexualized), to what degree, for how long, and how immutably. Whether the determining agents of homosexuality are innate and biological or acquired is beside the point. The point is that they are *determinants*, no matter *where* they come from, or *when* they occur.[12]

We will leave it to the researchers to continue to explore the theories and come up with more definitive answers. Families cannot put their lives on hold until we have those answers. Money's important point is that homosexuality and heterosexuality is *determined*, not chosen, and that is what we have to keep in mind.

## Can homosexuality be cured?

Once again, I want to distinguish between homosexual orientation and homosexual behavior. There is divided opinion that homosexual orientation can be changed. There are a few psychologists like John Harvey, O.S.F.S., who say that if the homosexual can be made to desire such a change, change can take place. The actual numbers of gays or lesbians who claim to have changed their orientation are quite low in this regard. However, the majority of psychologists and sexologists argue that sexual *orientation* is never changed. They maintain that what is being changed in these situations is actually sexual *behavior*.

It is well known that psychotherapy has had little success in attempts to change homosexuals to heterosexuals. The current thinking by the majority in the health-care professions is that the best approach for therapists to take with gay and lesbian patients is to promote *self-acceptance.* That is, to affirm the homosexual as a person, help them discover their self-worth, and aid them in learning to cope with the social ramifications of their homosexuality. In this respect counseling for the young homosexual and his/her family may be useful. Such counseling may aid in accepting and adjusting to the impact this discovery may have on the family system.

### Should I tell the rest of the family?

This is a decision that should be made in consultation with the homosexual person. Gay and lesbian people need all the support they can get. Who better to give this support than one's own family? It is from the family that the gay and lesbian person can draw the strength to live a stable and well-adjusted lifestyle. However, the homosexual should be the one to make this decision. Rejection by people one loves the most is devastating.

### Do people choose to be homosexual?

No. One thing we have come to learn about homosexuality over the years is that orientation is set at least by the time we are four years old. (Many researchers say two years old.) Just as people do not wake up one day and say, "I've decided I'll be heterosexual," neither do they decide, or choose, to be homosexual. They just are. As a matter of fact, I doubt anyone would choose an orientation that makes them the subject of constant ridicule, crude jokes, open hostility, and even violent abuse. The matter of whether we are homosexual or heterosexual is out of our hands. What can be chosen or rejected by every individual is sexual activity and behavior as to how they will live out their sexuality.

### What does the church say about homosexuality?

Christian churches today have divided opinions regarding homosexuality ranging from complete acceptance and blessing of gay and lesbian marriages to complete rejection of the homosexual person. Most churches are somewhere in between. Some have created special ministries to work with their gay and lesbian populations, and many are currently studying and dialoguing to gain a better understanding of the homosexual orientation.

The Catholic Church says that there is no sin in being a homosexual person. Objectively speaking, there is sin in genital sexual activity between homosexual persons. Objectively then, as stated in the recent document titled *Human Sexuality: A Catholic Perspective for Education and Lifelong Learning,* the Catholic Church calls homosexuals to a life of self-imposed celibacy.

At the same time, the church distinguishes between *objective* and *subjective* morality. Although I do not want to get overly theoretical, I feel this is an opportunity to clarify some important information regarding Catholic teaching here. This distinction between *objective* and *subjective* morality is an important one. Moral evaluation depends upon this distinction. The difference between the two is this: *Objective morality* is the ideal, the goal, the norm as it should be understood and lived. For example, objective morality says it is always wrong to take a human life. *Subjective morality* is the individual's attempt to follow the ideal. The individual's understanding of morality is *subject to* the ideal as the individual understands it.

Subjective morality considers the *ability* of the individual to follow objective morality. Subjective morality says although it *is* immoral to take a human life, *you* are not immoral if you kill someone threatening your life. In other words, it would be ideal, it would be best, if you did not have to take this life.

Let's look at another situation involving the same moral law. Killing a human is always objectively wrong. But in some primitive religions offering a pure and innocent baby was seen as a perfect sacrifice, one that would greatly please the gods. When the missionaries faced such a situation, they had to consider that the natives *objectively* were performing an immoral act. At the same time, *subjectively,* because of their lack of education and exposure to civilization, the natives were not fully responsible for performing this immoral act. Although the act was immoral, the person performing the act was not fully able to act morally in this circumstance.

Confessors evaluate moral behavior by taking *both* factors into consideration. For example, a confessor might say that objectively homosexual acts are wrong. But in this case, and given this person's orientation, this is the best s/he can do. The confessor would then try to encourage the individual to cultivate as many virtues as possible within these admittedly limited circumstances.

This is not a new teaching in the church. This has always been a part of the Catholic approach to morality.

In the area of pastoral care efforts are made toward healing and comfort. The 1976 document from Catholic bishops, *To Live in Christ Jesus*, states:

> Homosexual [persons], like everyone else, should not suffer from prejudice against their basic human rights. They have a right to respect, friendship, and justice. They should have an active role in the Christian community.[13]

In a 1986 document from the Congregation for the Doctrine of the Faith entitled, *Letter to the Bishops of the Catholic Church on the Pastoral Care of Homosexual Persons*, the following was observed:

> It is deplorable that homosexual persons have been and are the object of violent malice in speech or in action. Such treatment deserves condemnation from the Church's pastors wherever it occurs.[14]

Not all churches take this view. Some deny homosexuals membership. However, in many churches there is much discussion and reflection on the topic of homosexuality. In an effort better to understand and minister to the needs of their gay and lesbian members, many churches are making efforts at educating and updating the views of those under their care. There is a greater effort toward dialogue with the gay and lesbian community than ever before, and clergy and religious alike are trying to keep abreast of the most current scientific and behavioral information on homosexuality available today.

The Evangelical Lutheran Church of America took educational steps to promote a better understanding of the biblical passages deemed to refer to homosexuality. In the first draft of a social statement titled, *The Church and Human Sexuality: A Lutheran Perspective*, there is a careful and concise examination of these specific Scripture passages and the possible interpretations given by modern theologians. Following this thorough exploration are three possible responses for members of the Lutheran Church. These responses can be briefly summarized as follows:

*Response 1:* To love one's neighbor who is homosexual means to love the sinner but to hate the sin. Our church should be loving and accepting of persons who are homosexual, welcoming and encouraging membership, but clearly opposing sexual activity. Those holding this position usually view homosexuality as a disease or a serious distortion resulting from the Fall. Because of this, it is felt that homosexual persons cannot responsibly live out their Christian freedom through sexual activity, even in a committed relationship. Lifelong abstinence presents the only moral option.

*Response 2:* To love one's neighbor means offering compassion to gay and lesbian persons and showing an understanding of the dilemma facing those who do not possess the gift of celibacy. It is not loving to demand lifelong abstinence from all homosexuals whose orientation, through no choice of their own, is an integrated aspect of who they are. Those holding this position usually view homosexuality as a defect or example of brokenness in God's creation. More in keeping with God's intentions would be to live out one's homosexuality in a loving, committed relationship rather than through loneliness or casual sexual encounters.

*Response 3:* To love one's neighbor means to affirm openly gay and lesbian persons as well as their mutually loving, faithful, committed relationships. These relationships are the appropriate context for sexual activity that can be expressive of love for one another. Those holding this position usually view homosexuality as another expression of God's creation. Homosexuality should be lived out with qualities, boundaries, and structures which are consistent with those that apply to heterosexual persons. The church should move in the direction of blessing committed same-sex unions.[15]

While each of these responses is based on accepted interpretation of Scripture, each differs over which texts are most relevant and how these should be understood and applied. All three responses are supported biblically and theologically by some members of the Evangelical Lutheran Church.

It would be ideal if all churches would follow the example of the ELCA and its willingness to seek input from the lived experiences of the faithful, giving consideration to various responses, providing thorough explanation and clarification for controversial issues, and pursuing growth through education. One can applaud and encourage the fine efforts at Christian understanding that have taken place in the initial draft.

In chapter 5, I made a reference to the recent report from the Rabbinical Assembly's Commission on Human Sexuality. I refer to that document again now. Regarding homosexuality the commission did not take a definite stand, but rather asked the law committee to examine the tension that exists between the traditional teaching that views same-sex relations as an abomination and Conservative Judaism's commitment to civil rights for homosexuals.

It is important for us to remember that there have always been controversial issues in the churches and there always will be continually uncovering of new sources of information and new ways of understanding old issues.

Decisions by church officials affect the lives of millions of Christians worldwide. I had occasion to visit Rome with my son. We were part of a group of 7,000 people from all over the world who participated in the Pope's weekly audience with the public. Because of the large crowds, and because section seating is on a first-come, first-served basis, my son and I arrived an hour and a half early. As I sat and waited I became awed at the immensity and diversity of the church's presence in the world.

There were children and adults of all ages. There were clergy and religious and lay people—all joined by faith. Watching the various groups enter the hall, many in their native dress and costume, I realized more fully the powerful responsibility the governing body of the church has. Gathered here were only a minute sampling of the races, cultures, and ethnic backgrounds the Catholic Church serves. The governing bodies of all faiths have a serious responsibility to all their people.

We in the United States are so fortunate. We have at our disposal some of the most up-to-date technology and education in the world today. We have this available at the turn of a knob, the push of a button. Some of the world lives a slower pace. When the governing body of any church embarks upon the decision-making process, they must consider input from all of these diverse groups of people, each with their own understanding due to the information and education they have at their disposal. They must gather data and information from all over the world and consider how this data reflects the people, their customs, and traditions.

This is one reason churches move so slowly and proceed with such caution. We in the United States must remind ourselves of this. That is not to say that we cease to give input, to challenge and monitor the direction, and encourage the pace of the governing bodies. This is our right and role as laity and our responsibility to our faith. Nonetheless, we do this with the understanding that we are but one part of the mystical body of Christ and we show patience and understanding to the entire body.

This is not to say all churches will ever change their teaching on sexual activity between homosexual persons. I do not wish to give false hope to those who would see an end to their suffering. I simply have no idea what direction this understanding will take in the future. I do, however, have trust and confidence in the Holy Spirit. I have confidence in the power of education. I have confidence in the ability of the social and behavioral sciences to study meticulously the conditions of the human body. I have confidence in Christians as they continue to educate themselves in their role to be responsible to the gospel values. I have confidence in the thousands of gay and lesbian Christian laity and clergy that their devotion to their faith will aid them as they struggle not to lose heart. I pray that they will continue to nudge gently their church to continue the investigation of this issue of homosexuality.

### Should my gay child "come out?"

"Coming out" means openly declaring one's homosexual orientation. Many a gay or lesbian child has been disowned and kicked out of the family home when they have told their parents about their orientation. Our society has little tolerance for anyone who is different. Because of this, many homosexual people have become nonpersons. No one knows who they really are. They have to deny who they are as a person to all but a few. This does not allow the homosexual person to grow and develop in a holistic manner. When you cannot talk about your life, your friends, and your activities with openness and enthusiasm, you may live a life of continual denial and deceit. When you must keep all your feelings locked up inside it becomes difficult to grow and thrive as a human being.

Denial and repression are not mentally healthy for anyone. Yet this is the reality of the situation for many gay and lesbian people. Knowing they would be rejected and avoided, they hide who they are from family, friends, relatives, and coworkers. They live a life of constant denial and isolation. They force themselves to laugh at the gay and lesbian jokes told by others while they hurt inside. They make up stories about boyfriends and girlfriends so their family will quit asking them, "When are you going to get married? Whom are you dating?"

One of the most devastating consequences of this secrecy and hiding is that young gay boys and lesbian girls have no role models to pattern their lives after. You may remember earlier that I identified sexuality as one of the most important components of our personality, one that involves the spiritual, emotional, intellectual, social, and physical aspects of our personhood. Because homosexual children feel so different, many do not know where they fit into society. When both church and society close doors to them, many do not know where to look for what or whom they can become. Until we can eradicate the fear and discrimination that the homosexual is forced to live with there can be few healthy and admirable role models presented to young homosexual children. As one mother of a gay child observed, "Homosexuals are the only minority I know of where the parents and children are not a part of the same minority."

This deprives gay and lesbian children of adequate role models. They know they cannot grow up to be like mom or dad. They know they cannot look forward to marriage and raising a family. Who then can they be like? As they begin to search for identities and examples during their youth, they find few healthy examples. So few homosexual persons have publicly acknowledged their orientation, the gay or lesbian child sees no heroes, no models of "what I can become," no examples of public aspirations. Instead, they come to realize that if they are to be successful and accepted in our society, they will have to deny who they are, keep it hidden. The message is "Fake it! Never let the *real* you be known."

Often, the recognizable gay or lesbian person, the one who makes the papers, is one who is *not* representative of the homosexual community at large. That is to say, the kind of homosexual often represented in magazine articles and depicted in newspaper columns is bizarre, is an extremist, a publicity seeker who loves the limelight and tries to shock the public. This is not the typical homosexual person. Homosexuals themselves despise this type of representation.

Were all gay men and lesbian women to identify themselves publicly, the shock to our society would be great. So, too, would be the rewards. Well-loved friends, well-known professionals, government officials, doctors, clergymen and women, scientists, educators, religious leaders, lawyers, businessmen and women, athletes, artists, writers, and public figures of every kind and in every profession would be seen for who they are: successful and responsible gay and lesbian people. The great fear of the "dyke" or "homo" would cease to exist. Our country could come to know and respect the contributions homosexual men and women in all walks of life have made to this wonderful "melting pot" of ours. People would also find that the homosexual community is remarkably like the heterosexual community.

People might come to see that sexual orientation does not make you a "good" or "bad" person. We might recognize that sexuality is a "given";

our choice lies in how we live out our sexuality. It might be acknowledged that sexual orientation is a *personal* issue, that we *all* have homosexual family members just as we *all* have heterosexual family members. The identification of the "problem" as "out in San Francisco or Washington" might be corrected. Instead, we could accept the fact that homosexuality is a part of life that we cannot change and need to better understand. This has been the case with every racial and cultural prejudice that we, as a country, have had the courage to face.

Parents could openly look to one another for information and support, as they learn together how best to raise lesbian and gay children, how to help their children with their homosexual orientation. All of society could benefit from the caring and sensitive nature of many homosexual persons, which comes, perhaps, as they learn to live with the pain of their orientation.

Should your gay son or lesbian daughter let it be known that they are homosexual? I cannot answer that question for you or them. I do know, however, that as long as we are unable to identify the stable, well-adjusted, loving, caring, sensitive, and productive gay and lesbian members of our society, the cycle of deceit will never be broken. If gay and lesbian persons were accepted members of our society, of our churches, we could all grow toward the unity of humankind to which we are called as Christian people. As it has been aptly put, "We are *all* part of the mystical body of Christ, and part of our body is homosexual."

## Should I talk to my child about abstinence, AIDS, and condoms?

By all means! Homosexual and heterosexual children need the same information on these issues. A Christian homosexual will need to consider all the ramifications of becoming sexually active just as Christian heterosexuals do. Teachings of the church, state laws, psychological and physical issues all need to be carefully thought through.

Abstinence is a lifetime issue for all people, heterosexual and homosexual alike. There are periods in everyone's life when postponing or deciding to abstain completely from sexual intercourse is the very best course of action. There are certainly sincere, faith-filled Christian gay men and lesbian women who have chosen to live a life of abstinence in accord with the teachings of their church. In our society today we are given the impression by the media and society at large that such an undertaking is entirely out of the question for a layperson. But this is not so. By all means this is a difficult and challenging undertaking, but not an impossible one.

The universe does not revolve around intercourse as many would have us believe. Our sexuality is lived out in many ways, only one of which is sexual intercourse. One can find meaningful sexual expression in relationships that do not have to culminate in physical intimacy. Indeed, many of us experience several such relationships in our lifetime.

Presenting abstinence as a negative, an unachievable reality, is unjust and unfair to our youth, both homosexual and heterosexual. Let us then present it in a positive way, with realistic expectations and guidelines and leave it to the individual to choose or reject it as their conscience, in accord with their faith, sees fit.

All young people today should have a thorough understanding of the HIV virus and AIDS and how it is transmitted. For a parent to neglect this education is unfair and unjust. There are just too many possible situations that may put your child in danger for you to ignore this serious issue. Information regarding condom education is given in chapter 9.

One of the saddest situations witnessed today by many counselors and health-care workers is that of the family who finds out their child is homosexual *and* dying of AIDS. This is a situation that could be avoided if children felt they were able to talk about what it means to be lesbian or gay with their parents. However, the majority of gay men and lesbian women feel they are not free to do this. The rejection they have faced from society at large is bad enough, but to risk rejection from their own parents is an unbearable thought for most, and so they wait till they have nothing more to lose. Some never do tell their parents; they die alone.

## How Can I Help My Gay or Lesbian Child?

Your love and support is the best help you can give your child. Being willing to listen as s/he relates struggles, joys, difficulties, adjustments, accomplishments, and concerns is a big step in the right direction. Provide for professional counseling if your child is willing. Don't ask questions that imply judgment on your child's behavior.

Accept and show a positive interest in his/her friends. If you are suspicious of every friend s/he spends time with, or brings home, your child will eventually keep friends and activities from you. Don't assume your son or daughter is sexually active. Respect your child's right to privacy. Let him/her know you are available to help in any way possible. Share all the current correct medical information you have access to.

Treat your homosexual child the same way you treat all your children, with respect and integrity.

Learn how to deal with your anger, find out where it is coming from. As one parent suggested: "Ask yourself, am I angry because others will think I'm a failure as a parent, that I'll lose my image because I have a gay child?" Which is more important, your embarrassment, what others think, or the daily pain and rejection your child is living with?

There is no need for parents to live alone with this secret, or to live in despair. There *is* a need for you to become educated. Keep yourself informed and updated with the current information relevant to homosexuality by reading appropriate materials, watching pertinent TV programs, and attending workshops and lectures. Put your child in touch with a religious support group such as Dignity or Courage, two different groups with two different approaches. Join a parents' support group, such as PFLAG (Parents and Friends of Lesbians and Gays): their national hotline number is 202-638-4200. Do all you can to encourage responsible, moral behavior in your child.

Invite your child to sexual morality. Reverend Paul Dinter is a chaplain at Columbia University. In an article in *Church* magazine in 1987, he had this important and pointed message for church leaders and educators. I think it applies to *all* parents as well:

> Too often, we attempt to control young people's use of their sexual faculties, instead of helping them to get to the point where self-control is an outgrowth of their self-esteem. To do this we must be adults who show them how to love themselves so they can love (and not use) their neighbors.[16]

Allow yourself to discuss this topic openly among trusted friends, as you become able. Others need help too and may be struggling with the same issue. Still others can come to see that this could happen to them as well, that it is not a matter of choice. If we do not come to accept that gay and lesbian children are a reality, then we are contributing to the world of unhappiness and rejection in which they live. Besides, parents need support too. Sharing your concerns with friends can be a source of that support. It is only by educating others that we will bring about understanding, acceptance, and better treatment for all homosexual people. As a courageous member of PFLAG suggested, "Try not to change your child, try to change society instead."

Excellent advice! If others know and like your child, if they have admired and respected your child as a person over the years, then to know that this child is lesbian or gay is to come to realize that many of the stereotypical remarks they have believed over the years are not true. Let others know that there are chaste gay and lesbian relationships. Educate them to the reality of monogamous, committed gay and lesbian relationships that have lasted for twenty or thirty years or more. Pray for all your children.

In conclusion, I would like to quote a beautiful passage from the book entitled *Unconditional Love* by Father John Powell, S.J. This passage applies to all parents and all children, but I think it is an especially appropriate ending to our discussion:

### THE MESSAGE OF UNCONDITIONAL LOVE

The essential message of unconditional love is one of liberation. You can be whoever you are, express all your thoughts and feelings with absolute confidence. You do not have to be fearful that love will be taken away. You will not be punished for your openness or honesty. There is no admission price to my love, no rental fees or installment payments to be made. There may be days when disagreements and disturbing emotions may come between us. There may be times when physical miles may lie between us. But I have given you the word of my commitment. I have set my life on a course. I will not go back on my word to you. So feel free to be yourself, to tell me of your negative and positive reactions, of your warm and cold feelings. I cannot always predict my reactions or guarantee my strength, but one thing I do know and I do want you to know: I will not reject you! I am committed to your growth and happiness. I will always love you.[17]

Good luck and may God bless you as you live out this message with all of your children.

# Chapter 8

. . . . . . . . . .

~

# Do As You Say

Much of what our children learn from us comes not from what we say, but from what we do. Much of what they learn from us comes through nonverbal communication. We have a responsibility to try to live what we teach. How we treat each other in our homes will say more to our children than the lectures we give them on respect. If we do not treat our children with respect, we cannot expect respect from them. If we ourselves use obscene language, we can expect that they will also. If we do not treat each sex with equality, then our children won't either. If we make crude jokes about sex, then they will not have the proper respect for sex within their own lives. If we lie or cheat, we can expect them to do the same. If we never go to church, they probably won't either.

On the positive side, if we show patience and understanding toward all family members, so will our children. If we participate in our parish community, show love and respect for our faith, and attend church regularly, chances are very great that when our children are on their own, they will do the same.

As we try to present values about sexuality, we need to do so in a positive manner, both verbally and nonverbally. If we don't our sexual warnings may backfire.

Research involving parent-child communication about sexuality yields interesting and helpful information. Dr. Jean Van De Polder, Director of the Child Psychiatry Clinic at the University of Colorado Medical Center, has studied this topic in depth. Some important findings of this research as presented in an article in *Medical Aspects of Human Sexuality* are:

> Sexual warnings given in an anxious or angry tone of voice using judgmental language imply suspiciousness, distrust, and a fear of sexuality which the adolescent may greet with outright anger, oppositional behavior, or total social withdrawal from appropriate interaction with peers.[1]

Dr. Van De Polder finds that parents' sexual warnings often carry covert messages that encourage the very behavior they are condemning. In such situations the adolescent hears and carries out an invitation to do what the parent seems, on the conscious level, to be saying not to do. In this type of scenario Van De Polder finds that the parents have ambivalent feelings about themselves and their own sexuality.

Such feelings are intensified in problem situations. When parents hate or find their own sexuality disgusting they will have difficulty in accepting sexuality in their adolescent children. For example, a mother who finds her own sexuality bad, dirty, or disgusting, may see her child's sexuality as bad, dirty, or disgusting. If the mother does not get in touch with her feelings and resolve them, she in turn says, unconsciously, to her child, "You are the one who has bad, dirty sexual thoughts, not me. You need to be controlled and punished."

Although this is an unconscious message on the part of the mother, it can nevertheless cause the adolescent to actualize, or carry out, the negative identification with the mother, no matter what the conscious message may be. Children identify with their parents and to a certain degree accept their parents' conception of them. In this way the negative cycle remains unbroken and continues for yet another generation of dysfunctional sexuality.

Parents may convey this same message by removing themselves emotionally from anything to do with their child's sexuality. Fathers who ignore their daughter's budding sexuality and eliminate hugs and other signs of affection toward their child subtly convey the message that sex is bad or disgusting. The daughter more than likely will internalize the message as "I'm bad. I'm disgusting." She may try to find someone else to love her to prove to herself she is lovable, or she may accept this unconscious message and withdraw socially and/or emotionally from her peers.

Van De Polder notes that in still other situations, warnings that backfire may come out of the parents' own unconscious desires to experience vicariously the adolescent's sexual encounters. This type of situation occurs with parents who wish they would have had more sexual experience. Because of their unconscious regrets, they often identify with their teens increasing sexual drive. They may ask for intimate details of their teens experiences and sexual encounters. They may consciously give a weak warning to their adolescent about sexual behavior, but they seldom set appropriate limits.

Nor do they discourage or identify inappropriate sexual behaviors for their teen. So while their verbal message may be "don't," their unconscious nonverbal message is "do." The adolescent will pick up on this unconscious message of approval and may be angry or resentful toward the parent, without quite knowing why. At some point in time, the adolescent may come to the realization or feeling that s/he was exploited. "Mom pushed me into dating relationships too early. I wasn't ready for it!" "Dad got a kick out of my 'conquests.' He seemed pleased to have a son who could have his way with women."

When such situations exist, the sexual warnings given by parents backfire. In an additional commentary on this subject in the same article, Dr. Elissa Benedek, Director of Training and Education in the Center for Forensic Psychiatry at the University of Michigan School of Medicine, remarks:

> "Warning" in itself conveys the message that all sexual behavior is dangerous and inappropriate. Warnings fail because adolescents know that despite the risk of sexual behavior there are benefits. It's fun. A more objective analysis at a rational time would in all probability be more successful.[2]

Dr. Benedek reminds us that adolescents do want to talk about their sexual behavior and have questions answered by parents and other trusted adults. They look to adults as a source of wisdom and support. But the parent who "warns," or points fingers, will be the parent who is excluded from the process. When this happens such a parent loses one more opportunity to share with his/her child. A lost opportunity that can never be regained.

None of the scenarios above are healthy for *any* of the parties involved. Pain and frustration result. Often the damage goes unattended for years, but causes great harm in the meantime. Only with conscious and determined effort on the part of the parent can such dilemmas be solved and resolved in time to benefit one's children.

The best way for children to learn about the place of sexual expression in a relationship is through observing a loving, caring relationship at home. Parents, secure and in touch with their own sexuality, can model a loving relationship. They set an excellent example when they talk about sexuality respectfully, openly, comfortably, even playfully. It is good for children to see their parents hug and kiss, hold hands, snuggle on the couch. This gives children many positive messages about sexuality, one of which is: intercourse is only *one* way to express sexual love; there are *many* other ways.

On the other hand, when children see sex abused or misused, when they witness sexual manipulation or hear crude, disrespectful conversation about sex, they will have great difficulty appreciating sexuality as a treasured gift. If they see dad physically strike or verbally abuse and put down mom, if they see mom sexually manipulate dad or flirt with other males to get what she wants, they get a clear message that it is OK to use sex to get what you want. If these same parents adhere to a double standard for their children, the messages will be confusing and young people will have trouble integrating them into their personal belief system.

All children go through a period of rebellion when they reject many of the things their parents hold dear. But if the parents can keep calm (my son would say "chill out") and be patient during this trying time, most young people will end up accepting most of what their parents try to offer them. They simply need the time and space to step away, consider alternatives, and reclaim as their own that which they observed and decided is true.

This topic brings to mind one student I had back in the seventies who gave his parents many sleepless nights. He was the oldest child and very intelligent. So intelligent, he questioned everything his parents did. His father and mother were quite conservative in the practice of their faith, following church teaching to the letter of the law and imposing very strict rules and regulations on their children.

My young friend was endlessly challenging his parents about every aspect of life issues imaginable, especially religious rules and practices. His challenging sometimes took the form of experimenting with drugs, alcohol, and sex. When he graduated from high school he quit going to church, grew his hair long, and dropped out of the "system," as he called it. No Oxford shirt and tie for him, thank you. He was into torn jeans and American flag T-shirts. He even changed his name to show he wanted no connection with the world of his parents. He had, he thought, rejected their values and attitudes.

In his early twenties this young man took to the woods and lived in a tent. He began making his own soap and canning his veggies. He grew all of his own food. Before long he had built himself a log cabin, gotten married and, after a time, had four beautiful little daughters. Gradually, he began to change his attitude about religion, politics, drugs, "wild living," and the like. In time, he cut his hair, shaved his beard, and became a "pillar" in his church. He did not return to the church of his parents, but became equally, if not more so, as active in the church he and his wife chose to attend. Today he is responsible for a religious newsletter he edits and publishes informing concerned citizens of government policies.

Some education is more "caught" than "taught." After going his own way, and checking things out, he returned to many of the values he observed at home. Even though he would deny that he is anything like his parents, he has in fact copied many of their attitudes toward religion and government. With a few exceptions and modifications (some more conservative than his parents), he reclaimed their views as his own. This hope that the lessons taught will not ultimately be without effect has been expressed by one religious conference:

> Christian parents must know that their example represents the most valid contribution in the education of their children. . . . If they match their words with corresponding actions, the message rings "loud and clear" that this is an important value for them, for this family, and for the young learner. . . . Attitudes often speak louder than words.[3]

Not all teens go through the same degree of rebellion as my young friend did. But, in truth, most children to some extent eventually reclaim the values they absorbed at home, sometimes to the embarrassment of the parent. All parents do give messages to their children, verbally and nonverbally. Being aware of this and carefully choosing the messages we wish to impart can help us to avoid sending undesirable messages.

There was an excellent letter published in Ann Landers's newspaper column some years ago that beautifully illustrates this point. The author is unknown, but the message is quite clear:

### It's OK, Son, Everybody Does It!

> When Johnny was 6 years old, he was with his father when they were caught speeding. His father handed the officer $5.00 with his driver's license. "It's OK, son," his father said as he drove off. "Everybody does it."
>
> When he was 8, he was permitted to sit in a family seminar, presided

over by Uncle George, on how to shave points off an income tax return. "It's OK, kid," his uncle said. "Everybody does it."

When he was 9, his mother took him to his first theater production. The box-office man couldn't find any seats until his mother discovered an extra $2.00 in her purse. "It's OK, son," she said. "Everybody does it."

When he was 12, he broke his glasses on the way to school. His Aunt Francine convinced the insurance company that they had been stolen and collected $27.00. "It's OK, kid," she said. "Everybody does it."

When he was 15, he made right guard on the high school football team. His coach showed him how to block and at the same time grab the opposing end by the shirt so the official couldn't see it. "It's OK, kid," the coach said. "Everybody does it."

When he was 16, he took his first summer job at the neighborhood supermarket. His assignment was to put overripe tomatoes in the bottom of the boxes and the good ones on top where they would show. "It's OK, kid," the manager said. "Everybody does it."

When he was 19, he was approached by an upperclassman who offered the test answers for $3.00. "It's OK," he said. "Everybody does it."

Johnny was caught and sent home in disgrace. "How could you do this to your mother and me?" his father asked. "You never learned anything like this at home." His aunt and uncle also were shocked.

If there's anything the adult world can't stand, it's a kid who cheats.

## Monitoring the Tube

This is sometimes an unpleasant but very necessary responsibility. Just as our children learn by what they see at home, they also pick up values and attitudes from what they watch on TV. This is especially true if they like and identify with the character they are watching. Today, it is not only cable TV we have to be wary of; even the commercials and programming on regular TV can be sexually suggestive.

We have to set guidelines for our children as to what is acceptable for them to watch. This can become increasingly difficult as they become older, especially if they have younger sisters and brothers. While a personal TV for an older child (late high school on) is acceptable, I do not think it is wise to have a TV in each child's room, especially younger children. This tends to isolate a family and to discourage the good communication that can come from watching a show together as a family.

For those looking for help with guidelines in this area, the Center for Population Options has a fine pamphlet available to help with guidelines and conversations about television shows: "Talking with TV," can be obtained for a small fee by calling (202) 347-5700. The Center for Media Literacy also has materials available for parents at reasonable costs. Their magazine *Media and Values* is an outstanding resource for parents. You can call them for more information at (310) 559-2944 or (800) 226-9494.

The best approach is to make the time to watch television with your child occasionally. You might even watch a show with your family that you feel is objectionable. After the show, in a nonthreatening way, ask how they felt about the show and explain in what ways you felt the show violated the morals and values you are trying to instill in them. Listen with an open mind as they respond to your criticisms, try to see the show as they did—through younger, less experienced eyes. Remember they are not looking at the show with the same background of experience you have. What may seem obvious to you may not be noticed at all by them.

If there are shows you do not want your child to watch, be sure you remember to explain *why* that particular show is off limits. With your older children you might compromise once in awhile. For example, if you are home they can watch the show in question, or if you watch it with them they can view it, but if not, they can't.

Obviously this is going to be difficult to enforce, and trust is an essential element. Even if they watch the show at a friend's house, at least you have given them an example and stated your moral principles to them. While it may not seem like much of a victory at the time, what you have said will be respected by them as time goes by and they see that you stand up for what you believe in, even when it is difficult or unpopular. It doesn't necessarily mean they will ever agree with you.

*Give your children alternatives.* If you have a VCR, perhaps you could let them invite a few friends over and rent a movie that is mutually agreeable. Allow them to pick the movies that the family will watch from time to time. You may not always enjoy them but you will be keeping in touch with the world your child lives in. Don't get too hung up on control. You cannot be with your child all the time, everywhere. It is better to express the *reasons* for your thinking or your *reasons* for objecting, rather than set down rules you cannot enforce. This will leave them with something to think about and mull over later, when you aren't there. It's been said and I believe it's often true, "Rules without reasons lead to rebellion."

I remember quite well a typical example of our lack of ability to control everything our child does, much less what they watch on TV when they are out of the home. When cable TV first came out in our neighborhood our children were pestering us constantly to get it. My husband and I decided that we would not get cable until our children were out of high school. We explained that we didn't want to have a lot of arguments and rigid rules over programming. We felt there was enough to watch on regular TV and we were concerned about the movie channels on cable.

We told our children that many of the movies were adult material that we did not feel they were quite ready to experience. Also, there were movies we did not want coming into our home because we felt they were degrading to men and women, channels we did not want to support financially. Rather than have ongoing discussions about which movies were OK or blocking programming, we simply decided that cable was nonnegotiable until high school was over. (*Nonnegotiable* was the term we used to let our kids know this was not an issue we were going to change our minds about. I should add we used the term sparingly over the years and that increased its power.) In addition, our children were involved in high school activities and there wasn't enough time to watch enough cable TV to justify the additional cost. Cable TV was not an essential. There were other things they wanted to do where we felt our money was better spent.

All of our children were in high school at the same time; none of them were happy with our decision. We were "out of it" as parents. We did not love them. We were unfair and unreasonable. Worst of all, we "didn't trust them"!

About that time the pastor of our church was looking for high school students to answer the phones at the rectory, and both of our sons began working there regularly. A month or so after they had begun work at the rectory, I overheard one of my sons talking to a friend about cable TV. He talked knowledgeably and at great length about the programming. Later, I asked him about the conversation.

"How is it you know so much about cable?" I quizzed.

"They have cable up at the rectory, mom. The TV is in the same room as the desk. I watch it all the time when I answer the phones. Now mom, you didn't say we could *never* watch cable, you just said you wouldn't get it here at home. Right?"

So much for control! The pastor and I were able to laugh about my son's solution to the problem of "out-of-it" parents. Still, I didn't regret my decision nor did I try to place any restrictions on what the boys watched at the rectory. (I am sure our daughter had found a similar solution. Being the oldest, she was smart enough to keep it to herself!) It was enough that our children remembered what our objections were and considered them, however unconsciously, as they watched cable elsewhere. They were learning to discern, and that, after all, was our goal in the first place. (For those of you who are curious, when our youngest son was in his second year of college, someone remembered our agreement about cable. We got basic cable that year and enjoyed it, especially the sports channel!)

Someone once told me that to be a good parent you have to get comfortable with being hated once in a while. I have found that is true, but I have also found that more times than not *eventually* your children respect your ability to really *be* a parent to them, even when it means being unpopular. Kids have plenty of pals. *Only you can be their parent.*

Of course, everything I've said about TV goes for movies too. Sometimes the best way to talk your child out of seeing a movie you don't want them to see is to offer to go with them. (This works only at certain ages!) As with television, always try to state the reasons for your objections. Children are intelligent and they deserve intelligent reasons if they are to respect adult views. They can't consider and internalize what they aren't told.

This may mean you have to see a particular movie you don't want to in order to explain your objections to your child. Sometimes you may decide the final message of the movie is so important that it outweighs any potential harm to your child. Kids are smart; give them credit when they deserve it. You may say, "I saw this movie and I'm going to let you see it on the condition that we talk about it after you see it." Then take your child to lunch and have a movie review. Be creative and don't lose your sense of humor.

## Hugs—And Lots of Them!

No matter where we are in our lives and no matter where they are, we all need affection and affirmation. This tells us that we are loved, that we are valued, just as we are. Our children *always* need our affection. Take care not to let expressions of affection diminish as your child ages. It is easy to hug a baby. We can kiss and cuddle them all day long. But we never seem to be able to catch up with our young teens long enough to hug them, and yet adolescents are in *great* need of affection. They are at one of the greatest periods of insecurity in their lives. They often feel rejected by their peers, are emotionally upset, sick of school, tired of always seeming to do the wrong thing, bothered by acne, worried because they are not growing, or scared because they are. The list goes on and on. Teen years are a time when the love and reassurance that only a family can give is desperately needed.

One of the saddest days in my teaching career came over such an issue. I had been teaching human sexuality to seventh and eighth-grade boys for several years, when this incident occurred. One of my eighth-grade students was having a lot of problems in school. He was getting into fights frequently, getting kicked out of class for being disruptive, arguing with his classmates constantly, being disrespectful to everyone, falling behind in his grades, falling asleep in class, you name it. In short, he was in deep trouble.

He was a "tough guy" and proud of it. He didn't want or need anyone's help. However, he came in to talk to me one day after school. He had been in trouble again and wanted to talk about it. As we talked, he revealed that his parents were getting a divorce and that he was caught in the middle of frequent, all-night fights between his mom and dad. He loved them both and couldn't understand why they were breaking up. Like most young people in his position, he had been unaware they had been having trouble for some time. Unfortunately, they were both too involved with their own hurts and decisions to see how serious the damage their tug-of-war approach to the situation was doing to their son. (I am not placing blame, merely relating my observations.)

During the conversation the young man related his difficulty in getting along with his dad. He said he loved his dad but that his dad didn't understand him. As we talked, I tried to reassure him. I told him that I was certain both his parents loved him very much—they were going through a tough time and didn't see how much he was hurting for them. "In time," I said optimistically, "things will get better. I don't know your parents well, but there are things I have observed that tell me they care deeply for you."

"Really? You're right, you don't know them!" He looked me straight in the eye—angry and hurting desperately. His eyes were filling with tears but he fought to appear unmoved.

"You think you know my dad? You think my dad loves me? Ha! Let me tell you about him. I'm fourteen years old now, and not once— NOT ONE SINGLE TIME—has my dad ever said he loves me. Not even when I was a little kid! I can't ever remember him saying to me 'I love you.' Not once, not ever." Then he broke down.

I will never forget that experience. I have seen that same mixture of anger and hurt on many faces since then, but when I saw it that day, it was for the first time. It reminded me how desperately *we all need to hear the words*, to feel touched, connected, to be told *openly, frequently* that we are loved. There was nothing I could say to take away the hurt, but this young man's dad could have done so with just three words. I know he would have meant them, too, if only he would have realized how much hearing those words mattered to his son. Many feel that actions are a more important reflection of care, and that is often true. But as parents we need to provide for our child with both actions and words. We can never assume they know how we feel about them. Sometimes we all just need to *hear* that we are loved.

After thirty plus years in education, I have found that many times the problems that are tearing a family apart could be made much less painful if each of them took just a minute to hug, kiss, or just give each other a pat on the back.

Men and women, boys and girls, have the need for affection all of their lives. If your children don't get hugs from you they may look for them elsewhere. Not a comforting thought, is it? Sure, they may toss you off or pull away. They may even say they don't need your love sometimes. But don't stop hugging them. That's when they need your love the most. Don't be surprised if you start a trend. What a wonderful feeling it is to get an unexpected hug—just because you are loved!

One day many years ago I was feeling down, and my perceptive ten-year-old son picked up on it. "Mom," he said, "you need the hug of the day," and he gave it to me! I will never forget that day and what a pickup his gesture was for me.

From that day on the whole family took up the tradition of giving every family member at least one "hug of the day." Grandparents, relatives, and friends also became recipients of this gift on various occasions. It was not that we didn't hug before, but my son's catch phrase made us aware that even though we thought we were affectionate, there were special times when we needed to be even *more affectionate*.

Later the "family hug" became a variation of the "hug of the day." My children are all in their twenties now. We've faced some tough challenges and been through some difficult times, yet nothing keeps us from joining in a family hug whenever we can. What a wonderful feeling it is for all of us, a reassurance to know that we have been and always will be, on good days and bad, there to love and support each other.

## Good Is Good

It is my belief that we ought to be striving for good families and not perfect ones. As a counselor friend once reminded me, *good is after all good.* I had just given a lecture the previous week to a group I had never worked with before. Coming off a dry spell of having given no lectures for a couple of months due to surgery, I was disappointed at my delivery and lack of energy, and was explaining this to my friend Barbara Cummings. She listened quietly while I went on and on about my "failure." When I stopped for breath, she looked at me kindly and asked, "Was your lecture dismal? I mean, do you feel the group learned anything from you? What was their response when you were finished?" I told her that the audience seemed to appreciate my efforts. They showed interest and participated throughout the session; and there were several who came forward afterward with questions and congratulations.

"Well," she asked slyly, "would you say it was *good,* even though it wasn't as perfect as you would have liked?" "Yes," I said haltingly, "I guess it was good. But I have done much better." "Pat," she scolded gently, "you can't give the best talk of your life *every* time you present one. Don't be so hard on yourself. From what you have said the audience did learn some new things and responded well to your presentation. *They* didn't know it wasn't your best night. To them your presentation may have been wonderful. At the very least it was good. But after all, let's not forget, *good is good!*"

What a wonderful gift Barbara's response was. Many times since then, when I haven't been perfect or wonderful, I ask myself if I was good. If the answer is an honest "yes," I smile and relax and remind myself that after all is said and done, good *is* good! I have also tried to pass this reminder on to others who, like myself, get too hung up on *perfect* to recognize *good.*

When we strive for perfect we set ourselves up for failure. When we demand perfect from our children, they grow up feeling they are never quite good enough, perhaps not as perfect as mom or dad, that somehow, in someway, they have let us (their parents) down.

Many years ago I came upon a quote I thought made a lot of common sense. I read it frequently to keep my sense of balance. It was written by statesman Carl Schurz, and was a part of the address at Faneuil Hall in Boston in 1859. It goes like this:

Ideals are like stars; you will not succeed in touching them with your hands. But like the seafaring man on the desert of waters, you choose them as your guides, and following them you will reach your destiny.

We cannot be perfect people, but we can be good people. We can model goodness to our children. We can model balance. We can create a happy family, a holy family.

In a recent message to families, the Catholic bishops of the United States remind us:

Remember, a family is holy not because it is perfect, but because God's grace is at work in it. . . . Wherever a family exists and love still moves through its members, grace is present. Nothing—not even divorce or death—can place limits upon God's gracious love.[4]

# Chapter 9

. . . . . . . . .

∿

# The Reality
# of Sexual Abuse

In 1984, *Life* magazine reported that there were currently thirty-two million adult women in this country who were victims of sexual abuse when they were children.

In 1979, one in five girls and one in eleven boys responding to a college questionnaire reported having had a sexual experience of some kind with a much older person during childhood.[1]

In 1992, one in four girls and one in six boys reported that they had been sexually assaulted. Recent studies report much higher rates of sexual intercourse among teens who have been abused, including higher rates of pregnancy and multiple partners.[2]

Twenty-nine percent of all rapes occurred when the victims were younger than age eleven, with sixty-one percent of all reported rapes occurring before the victim reached age eighteen.[3]

At least thirty percent of the time the child molester is a relative (expert opinion is that this percentage is higher, but because incestuous incidents are the least likely to be reported, it is difficult to prove this statistically).[4]

Of 160 women treated for sexual dysfunction it was found that ninety percent had been raped during childhood, twenty-three percent by fathers or stepfathers.[5] Evidence confirms that molestation by a trusted caretaker is one of the most damaging forms of childhood sexual abuse.

Seventy-five percent of prostitutes were sexually abused as children.[6]

According to a 1985 study by Ruth and Henry Kempe, two million children run away from home each year, and up to half of them do so because they have been abused, primarily sexually.

Research confirms that thirty percent to forty percent of all children are sexually abused in some way before the age of eighteen.[7]

Almost every family is in someway touched by the crime of sexual abuse. Unpleasant though it is to discuss, we must do so if we are to bring about much needed change in our society, and protect our children from a serious, potentially life-altering tragedy.

Is child sexual abuse something new? No, unfortunately not. History is filled with reports of the sexual mistreatment and molestation of children. The "good old days" were not *all* good. Lest we fear that talking about sex has brought on these problems of sexual abuse, we need to remember that silence about sexuality has never meant society was free from sexual problems.

In 1860, the dean of forensic medicine in France, Ambroise Tardieu, published an exposé entitled "A Medico-Legal Study of Cruelty and Brutal Treatment Inflicted on Children." In so doing, he identified what would be known 100 years later as the "Battered Child Syndrome". At the time he published his report, however, his peers totally ignored it.[8] In 1870, Josephine Butler crusaded for the abolition of child prostitution. She bitterly accused the men in high station who exploited such children. Were her efforts rewarded? No, instead she was denounced and treated obscenely by London police and brothel keepers. When a well-known editor of the *Pall Mall Gazette* supported her cause, he was sent to jail for three months.[9] These are but two examples; there are countless others, too numerous to mention. My point is to affirm that sexual problems are not new to society. All too often we ignore history and fail to learn from the past.

Many factors have brought about our increasing awareness of sexual abuse today. (I will not go into detail nor list all of these. Rather, I offer a few of them for the sake of perspective.) To begin with there is the phenomenon of instant communication. In times past, there was not the mass-media coverage of issues there is today. Next there is the factor of an increased willingness to discuss sexual matters, both privately and in the public sector. In the past there has been secrecy and fear about discussing sexuality, a reluctance to discuss *any* intimate issue. Another factor affecting our rising knowledge about sexual abuse is our increasing willingness to listen to children and uphold their rights. Years ago a child dared not accuse an adult of impropriety. Children were "to be seen and not heard." The authority equated with adulthood was unquestionable. Parents were never openly challenged by young children. Child labor was accepted by our society; children were property and did not have "rights."

These factors and others have contributed to the recent focus on childhood sexual abuse. As a society, we are beginning to realize that this is a problem we must face. Parents cannot wait for society to find a solution to this problem. Our children are at risk now. Parents must face the reality of childhood sexual abuse and communicate with their children honestly and openly, thereby providing their children with the knowledge and awareness that may save them from this tragedy.

Often parents ask, "How would I know if my child has been abused by someone?" My response is to ask if the parents notice any new or unusual sexual behavior manifested by their child. Unusual or exaggerated behavior is often an indicator that something is wrong.

The following is a list of behaviors parents and educators need to pay attention to in order to detect possible sexual abuse. This list comes from the Sex Information and Education Council of the United States (SIECUS).[10] If your child displays one or more of these behaviors, you probably would want to seek professional help in determining whether there is need for concern and/or counseling. The American Association of Sex Educators, Counselors, and Therapists (AASECT) could put you in touch with a sex therapist in your area who specializes in working with children who have been sexually abused. Their number is (312) 644-0828.

Should you recognize any of this behavior as applicable to your child, please don't panic. Your anxiety and discomfort will only worsen the situation for your child. Instead, seek professional help and follow the advice you are given. The sooner you deal with this problem, the sooner your child can heal. The longer you wait to deal with this problem, the more difficult it will be for your child to cope and heal.

To ignore sexual abuse is to expose your child to a life of troubled relationships, an increased risk to drug and alcohol abuse, poor psychological adjustment, as well as the possibility of Post-Traumatic Stress Disorder, and a greater degree of mental-health problems.[11] Don't be afraid to face the issue and take action if necessary. Help is available for those who ask.

According to the SIECUS guidelines: "When Children's Sexual Behaviors Raise Concern," these are the behaviors to watch for:

1. The child focuses on sexuality to a greater extent than on other aspects of his or her environment, and/or has more sexual knowledge than similar-aged children with similar backgrounds who live in the same area. A child's sexual interests should be in balance with his or her curiosity about, and exploration of, other aspects of his or her life.

2. The child has an ongoing compulsive interest in sexual or sexually related activities and/or is more interested in engaging in sexual behaviors than in playing with friends, going to school, and doing other developmentally appropriate activities.

3. The child engages in sexual behaviors with those who are much older or younger. Most school-aged children engage in sexual behaviors with children within a year or so of their age. In general, the wider the age range between children engaging in sexual behaviors, the greater the concern.

4. The child continues to ask unfamiliar children, or children who are uninterested, to engage in sexual activities. Healthy and natural sexual play usually occurs between friends and playmates.

5. The child, or a group of children, bribes or emotionally and/or physically forces another child/children of any age into sexual behaviors.

6. The child exhibits confusion or distorted ideas about the rights of others in regard to sexual behaviors. The child may contend: "She wanted it" or "I can touch him if I want to."

7. The child tries to manipulate children or adults into touching his or her genitals or causes physical harm to his or her own or other's genitals.

8. Other children repeatedly complain about the child's sexual behaviors—especially when the child has already been spoken to by an adult.

9. The child continues to behave in sexual ways in front of adults who say "no," or the child does not seem to comprehend admonitions to curtail overt sexual behaviors in public places.

10. The child appears anxious, tense, angry, or fearful when sexual topics arise in his or her everyday life.

11. The child manifests a number of disturbing toileting behaviors: she plays with or smears feces, urinates outside of the bathroom, uses excessive amounts of toilet paper, stuffs toilet bowls to overflowing, or sniffs or steals underwear.

12. The child's drawings depict genitals as the predominate feature.

13. The child manually stimulates or has oral or genital contact with animals.
14. The child has painful and/or continuous erections or vaginal discharge.[12]

Be careful when choosing baby-sitters and day-care providers. Be sure to visit unexpectedly in order to get a "true picture" of the place or person you are considering caring for your child. Keep in mind that most children are abused by a relative or someone they know. I understand it is not easy to imagine any of your loved ones causing harm to your child. Yet very often, that is exactly what happens. Trust your child until you have substantial reason to do otherwise. Seek professional help if you are confused or suspect your child may be confused. Do not discount their stories before you have thoroughly checked them out.

One young mother told me of her horrifying discovery that her younger brother had molested her four-year-old daughter. It seems the mother had asked her brother to baby-sit while she worked part-time. He had been out of a job for a while and she wanted to help him out. In addition, she thought it would be great to have her children with a relative while she worked. One day she was able to leave work early and arrived home unexpectedly to find her daughter hysterical, in tears and bleeding from the vagina. To her shock she learned that her brother had molested her daughter. The mother was beside herself. How could this have happened? How could her brother, whom she loved so dearly, do such a thing? She was devastated and felt betrayed.

A teenage girl at a private school where I was doing some counseling was brought to me by her friends. "Katie can't stop crying and she won't tell us what's wrong. Will you talk to her please? She's really upset!"

I did talk to Katie that day and for several months after. It seems she had been having crying episodes since she found out her stepbrother was returning home after being away for several years. At first she could not identify why that should upset her so. Gradually, she began to have flashbacks of his visits to her room when she was five or six years old. He, then about sixteen years old, would come into her room after her parents were asleep at night and lie next to her, fondling her and masturbating. He would then sneak back to his own room for the remainder of the night.

Katie had tried to tell her mother as best she knew how. She said she was afraid of her stepbrother and wanted him to move away. She told her mother he "hurt her at night." She begged to be able to sleep with her parents. She tried to put furniture against her door so he could not get in.

Her parents talked with their son. He said he was just "playing around" and that Katie was exaggerating. He promised to stay out of her room at night. But he did not. His nightly excursions continued, but not quite as often.

When Katie continued to complain the son continued to deny the episodes. Her parents thought Katie was simply having trouble adjusting to their marriage and dismissed her fears as "wild imagination" and "jealousy of her new brother." A small frightened child, she didn't know how to fight back or get them to believe her. Finally, after meeting with no success, she stopped saying anything. Her stepbrother's visits to her room continued until he moved away about two years later.

Now he was coming back and even though she was much older, her panic returned. In addition to the old fears and anxieties, she had new concerns. As she had grown older she began to wonder why her mother didn't believe her when she tried to tell her about the abuse. Why had her parents continued to let her stepbrother stay in the house when they knew Katie had such a terrible fear of him? Surely they must have heard him at night. Why did they not do something? Why had her mother never mentioned it again?

She was hurt and depressed. Her self-esteem was low and she couldn't stay focused on her schoolwork. She was having trouble sleeping and had begun to drink on weekends so she could "relax a little bit." She stayed out late and began showing up late for work and school.

She and her parents were not getting along. There were frequent, violent fights. Did her mother not love her or care about her? Why would she not believe Katie now that she was older? Why didn't her mother simply refuse to take the stepbrother back? Finally, things became so severe Katie had to be admitted to a treatment center for more intensive therapy.

As she dealt with these difficult questions in her counseling sessions, Katie began to experience emotional flooding and detailed flashbacks. She identified smells that reminded her of her stepbrother only to burst out in tears in front of puzzled friends. She remembered an episode with her stepbrother that took place on a visit to her grandmother's. While her mother visited inside, she was told to play outside. Her stepbrother took her into a grove of trees and fondled her until her mother called them into the house. After that she was aware of always feeling uneasy around woods, but up to this point hadn't been able to identify why. She cried and cried. She felt restless and angry.

As she slowly put the pieces together, she learned to forgive herself. She began to understand that even though she had repressed these memories, because they were too horrible to think about consciously, they were nevertheless affecting her life. She tended to date boys who degraded and used her. She didn't think a really nice guy would want to go out with her. Her low self-esteem was keeping her from believing she could go to college and have a successful career.

Fortunately, Katie was a fighter. She was determined to take charge of her life and not let this traumatic childhood experience ruin her. She wanted desperately to deal with it and get on with her life. Gradually, she recognized she had felt guilty and ashamed because the touches felt good to her. She was finally able to understand that she had no reason to assume any guilt or accept any blame for what happened. In time, she was able to accept that she was only a child and that as a child, she was not responsible for causing her stepbrother's problem or the abuse that accompanied it.

Unfortunately, Katie had to deal with all this alone. When I brought her mother in for consultation, I was saddened and disappointed. The mother was in complete denial. "Couldn't Katie have imagined all this? . . . What am I supposed to do? . . . I don't want to lose my husband over this! . . . How can I tell him his son isn't welcome in our home? . . . But we all have to have Christmas together; we're family!"

Such were the comments I heard on that and subsequent days as I tried to help Katie's mother understand the effect her behavior was having on her daughter. Missing was the loving concern for her daughter and the terrible emotional struggle she was going through. Trying desperately to keep up her grades, hold her job, and graduate on time, Katie was dealing with rejection by her mother on top of everything else.

After several visits, Katie's mother broke down and admitted that she too had been abused by a relative when she was young. Because no one had helped her to deal with it, she took the approach, "These things happen in every family; she'll get over it—I did; it's not the end of the world; there's really nothing you can do about these things." By denying the abuse that Katie had experienced, she was denying the abuse she too had suffered.

It took a long time for Katie and her mother to work things out between them. Were it not for Katie's strength and determination to do so, it never would have happened. Her mother did not have the strength or the desire to take charge of her own life, let alone help her daughter to do the same. She could not bear to examine her own abusive situation and identify how it had influenced, and continued to influence, her life in negative ways.

Denial and repression are a common way to handle painful experiences, especially those that occur early in life. The energy needed to face and work through such tragedies is phenomenal. Counseling takes strength, dedication, and hard work. How much better it would be if we parents could establish positive communication patterns from early childhood on that could allow us to deal openly and honestly with negative situations as they arise in our families and personal lives, rather than wait for a crisis to force us into doing so.

Abuse can happen to anyone at any age, but children are particularly vulnerable. The perpetrator is usually not some stranger hiding behind the bushes. As we see from these two cases, it is often someone trusted, someone very close to home. It is important to remember that the perpetrator too has been wounded, probably early in life, and may suffer terrible feelings of guilt and helplessness at his/her dysfunction. The gospel approach is to seek help for *both* the perpetrator and the victim, not revenge. *Forgiveness is part of recovery.*

Let's now take a look at some things you might say to your young child to help protect him or her from falling victim to sexual abuse. The first lesson to teach them is that no one—adult or child, family member or stranger—has the right to harm them sexually or otherwise.

Remember our goal is to help the child become aware of potentially harmful situations and to give the child permission to tell us if such a situation should arise. We do not want to create a distrust of all family or friends; we do not want to arouse fear and anxiety over new situations or new people. We do not want to give rise to a fear of sexuality or foster the attitude that sexuality always causes pain and problems, and thus lead to the conclusion that all sexual feelings must be bad.

In order to avoid such pitfalls, it is important that we talk with our young children in a tone that is calm and gentle. It is best to have such a conversation when you are going to be around for awhile, should your child become anxious or have questions requiring further discussion. Here is how a conversation might go:

*I want to talk with you about something very important. Come sit by me for awhile. Have you ever heard of the word "abuse"? What do you think it means?* (Allow child to answer and then continue.)

*Our hands and feet and legs are uncovered most of the time, aren't they? Everyone can see them. There are other parts of our body that are covered up most of the time. We call these private parts, because they are parts that we don't want everyone to see. Some private parts are the breasts, the vulva, and the penis. These are very special and personal parts of our body. No one should touch these parts of our body unless we tell them it is OK.*

*But there are some people who try to touch the private parts of children's bodies, even when the children ask them not to. Sometimes they tell kids to* keep this a secret. They may even say, "Don't tell anyone about this, or I'll hurt you." This is very wrong. If anyone ever tries to do this to you, you should tell them "no." You should tell them that you will tell me about it. This is called sexual abuse and sexual abuse is wrong. It can hurt kids very much. It can make them very unhappy. Have you ever heard of someone being sexually abused? How did you hear about this?

Honey, if someone should touch you when you don't want to be touched, I want you to tell me right away. If I am not nearby, tell another adult, someone that you trust. That person will know what to do. He or she will help you.

I know this may be hard. Sometimes the people who touch us in the wrong way might be people we love. We don't want to make them mad at us, do we? We don't want to hurt them. But a person who tries to abuse your body by touching your private parts when you don't want them to is sick. And no matter who they are they need to get help. If you tell me, or another grownup, about the person who abused you, you could help that person to get better. This takes a lot of courage doesn't it? Yes! I know it does. And I know it would be hard. But it is very important that you tell me if anyone ever tries to touch you when you don't want to be touched.

Now please don't be confused.

Can you think of anyone who might need to touch your body to help you or examine you? Yes, a doctor or a nurse might need to. They may need to do this to make sure you aren't sick. That's not abuse.

What about if your teacher or a neighbor gives you a quick, friendly hug or pat on the back? Is that abuse? No, that would not be abuse either.

Abuse usually happens in secret. If someone is going to try to abuse you, they might try to get you alone, away from others. They may want to go someplace where no one else can see you. They might even say, "Let's keep this a secret. Don't tell anyone what we did." Abuse often makes you feel uncomfortable or ashamed.

Most of the time it feels good to touch our bodies and to be touched by someone else. We love to be hugged and kissed. God gave us these good feelings. But when you don't want to be hugged or kissed or touched in any way, I hope you will say "no."

I hope that you will respect others too. If you want to hug them and they don't want to be hugged, I hope you listen to them and respect their right to say "no." Remember, sometimes you just don't feel like being hugged and sometimes other people don't feel like being hugged either!

It's very important not to laugh or joke about this. When you tell someone "no," you should look that person straight in the eye. Be sure you don't laugh. Look mad. The person has to know that you are not joking around. So be *very strong and say your "no" loud and firm, like this: "NO." Try it with me now: "NO."*

*Now one more thing. If you have a friend who you think is being sexually abused, what should you do? You could tell me, or your teacher, school counselor, or nurse, or some other grown-up you trust. You will be helping your friend, even though it may be hard for you.*

*One of our most special gifts from God is our wonderful bodies. Our Creator made our bodies special and important. I hope you won't let anyone hurt your body.*

Later, you might go over the main points of your conversation. Encourage your child to practice being assertive:

- *If you don't want to be touched, what should you say? Right! You should say "NO."*
- *When you say "NO" where should you look? That's right! You should look the person straight in the eye.*
- *When you say "NO" should you laugh? No, you should not laugh. You must look serious, like you really mean what you say.*
- *If someone does touch you, even after you said "NO," what should you do? Very good! You should tell me or an adult that you trust.*
- *What should you do if one of your friends tells you that they are being abused? Correct! You should tell me or another grown-up you trust.*

We need to give our children the words to say and the confidence to say them. In this way, they know they have our support and trust.

Discuss with your child whether s/he has ever experienced any type of sexual abuse, and if so, who was involved. Assure your child that s/he will be protected, not harmed, by telling you. Depending upon the situation, you may wish to consult a physician as to the advisability of counseling for your child.

With an older child you might want to discuss in greater detail how you would want them to handle a situation should someone try to abuse them. Talk with them about situations that may be potentially dangerous. For example, hitchhiking, accepting a date from someone they do not know, going somewhere unknown, or drinking or using drugs at parties. Explain to your child how drugs and alcohol change some persons' personalities. Tell them how to get away from someone who might be threatening them. Here are some points to stress:

*Don't be alone with someone who makes you feel uncomfortable, even if it is a relative or family member; if you must be around them, try to have someone else with you. Otherwise, avoid them and tell me about it.* (Sometimes a young person has to be in the company of someone that makes him or her feel uncomfortable. Perhaps a relative or neighbor who hugs them "too close." We need to give them skills for handling such a situation, permission to leave such a situation, or permission to avoid it in the first place.)

*If someone is making advances you don't like or feel comfortable with, tell them so. Make your feelings known very clearly and firmly. Tell them you will report them to me or the police if they try anything improper. If they continue to make you feel uncomfortable, you may have to be rude or even call the police. If you are feeling nervous, leave at once.*

*Avoid going places alone. Always let me know where you are going and whom you will be with.*

*It's important for you to dress modestly and use appropriate language. You don't want to give anyone the opportunity to misunderstand your intentions or desires.*

*Avoid going places where you feel uncomfortable or in danger. Even if the abuse involves someone in our family, you should come and talk to me about it. I will stand by you and help you. If you don't think I can help you, you have my permission to go talk to someone you think can.*

*If anyone threatens you in any way, leave. Come home immediately and if I'm not home, lock the doors, call me or the police, and don't let anyone in the house until I, or the police, get there.*

*If this should ever happen with a boyfriend or girlfriend, stop going out with them. They will never respect your feelings. Ending the relationship is the only way you can retain your self-respect.* [12]

Help your child understand that sexual abuse can happen to anyone. No one has the right to make them do something they do not want to do. No one has the right to use them for their own pleasure. They have the right to say "no" and to have that right enforced.

In 1989 I released a video and print sexuality series for junior high students titled *In God's Image: Male and Female.* Several months ago I received a phone call that made all the work I put into that series worthwhile.

The phone call was from a sales representative who was handling sales of the series. It seems a customer had called to relate a story involving one of the schools using *In God's Image*. The story was about a student who attended that school and her parents.

The girl had been in classes using "*In God's Image* from fifth grade on. She was in eighth grade when the following incident took place. The girl was an only child and both her parents worked, so she came home each day to an empty house. One day when she arrived home, there was a note on the door that UPS had tried to deliver a package and, since no one was home, had left the package next door.

Shortly after she was in her house, the next-door neighbor called and asked her to come over and get the package for her parents. She said she would be right over and within a few minutes was ringing the neighbor's doorbell. The neighbor invited her in and told her the package was upstairs. The girl had babysat for this man and his wife several times and knew that the only rooms upstairs were bedrooms. She was puzzled and a bit alarmed, so she said, "UPS doesn't deliver things upstairs in houses." He insisted the package was upstairs and moved toward her to guide her upstairs. She resisted and said, "There's nothing upstairs but bedrooms! I'm not going up." With that she dashed toward the front door. The man tried to tackle her and force her to the floor, but she wiggled away and ran out the door.

When she got in her house she locked all the doors and called her mother at work. Without hesitation her mother said, "Stay inside and don't let anyone in. I'm going to put my coworker on the phone with you while I hurry home. I'll be there in ten minutes. Stay on the phone with her until I get into the house. I'll call the police and tell them what happened."

The coworker talked to the girl until her mother came home. When the police arrived and the investigation got under way, it was discovered that the man had been abusing his two young daughters as well.

The mother told the sales manager, "I'm not sure my daughter and I would have handled this so well had it not been for the sexuality program she was in. Because there was a video on sexual abuse, and because the parent worksheet advised talking with my child about what to do in case of an abusive situation, my daughter had talked with her father and me about what we would want her to do. *Because* we talked with her about it, she felt confident and knew exactly what to do. So did I. To be honest, had we not done so, I'm afraid I might not have handled it so well. My husband or I might have questioned my daughter's interpretation of the events. After all, we knew this man so well. My daughter had babysat for him and his wife so many times! There was never a reason to suspect anything like this would happen.

"I might have said, 'Are you sure you didn't misunderstand him, honey?' or 'Are you certain he was coming on to you?' That would have really hurt my daughter and confused her. I'm so glad we talked beforehand. It made a terrible situation a little easier to manage because we both knew what to do. Afterward, we knew we had done the best thing we could."

I can't tell you what a good feeling I had after hearing this story. Advance communication *can* and *does* work. Planning how to handle a dangerous situation can be helpful. *Anything you can do to empower your child is worth your time.* You might even want to enroll in a self-defense class with your daughter or son. (Remember, boys get abused too. So be sure to have this conversation with both daughters *and* sons!)

Plan in advance exactly what to do in case of an emergency. Do it today, do not wait. We cannot control every situation, but we can encourage skills and present information that can lessen the effects of a crisis should one occur. You never know when such information will be useful for your child or for yourself. Hopefully, you will not have to use it, but if you do, you will be awfully glad you took the time.

One final comment. Sexual abuse is a reality. *Don't overlook the possibility of it happening in your home.* Don't blind yourself to signals or cues your child may be trying to give you. Please don't turn a deaf ear to cries for help. If you don't know what to do, get help! It's as near as your phone. There are support homes and hot lines in every city. You are the only one who can protect your child from this crime. If you don't who will? If you don't, you will have to live with the knowledge you might have helped prevent your child's pain, but instead looked the other way.

There are many women and men today who suffered the additional burden of having been abused *twice:* once at the hands of the offending parent and once by the parent who refused, for whatever reasons, to acknowledge that there was something terrible going on in their home. Please don't let this happen in your home, to your child. Prepare your child for the possibility of dealing with sexual abuse, and be prepared to deal with it yourself.

# Chapter 10

. . . . . . . . .

~

# Avoiding the Tragedy
# of Date Rape

During the last ten years, a new word has become part of our sexual vocabulary. The word is *date rape* and it has become a grim reality. The term is new; the issue is old. Date rape occurs anytime one person, friend or acquaintance, forces himself physically and sexually upon another person. FORCE is the key word. We are not speaking here of seduction, which at some level implies consent. We are speaking of *unwanted* sexual activity, specifically forced intercourse.

The use of force is what defines rape, not the relationship between the two people involved, or the presence or absence of a weapon.[1] Throughout our entire discussion please bear this definition in mind, because it is the force, and lack of consent, that is the focus issue here. *We are not discussing sexual activity among consenting adults; we are discussing an act of violence.*

*Webster's New Universal Unabridged Dictionary* describes violence as "unjust use of force or power, as in deprivation of rights." What makes date rape so very wrong is that the rapist takes away or denies the victim's freedom to refuse. We are discussing an act of coercion, an act of physical force used to damage or injure, an unjust desecration of a person's mind and body.

Date rape is a major problem on our college campuses. Currently one in four college women reports being raped or having rape attempted on her by her senior year. Nationally, the incidence of date rape is highest among women in their first year of college. Seventy percent to eighty percent of these women will know their perpetrator. According to the FBI one in fifteen college men admit having attempted or completed date rape by their senior year.

Many of you will have sons and daughters attending college. Presumably, you will talk with your young adult about some of the realities of living campus life, whether they live at home and commute or actually live on campus. I hope you will take the time to include the topic of date rape in your list of "important reminders."

Date rape is not limited to the campus. Most of you will have sons and daughters who will date, whether they attend college or not. By talking honestly and openly about rape and what it means to both men and women, you can help your adolescent avoid becoming a statistic.

To be effective, I think this talk should take place before your adolescent ever begins dating. Some studies are now showing a rise in high school date rape. In order to prepare your daughter or son to avoid this tragedy, your discussion should take place several times during the dating years, beginning in junior high.

To better understand the problems encompassing the date rape, we need to take a good look at our own American culture. Who have our heroes been? If dollars at the box office are any measure of popularity, it is interesting to note that many of the most popular stars at the movies and on TV, especially in the past, are men who have made their fortune portraying violent, aggressive men.

Men like Clint Eastwood, Chuck Norris, Bruce Lee, Avery Brooks, Sylvester Stallone, John Wayne, David Michael Thomas, Howard Rollins Jr. and Charles Bronson, just to name a few, have become well-known national figures while portraying distant, aloof, violent, aggressive, unattached loners who face the world defiantly and use force to get what they want from others.[2]

As a country, we Americans have a love-hate relationship with violence and aggression. Statistics show that when compared with Australia, France, Poland, Sweden, and Austria, Americans kill one another *ten times* more frequently. When compared with Spain, Denmark, Norway, and Greece, we kill one another *twenty times* more frequently.[3]

Sadly enough we Americans expect our men and boys to be tough and aggressive on supposedly appropriate occasions. "Sugar and spice and everything nice" describes the popular idea of a young girl. Mothers tell their sons to use force in order to "stand up for themselves." Fathers tell their sons that they should "act like a man" and "don't run from a fight like a sissy!" Coaches tell their players that injuring others is "part of the game," "all's fair in love and football," "pain is pleasure," "agony is ecstasy," to "develop the killer instinct" and to "take it like a man."

Relatives tell the little girls in their families, "You're too pretty to play soccer," and, "Why would your daughter want to play on a co-ed team with those rough boys? She should stick with the girls!" A father encourages his daughter, "Just cry a little, you'll never get a speeding ticket." "Just bat those beautiful eyes of yours and you'll get an A."

## Who "Wears the Pants" in Your House?

Somehow we clearly teach our young men that their initiation through violence is part of a rite of passage into manhood. All the while we give conflicting messages. When boys are young we caution them to "turn the other cheek," and admonish them "not to hit girls." But as time progresses domination and control are often seen as masculine virtues to be copied.[4]

Violence is not inborn; violence is learned. Rape is *not* an integral part of the male nature. Rape occurs in cultures characterized by other forms of violence. In a study of ninety-five cross-cultural societies, forty-seven percent were identified as rape-free, thirty-five percent were listed in an intermediate category, and only eighteen percent were classified as rape-prone societies.[5]

The United States is a violent and rape-prone society in which women are seen as subservient to men. This is borne out by the following facts regarding violence against women. These are taken from the video by Joan Chittister, O.S.B., *Women, Religion, and Peacemaking: Sexism and Militarism*:

- Two million women are beaten yearly.
- In two thirds of all marriages the woman is beaten at least once during the marriage.
- Twenty-five percent of all women in the United States are beaten weekly.
- Twenty percent of all medical emergency treatment is the result of a wife-beating incident.
- Twenty-five percent of female suicide attempts follow a wife-beating incident or involve women from battered homes.
- One in four murdered women are killed by their husbands or boyfriends in anger.
- In the United States one woman is beaten every eighteen seconds.
- Rape is the fastest rising violent crime listed in the FBI's *Uniform Crime Reports*.
- In the United States one woman is raped every three minutes.
- More than half of the rapes occur between people who have met before. These are called "date rapes."

These statistics are taken from *reported* incidents of abuse. Many women *do not* report physical and sexual abuse due to fear or shame. Therefore, officials estimate that fifty percent of all rapes go unreported, which means that the actual incidents of rape and physical abuse are much higher than the preceding statistics indicate.

Given this background of violence toward women in which to grow up, is it any wonder that young men feel they have the right to force their dates into sexual activity? Is it any wonder that other young men will stand idly by while a young man "gets what's coming to him?"

## What Does She Know, She's Only a Woman!

One significant predictor of a rape-prone society is the endorsement of the "macho personality." Another is the belief that women are inferior. In her book *Rape and Sexual Assault II*, Ann Burgess defines a "macho personality" as embracing the following three characteristics: 1) a calloused attitude toward women, 2) a conception of violence as manly, and 3) a view of danger as exciting. These three factors are significantly correlated with self-reported sexual aggression against women and are the best predictor of sexually coercive and assaultive behavior.

The parallels between the male American heroes and the "macho personality" are striking and obvious, as is our classification as a society prone toward rape. Sadly, the high rates of sexual aggression seen in college students support the claim that rape is a culturally sanctioned phenomenon in the United States.[6] Diane Russel, a researcher and writer on the topic of rape, explains it this way:

> Rape may be understood as an extreme acting out of qualities that are regarded as super masculine in this and many other societies: aggression, force, power, strength, toughness, dominance, and competitiveness. To win, to be superior, to be successful, to conquer—all demonstrate masculinity to those who subscribe to common cultural notions of masculinity. . . . Sex may be the arena where these notions of masculinity are most intensely played out. Particularly by men who feel powerless in the rest of their lives.[7]

Measured by these standards Jesus Christ would be seen as a wimp by many in today's American society. "Turning the other cheek" may be OK for girls and sissies, but a "real man" knows that is just so much mush.[8]

## Early Behavior Sets the Pattern

Research shows that from an early age, boys in groups communicate through domination and aggression, while girls communicate in ways that facilitate discussion.[9] Studies show that young girls are passive *only* when interacting with boys, not with other girls. It appears that the roughhousing engaged in by young boys makes it difficult for girls to interact with them, so they choose to play with members of their same sex instead.

Young boys do not respond to girls' commands to stop doing something. They do, however, change their behavior in response to demands made by other boys.[10] Numerous studies show that the most powerful reason that boys or men resist girls' or women's influence is peer pressure. It would seem that some men are afraid that if they allow themselves to be influenced by females their peers will see them as weak and less masculine.

Men have not been encouraged to be warm and caring or respecting and loving in their relationships. Young boys need warmth, cuddling, hugs, and tenderness just as much as little girls do. But they don't get it. ("Be a tough guy!" "You're not going to cry on me are you?" "Don't be afraid to get tough—it's part of the game!")

Such are the ways little boys are socialized into aggression. The result is that young boys assume a power-assertive style of interacting, in which they back up direct demands with force. This style of interacting is rewarded by others who see him as a "strong, tough little guy," and therefore reinforced, so that communicating in this manner becomes a way of life. Because of this style, from very early on, a girl senses and often directly experiences an element of fear in her interactions with boys and men.

The young girl, by contrast, seeks to communicate in ways that will please others and help her obtain what she wants at the same time. Girls' communication skills are associated with the ability to avoid violence and resolve conflict.[11] Because of this, girls have difficulty influencing boys and so tend to play with other girls whom they can influence, and to whose style of communicating they know how to respond. Studies show that young girls do respond to other girls' requests regarding their behavior as well as to requests made by boys.[12] Girls develop a style of relating to others based upon reciprocal agreement. They are rewarded for being polite, "good girls." Thus this method of communication is reinforced for them. Women have been discouraged from communicating assertively with men; this is often criticized and seen as "unladylike" behavior.

But being polite at all costs can cost women a lot as they grow older and continue this style of interacting. Women who were off-limits as little girls now become the primary targets for male aggression. Men are less likely than women to recognize subtle or nonverbal sexual refusals.[13] Because some women lack directness and assertiveness, men may feel that they are sending them a mixed message or that women don't know what they want as they try to tell men "no" in their less than direct manner.

## What Kind of a Man Is a Rapist?

Many people think that rape is something that happens only with a stranger who has a knife or a gun. Often if a woman knows or likes the man, she doesn't want to admit that she has been raped. We live with the myth that a rapist is a crazed, demented, psychotic individual. Sad to say, this is the exception rather than the rule. Psychologically, rapists are no different than most men.[14]

Men who rape women are men who like to dominate and control. They are men who are exceptionally jealous. They are men who do not respect or listen to women; they like to make all the decisions, control the whole date. They make demands on their date about who she can talk to, what she can wear. Men who rape women tend to be heavy drinkers. They make assumptions about what a man's rights are just because he paid for a date or is in a relationship with a woman. According to the FBI *Uniform Crime Reports* most men who rape are young, with sixty-one percent of them being under twenty-five. Men who rape are likely to believe that their sexual urges are uncontrollable. They believe in aggression and are likely to repeat their crime.[15] They are men who like to manipulate and humiliate women, men who enjoy making a woman feel guilty.

Aggressive men view wielding power as masculine; they believe that women enjoy sexual violence. They are callous and see themselves as superior to others, especially to women. They are insecure. They are very likely to have had more sexual partners and are "dramatically more" sexually active than men who are sexually nonaggressive. These men are more likely to regard heterosexual relationships as game-playing, and see women as being responsible for preventing rape. They are likely to have more sympathy for the rapist than for the rape victim.[16]

## A Look at the Myths

Researchers tell us that a society that accepts myths regarding rape is more likely to be rape-prone. The belief in these myths is one of the main causes most women decide not to report having been raped. In a recent nationwide college survey, eighty percent of the young women who had been forced to engage in sexual activity against their will stated that they had not reported the incidents due to fear they could not make a case against the man, that they would not be believed, or that reporting the incident would cause them to lose other friendships. Because these myths are held by many, rape victims are often treated with callous indifference or, worse yet, downright hostility. These rape myths produce damaging effects on the victim because they shift responsibility and blame for the act from the rapist to the victim. They also damage the victim because they deny or reduce the perceived injury to the victim.[17] Let us remember that, "Rape is an aggressive act perpetrated on another to show the dominance and power of the rapist."[18]

The following are some of the more prevalent myths regarding rape.

### Women enjoy sexual violence.

NOT TRUE: Virtually all women who have been raped report feelings of terror, humiliation, and degradation after their rape.[19] Psychologists report that women who have been raped by an acquaintance may suffer more because the incident causes them to lose confidence in themselves and their own judgment. Rape victims suffer extreme emotional distress and have many lingering symptoms such as flashbacks, emotional flooding, nightmares, loss of sleep, loss of sexual enjoyment, lowered self-esteem, and continual fear.

### Sex is the primary reason for rape.

NOT TRUE: *Power* and *anger* are the primary motives for rape. Researchers have found that rape is much more concerned with status, aggression, control, and dominance than with sensual pleasure or sexual satisfaction. This is supported by the high incidence of premeditated rape, which refutes the idea that rape is due to an uncontrollable sexual impulse.[20]

### Women are responsible for rape prevention.

NOT TRUE: Rape is the responsibility of the rapist, not the victim. A person wearing an expensive watch or carrying a lot of money does not expect or ask to be robbed. Nor are they told never to wear a watch.

A woman who dresses or acts in certain ways does not expect or ask to be raped.[21]

*Only certain kinds of women are raped.*

NOT TRUE: Research shows that rapists pick their victims for a variety of reasons, and that style of dress or character of the victim is seldom considered. In a study of rape victims in Washington, D.C., eighty-two percent of the victims were women with "good reputations."

*Women cry rape just to get even or cover up an unwanted pregnancy.*

NOT TRUE: In a 1985 study by Ehrhart and Sandler it was found that only about two percent of all rapes and sex charges have been determined to be false.

*Rape is sometimes justified.*

NOT TRUE: Rape is *never* justified. No matter how a woman is dressed, no matter if she is sober or drunk, no matter if she goes willingly to a man's apartment, there is no justification for rape. A woman may be guilty of using poor judgment, but that does not mean she is an object to be violated at will. Rape is a crime; it is an act of violence that carries with it the threat of death.[22] No one should ever be subjected to such violence. All people should have the right to change their mind. All people should be able to control their sexual urges. All people should respond appropriately to a "no."

It is up to us as parents to do what we can to break this cycle of violence and abuse. This is a problem that *can be solved.*

## What Parents Can Tell Their Daughters about Date Rape

It is true you can not control everything that happens, but if parents take the time to talk to their daughters about certain assertive behaviors, perhaps we could decrease the number of rapes generation by generation, until rape no longer existed in this country. It is helpful to women, in many situations, if they are assertive. Below are a few suggestions you might wish to talk about with your daughter. By following these basic precepts and using common sense, one can lessen the risk of being date-raped.

### Know your own feelings about sexual involvement.

Sexual intercourse should not be an accident. It is not something that "just happens." It is a special event that should be a choice, a conscious decision on your part. Examine your feelings carefully. Decide *when* you want to have sex and *with whom*. Determine the conditions clearly in your own mind. If *you* don't know what you want, no one else will either.

### Know your date.

Avoid getting picked up by men you don't know. Be sure you have spent enough time with a man to know his feelings about women and sex *before* you agree to go out with him. If you want to know how he feels about date rape, ask him!

### Learn to speak assertively.

Begin to practice being clear and assertive about the messages you send, the feelings you have. If you have doubts that others understand your position clearly, ask them what they think you said. This will give you some idea as to how you come across to others. Practice this in all your communications with others. Don't end your sentences by asking a question.

If you are saying "no," don't give a lot of explanation. Keep your message short and direct. Repeat it exactly as you first said it. If you are not getting your message across, don't hesitate to call the police. In order to speak assertively, you have to know what you want.

### Say what you mean.

If you don't mean it, don't say it! Men get confused and often angry with women who "lead them on" and then back off at the last minute. If you are not prepared to deal with the consequences, don't flirt! If you're not interested in a man, tell him so. Don't say "No" and then say, "Well, maybe later," or "Gosh, I'm not sure. I guess so. Maybe." This kind of communication makes you seem like an "airhead," a woman who can't make up her mind and doesn't know what she wants. It isn't cute; it's confusing. Be clear!

### Use assertive body language.

When you want to deliver a serious message to a man, look serious. Stand tall and erect. Keep your chin up and look him straight in the eye. Place your hands directly in front of you as a barrier to reinforce what you are saying. If you are saying "No," say "No" with your whole body. If you are not getting the results you want, do not stay and try to plead or argue. Turn around and leave at once.

### Always let friends know where you are and who you are with.

Don't leave a party or bar until you have let at least one of your friends know *where* you are going and *with whom*. Make sure your date/acquaintance is aware that others know whom you are with and where you are going. It is very risky to go off with someone you don't know well, to a place with which you are unfamiliar.

### Recognize your risk factors.

Young women must learn to realize that unfortunately they can't trust everyone. Coming from small communities and high schools where you are well known and know others well can lead you to the mistaken judgment that you are safe everywhere you go. This is not true. If you are walking late around campus, you are taking a risk. If you accept an offer to go to the room of a guy you don't know well, you are taking a risk. If you get drunk, you are taking a risk.

### Recognize that men are turned on faster physically than most women.

Sexual stimulation in most men is fast and physical. Men, in general, are turned on quickly by what they *see*. This is one reason some men complain of "mixed messages." If a woman is dressed provocatively and is flirting conspicuously, some men think she is sending the message that she is looking for a sex partner. In such a situation, some men will quickly become sexually aroused and feel that this is what the woman wants. This may not be at all true.

Because women are more likely to be turned on by what they *hear*, they need to realize that their clothes make a statement to men and may be a quick physical "turn-on." This is not reason for rape nor in any way justifies it. It is, however, important that young women recognize that what they wear, the way they speak, and how they act all send definite messages to men that may be misinterpreted. (If you are in doubt as to what you might be doing or saying that sends undesirable messages, ask a close male friend or relative for advice.)

*Use good judgment in accepting rides, dates, and offers for drinks.*

Think carefully before you accept an offer for a ride, a date, or a drink, even from someone on campus. Pay attention to the condition of the person asking you. Has he been drinking? Using drugs? Is he worked up or angry? Disoriented? Loud or rough? How well do you know him? Even the friend of a friend you know must be looked at carefully. Better to offend someone than to end up in a dangerous situation.

*Don't lose control by abusing alcohol or using drugs.*

If you want to be in control of yourself and have some control over what happens to you, you must avoid abusing alcohol or using drugs. You must be aware that alcohol lessens your inhibitions, clouds your judgment, and impairs your thinking. If you drink heavily or use drugs you are putting yourself at high risk; you are giving up control; you are taking a dangerous chance. Drugs and alcohol are two of the most frequent forms of force used to exploit females sexually.[23] You can't speak or act assertively if you're drunk.

Know your limits and stick to them. If you have trouble doing so, then ask a friend to help you out, to give you a helpful warning if you are exceeding your limit. If you need a few drinks to have a good time, you may well have an alcohol problem. Get help with it before you find yourself in a dangerous situation, one where you need to be sober and have all of your wits about you in order to come out in reasonable shape. You can't control everything that happens to you, but you can control your drinking.

*Remember you are in control of your own sexuality.*

It is up to you to decide how and when you wish to become sexually involved. If you do not want men taking advantage of you, you must behave, speak, and dress in such a manner that they will know you are not interested in a one-night stand. It is up to you to convey clearly to others what your thoughts and feelings are regarding sexual activity. This means you may have to go against the crowd or be the subject of teasing in order to stand up for what you believe in. Always remember, it is your right to set and follow your own standards.

### Avoid men who degrade or do not show respect for women.

This type of man is more likely than others to disregard a woman's wishes and commit date rape. Men who are loud and abusive in their behavior toward others, including other men, are trouble. *Stay away from them.* Pay attention to conversations, notice behavior, ask advice from others, listen to your inner voices. Avoid the use of sarcasm and/ or insulting remarks.

### Avoid men who abuse alcohol or use drugs.

Once again, men who abuse their own bodies by using drugs and/or drinking heavily are more likely to abuse women. Some men become violent when they drink; many drugs evoke violent behavior. A man doesn't have to be drunk to be dangerous. Drinking even one drink can change behavior in some men. This is an obvious danger signal, and one you can easily heed.

### Avoid men who are unusually jealous or manipulative.

Men who like to control you are more likely to rape you. If you are seeing someone who is abnormally jealous, follows you around wherever you go, tells you whom you can talk to, what you can wear, wants to control everything you do, always puts you on the defensive and makes you feel guilty, get rid of him. He is manipulating you and will likely continue to do so even more as time goes by. This kind of man feels inadequate in other areas of his life and tries to make himself feel important by controlling you. It's a potentially dangerous situation to put yourself in, and it's not going to get better.

### Learn how to defend yourself.

Bad things can happen to anyone. No matter how careful you are, you may find yourself in a situation where you need to protect or defend yourself from someone. Take a self-defense class. Learn some basic defense techniques. Be alert—learn how to recognize potential danger. Remember, rape is mainly about power, seldom about sex.

Mothers can model for daughters *how* to love men. Mothers can teach daughters to respect men. Parents, take the time to talk with your daughter to devise a plan of how to handle a situation should someone attempt to force intercourse on her. Follow the situation through to what she should do if she cannot escape from the perpetrator. Plan together whom she should notify and what hospital she should be checked out in. Hopefully, this is information that will never be used, but it will give both you and your daughter a feeling of increased security. In addition, should she need to use this information, having discussed it with you previously will enable her to act quickly with confidence, knowing you will support her.

## What Parents Can Tell Their Sons about Date Rape

Certainly the problem of rape is never going to be solved—and it *can* be solved—if women do not have the support of men. No husband or father wants to see his wife or daughter suffer the devastating and life-shattering effects of rape, and yet most men will be husbands and fathers, and some will be rapists. Many men who commit date rape do not think of themselves as rapists, but they are. It is extremely important to understand that *rape of any kind* is a crime, and any time a woman does not want to have sex with a man and the man *forces* her to have sex *against her will* is rape.

In order to eradicate the crime of rape from our country, men must become active and vocal in advocating the right of women to refuse sexual intercourse. If you believe that a woman has the right to refuse intercourse, then you must begin voicing that opinion to your male peers. Women cannot overcome this problem alone; they need men's help and support. *Men listen to other men.* What specifically can a man do to combat rape? Here a few suggestions you might want to share with your sons.

### Know your own feelings about sexual involvement.

Evaluate your attitudes and assumptions about your own sexuality. Having sexual intercourse should not be an accident. It is not something that "just happens." It is a special event that should be a choice, a conscious decision on your part. Examine your feelings carefully. Decide *when* you want to have sex and *with whom*. Determine the conditions clearly in your own mind. Make up your mind that you will never force anyone to have sex against their will.

### Learn to communicate clearly with women.

What should men do when they feel that a woman is sending a mixed message, or coyly suggesting sexual intercourse, while appearing to fend off his sexual advances? Men need to be comfortable openly asking a woman *exactly* what message she really wants to send. Neither male nor female should play guessing games or assume they know what the other wants. Just as women need to learn more about men and their perspectives, so too men need to understand better the female point of view.

There are only two sexes on this earth. We ought to try to appreciate each other's feelings so we can communicate effectively. Men need to encourage women to speak their minds openly and not be offended when they do so. Men should consider a woman's opinion when planning a date. If a man feels he is getting a "mixed message" from a woman, he should ask her to state clearly what she means or wants. Don't *assume* that you know what a woman wants; *ask* her instead. You will impress her with your willingness to listen and care about her feelings.

### Show respect when a woman says no.

No one likes to be rejected, but no one has the right to force their will on anyone else. If a woman meets your advances with a "no," back off. Show her that you respect her feelings. Give her time to get to know you better. If you force yourself on a woman you will lose her respect. You may even end up at the police station or in jail.

A few minutes of feeling like a conqueror is not worth facing yourself in the mirror or her hatred and fear the next time she sees you. Word travels fast, especially on a campus. When other women hear that you're out to use and abuse them, you'll be spending your Friday nights alone. On the other hand, when word spreads that you're the kind of guy who respects a woman's feelings, they just may line up at your door!

### Avoid telling jokes that degrade or humiliate women.

Have you ever been in a group when someone told a joke that put down your race, religion, or masculinity? Did it make you feel angry, uncomfortable, or embarrassed? Jokes that degrade women or call attention to their bodies are humiliating to women. Young women do not appreciate it when men use slang to describe the female anatomy. Slang is not something people use to compliment one another; its use is derogatory. You make yourself look insensitive and unkind when you make crude remarks about a woman's body.

*Stand up to your peers when they degrade or humiliate women.*

It has been previously pointed out that the biggest influence on men is their male peers. If women are going to be treated and respected as equals, then men have to be the ones to convince other men that this is as it should be. Have some guts! When you are in a crowd and some of your male friends begin to talk crudely about women, do not laugh. Better yet, speak up and say, "I don't really think that's funny." Walk away or in some way indicate your disapproval.

Once men begin to give each other permission to be thoughtful, once men begin to see that their masculinity does not depend on putting down women, then male abusive behavior toward women will begin to diminish. But it has to start with *men* creating an awareness in other men that this disrespectful, demeaning talk perpetuates abusive behavior toward women, and that this is no longer tolerable in our society.

*Defend a woman's right to speak assertively.*

If you want to prove you're a *real* man, speak out against date rape and all other forms of violence toward women. Tell your buddies that you admire a woman who knows what she wants and isn't afraid to say so. Be respectful and supportive when a woman is assertive and definite in her conversations with you. Encourage her to voice her opinion and reinforce her when she does. Women need to know that there are men who care about how they feel, what they think, men who will treat them as intelligent equals and encourage them to become the best they can be, men who are not afraid or threatened by a woman who can speak her mind. Women need the assurance that they will not be rejected as pushy or overbearing if they stand up for themselves.

*When you have doubts about what a woman wants, ask her.*

It is foolish to play guessing games that can end up awkwardly for both of you, when it's so easy just to ask a question. Men and women need

to learn to communicate comfortably about sexuality. Rather than operating on the assumption that a woman is out to pick somebody up
because of the way she is acting, why not ask, "Are you interested in
company?" That way you are both given the opportunity to get your
signals straight. But remember, if she says "no," let her alone.

*Never use force to get your way.*

Rape occurs when a woman *chooses not to have intercourse* with a specific
man, and the man *chooses to proceed* against her will.[24] Date rape is a
crime. Forced sex is *never* acceptable, even with someone you know
well. By resorting to the use of force with a woman, you show that you
are indeed weak, not strong enough to accept a "no," not strong enough
to control your own body, not masculine enough to walk away.

When you force a woman to have sex you take the risk of facing
arrest and possibly jail. To be practical, you face the risk of AIDS and/
or other sexually transmitted diseases, because you forfeit your right to
discussion. You become responsible for the probable emotional break-
down of another human being. You become, in fact, a criminal, prose-
cuted or not.

A woman is not rejecting you as a person if she refuses to have
intercourse with you. She may care very much for you but have other
reasons for not wanting intimacy at this time. If you pressure her into
having sex you may destroy the feelings she has for you.

*Teach your sons that real men treat women as equals.*

Most men will become husbands and fathers. Begin the end to the abuse
of women by treating your wife with respect and teaching your sons to
do the same. Never stand by and let them humiliate their mother or
sister. Teach them that *real* men treat women as equals. Your generation
has the opportunity to make the United States a rape-free society for
your daughters. *Carpe diem!*

*Realize that women respond differently to sexual arousal
than men.*

Because women respond more to what they hear than what they see,
they may look at dress and behavior differently than many men. What
a man sees as a real "turn-on," a woman may not. Most women do not
experience the immediate physical arousal that many men do. Sexual

arousal seems to take more time in a woman and is often triggered by different stimuli than men. (Many men respond to visual stimuli and direct touch; many women respond to verbal stimuli and gentle touch.) Because of this many women are not aware of the sexual stimulus they incite in men by sexy dress or dancing. Men need to be honest with women and tell them when their behavior or dress is overly provocative. It is only through honest communication that we can resolve our differences and come to a mutual respect of one another.

### Avoid women who pose a temptation for you.

If you are a man who feels he has little control over his sexual urges, then you would probably benefit from counseling. A healthy man should be able to control his sexual urges. It is not normal for men to lose control of themselves. If this is happening to you, you need to get help with this, and find out why you have this problem. It *is* a problem. To gain some immediate control over your impulses, avoid women who trigger them. If you feel yourself losing control, leave the situation at once. If you cannot rely on yourself to do this, ask a friend to help. You need not explain your situation in great detail. Indicate that at times you feel that you are losing control and if that happens s/he should take you home before you do something that could cause harm to someone else as well as yourself. This will take courage on your part. You will be showing your strength by leaving a potentially dangerous situation, whereas by staying and possibly forcing someone to satisfy your urges, you only show your weakness and lack of control. Real power comes from controlling yourself, not someone else.

### Do not abuse alcohol or use drugs.

Blaming your loss of self-control on drinking is a weak excuse. If you find you lose control more readily when you are drinking or high, *don't drink or do drugs!* One of the most important parts of growing up lies in learning your limits. You need to know how much is too much. You need to know at what point you are "out of it." Friends can help you, if you have the strength to ask for their help. They can tell you when you are pushing your limit if you are unable to recognize that yourself.

Don't do something harmful to another human being because you were too drunk to control yourself. You'll have to live with the knowledge that you raped someone for the rest of your life. Even if you could make it up to her, would you ever be able to forgive yourself? Remember you are in control of your sexuality. If alcohol can do that to you then you have a problem with drinking and need to get some help to solve it. If you feel the need to have power, have power over your drinking. If you want to conquer something, conquer your drinking.

Fathers, model for your sons how to love women. Teach your sons to respect women. Teach your sons to love and respect themselves. Talk with your son about the consequences of committing or attempting to commit date rape. Should he appear indifferent to the seriousness of this crime, counseling may help him identify his disregard for the rights of others and his inappropriate attitude about sexual intercourse.

## Working Together

Unlike many problems in today's society, the problem of date rape is one that we have answers to, as well as means to solve it. Now we have to work together, men and women, to put our knowledge and means to work. If rape continues rampant on the high school and college campus and in the United States, it is only because we are allowing it to happen. We have the power to control date rape. We have the necessary influence to make our campuses and streets safe for everyone. We can make high school and college social life fun again, not something to be feared. With the power that comes from men and women working together, we can ensure a better understanding and enjoyment of sexuality for all persons. Parents can begin this process by educating the next generation.

# Chapter 11

· · · · · · · · · ·

∽

# AIDS and Sexually Transmitted Diseases

No book on sexuality today would be complete without a discussion of AIDS and the implications of this disease for our young people. After consulting with parents of all ages, I felt it would be helpful to include a brief description of other sexually transmitted diseases prevalent in today's society as well.

Every year two and a half million United States teenagers are infected with an STD.[1] Experts tell us that there are about 27,000 new cases of STDs occurring each day. Adolescents between the ages of ten and nineteen constitute twenty-five percent of syphilis and gonorrhea cases today.[2] Many of us grew up in a time when syphilis and gonorrhea were the *only* venereal diseases (VDs) we ever heard about. At the time of this writing, there are over twenty-five *known* diseases that are transmitted primarily through sexual activity. Some of these diseases have no cure. Some are passed on when those infected transmit the disease to their child in childbirth. Some have no symptoms. Many have symptoms that are easily overlooked and go away if untreated. Even though the symptoms disappear, the disease remains in the body causing damage.

Before we begin, you may have wondered about the now frequently used term, STD. This term is preferred by educators and medical persons because "sexually transmitted" is more inclusive than "venereal." Not all sexually transmitted diseases are confined to the venereal area. I will use STD for the remainder of this chapter. There is not space to discuss all of these diseases, so I will focus on a few of the more common ones.

We will begin our discussion with acquired immunodeficiency syndrome (AIDS). I will be going into great detail here, as the topic is serious and the ramifications many.

AIDS: As of February 1990, fifty percent of those diagnosed with AIDS were twenty-nine and under. Since there is such a long incubation period for the virus, it is most probable that these persons actually were infected as teens. Among men aged twenty-five to forty-four, AIDS became the second-leading cause of death in 1989. AIDS kills young black men at three times the rate it kills whites, and it kills young Hispanics at twice the rate it kills whites.[3]

Here in the United States, women constitute the fastest-growing group of persons with AIDS. In New York City, AIDS is the leading killer of women between the ages of twenty-five to thirty-four. Owing to the long latency period between HIV and the onset of symptoms, most were likely infected as adolescents.[4] This puts teenage girls at high risk for AIDS. Research done by the United Nations Development Program states one reason for the high rate of infection among girls is that the genital tracts of girls are not completely developed. This leaves them more vulnerable to sexually transmitted diseases.[5]

At this time there is no cure for AIDS. The disease AIDS develops from the human immunodeficiency virus (HIV). From the time of infection, the disease may incubate, or remain hidden in the body, for up to ten years, possibly more. During this time the infected individual may have no symptoms, no indication that s/he is carrying HIV. However, during this time, this individual *can infect others,* even though this individual may be unaware that s/he may be doing so. The only way such a person would know if s/he were infected is if s/he had been tested positive for HIV. If one is tested too soon after initial infection, the virus may not show up. Doctors recommend testing be repeated six months after the original test to insure greater accuracy on diagnosis.

This means a young person could be infected at age fifteen or sixteen and not be aware they are caring the virus for up to ten years. During this ten years they have the potential of infecting everyone they encounter sexually. You can see just how dangerous and insidious this disease is, and how dangerous promiscuous sexual activity can be.

*AIDS is not a homosexual disease.* AIDS is a human disease. Worldwide the disease is sixty percent heterosexual.[6] It is a dangerous myth that unless you are gay or a drug user, you will not get AIDS. Unfortunately, it is a myth that is accepted as fact by many people, teens included. Many teens who are sexually active report that they have not changed their behavior regarding sex because they do not feel they are at risk. Many young people incorrectly see AIDS as a "homosexual problem."

Because there is no cure for this disease, it now ranks as one of the most serious diseases of the past fifty years. The World Health Organization (WHO) estimates that more than fourteen million adults and a million children are HIV-infected. If this rate of infection continues, it is estimated that by the year 2000, thirty to forty million people will be infected with the virus.[7] This warrants intense educational efforts on our part and must become a priority for parents. At this time, our young teens run the greatest risk of contracting HIV.

Because of experimentation with drugs, alcohol, and sex, our teenaged children are at high risk to contract AIDS. Teen use of illegal drugs is on the rise again in the United States. Surprisingly, this follows a decade of decreased use. Alcohol is highly associated with teen sexual activity. Because of these major cofactors, the HIV infection can occur indirectly from the chain of experimentation, by increasing heterosexual contact. Intravenous drug use provides a direct route for transmission of HIV. Noninjection drugs and alcohol often compromise and blur judgment, and reduce the likelihood that young people will make appropriate decisions about avoiding HIV. We need to tell our children clearly and openly that they are at *high risk* if they are engaging in any of these behaviors.

Parents need to explain to their children that even if they are not engaging in sexual activity, they are at high risk if they are sharing needles. Young people must be made aware that sharing needles for the purpose of injecting drugs, ear-piercing, injecting steroids, or tattooing will put them at high risk for contracting HIV. *The infected person probably will not know they are infected, but that is why the risk is so great.* Parents must get this message to their children.

Many young people are involved with gangs where tattooing and ear-piercing are commonplace. Often this is done by other gang members or friends. Ear-piercing is also popular throughout our society. Girls at slumber parties often share a needle and pierce one another's ears. *Infected needles are the problem.* Your children should be told that sharing a needle under any circumstances is totally unacceptable and potentially life-threatening.

Many teenagers are highly active sexually. Studies published in 1989 by the American Association of Counseling and Development show that by age fifteen, sixteen percent of boys and five percent of girls in the United States have had sexual intercourse at least once. By age seventeen these rates almost triple for boys and increase five times for girls.

By age twenty, eight of ten boys and seven of ten girls have engaged in sexual intercourse.[8] Studies done on large groups of youth who have been involved with the juvenile-justice system show an even earlier mean age for first intercourse: 12.3 years for boys and 12.9 years for girls.[9]

Young people who are sexually active are apt to have multiple sexual partners. A number of studies among college populations support this. Researchers found that nineteen percent to forty-nine percent of college women and forty-nine percent to fifty-seven percent of college men reported sexual experience with six or more sex partners. An astounding forty-six percent of the students indicated that AIDS had "no effect" on their sex life. It appears that for college students, "being more careful" about sex does not necessarily mean they are having fewer sexual partners.[10]

Because they do not believe they are at risk for contracting HIV; because many experiment with drugs, however briefly; because of the high rate of alcohol use; because they do not protect themselves against transmission of disease during sexual activity; and because they do not pursue health care on a regular basis, they are in a high-risk category.

As parents, we do not want to instill fear or panic. We do not want to equate sex with death. Information about HIV and AIDS needs to be given thoughtfully and carefully. We need to present our message in a positive manner, stressing it is the abuse of sex that causes pain and illness, not sex itself.

Sex is good; God created it to be a blessing. Sexual activity is only one way to contract AIDS. There are other behaviors that carry great risk. When men and women abuse any of God's gifts, great harm can result.

AIDS develops through HIV. HIV is transmitted in the following ways:

1) through the exchange of bodily fluids—blood, semen, or vaginal fluid;
2) through the sharing of infected needles;
3) through receiving a transfusion of infected blood (rare);
4) from mother to baby during pregnancy or birth from exchange of body fluids, and after birth from infected breast milk.

The symptoms of AIDS may include:

1) chronic dry cough;
2) persistent fatigue;

3) unexplained weight loss;
4) swollen glands;
5) red or purple blotches on or under the skin—these may be flat or raised;
6) fever, chills, night sweats;
7) persistent diarrhea.

As you may have noticed, the symptoms of AIDS are common to many other illnesses. Only testing can determine if a person is infected with HIV.

I would not advise parents to share this list of symptoms with young children, as they may become unnecessarily fearful and/or panic-stricken. It is far more important that they know *how* the virus is transmitted so that they can avoid these behaviors. When your child asks questions about AIDS, s/he should be given age-appropriate information. As s/he grows older the information should be expanded to include all aspects of the disease. If your child does not ask questions, then you may introduce the topic by saying: "Have you heard about AIDS? What do you think it is? Do you know how people get AIDS?" You may then proceed with necessary clarification and information. Remember to spread information, not fear. AIDS is hard to get and we know what specific behaviors to avoid.

One final thought before we go on. Parents have a responsibility as Christians to model acceptance and understanding toward all persons. It is wrong to single out individuals or groups and make fun of them or ridicule them. As the Catholic bishops advise:

> It is wrong to speak of HIV infection as any sort of "divine retribution" or to label its victims in any sense as "deserving" such a disease. Jesus confronted such a linkage between sin as cause and disease as effect when he told the crowd that the man born blind was not disabled because of his own sin nor that of his parents.[11]

Your children may be going to school with someone who has AIDS. They should be taught to respect such an individual, and not lay blame or shame on such a person. You have the responsibility to teach your child that AIDS is not caught through casual contact such as hugging, holding hands, or sharing a drinking glass. Simply being in the same class or in the same group with a person who has AIDS will not put your child in danger of transmission.

Children with AIDS need friends. They need compassion and understanding. Children with AIDS need to be treated like everyone else.

Parents form attitudes by modeling accepting and loving behavior toward all persons.

Catholic parents often ask, "Should I give my children information about condoms?" My answer to them and to all parents is most definitely "yes."

The Catholic bishops have clearly stated:

> Considering the widespread ignorance and misunderstanding about HIV infection and its modes of transmission, educational programs about the medical aspects of the disease and legitimate ways of preventing it are also needed.[12]

> Providing information that is both accurate and appropriate is a logical and necessary starting point. . . . Educational programs and public information campaigns cannot rely simply on fear as a motive.[13]

> Some people will not act as they can and should; they will not refrain from the type of sexual or drug-abuse behavior that can transmit AIDS. *In such situations, educational efforts, if grounded in the broader moral vision outlined above, could include accurate information about prophylactic devices.*[14]

If this advice is addressed to educators, surely parents have the right and responsibility to follow it as well. I am assuming that parents in such situations would be presenting a *total* environment that fosters the practice of the faith, and that this information would be given within that context.

AIDS is a public health issue. We are not talking about birth control here. We are looking at a serious disease, one for which there is no known cure at this time. Ignorance about AIDS will not save lives; knowledge can. Your child deserves to have all the information regarding this disease available. Such information may very well save your child's life. If you don't talk to your child, who will? Are you willing to take a risk and simply *hope* that they will not find themselves in a situation where they may have need of such information?

All of us make mistakes. All of us experiment with life to some degree at some time. Such experimenting is normal and natural. Knowledge and information have the potential power to reduce the destructiveness that may come from such experimentation.

Although it is true that condoms are not one hundred percent effective, they are eighty-six percent effective in preventing pregnancy. Latex condoms have been proven to be pore-free. This means not even water, one of the tiniest of molecules, can filter through them. The smallest microbes cannot pass through an intact latex condom. *Consumer Reports* notes: "So compelling is the evidence that since 1987 the U.S. Food and Drug Administration has let manufacturers list a roster of diseases that condoms, when used properly, can help prevent: syphilis, gonorrhea, chlamydia, genital herpes, and AIDS."[15]

Condom manufacturers claim only two percent of all condoms are defective. They say twelve percent of the condom failure rate is due to human error. In other words, *many people do not know how to use a condom properly,* or they fail, for various reasons, to do so. Some misuse is due to ignorance or misinformation, such as using oil-based lubricants that cause breakage. I think you would agree that eighty-six percent protection is better than none at all! The Surgeon General of the United States and the World Health Organization recommend condoms as one means to prevent the rapid spread of AIDS.

Parents are the best suited to talk about this personal issue with their child. You may say: "This is rather awkward. I've never really talked with anyone about condoms before and I'm embarrassed, but what I have to say to you is so important that I'm willing to be a little uncomfortable in order to say it."

Honesty is the best policy. If you believe intercourse should only take place in the context of a Christian marriage, say so. Once you have established the appropriate atmosphere, your conversation might go something like this:

*Honey, you know I believe that sexual intercourse belongs in the context of a committed, loving, and lasting relationship. I feel two people should be married before they have sexual intercourse. You also know that our church teaches that this is the way God planned for us to enjoy the gift of intercourse. I hope you will wait until you are married before you have intercourse. I pray for you, that God will give you the strength to wait.*

*We've talked about AIDS since you were little. You know how serious the disease is. The only way you can be sure you'll never get AIDS is by never sharing needles or using intravenous drugs. You also have to avoid becoming infected through intercourse. The best way to do this is to abstain from intercourse until you are married. The person you marry has to have avoided the same behaviors. Then you both have to remain monogamous and abstain from intravenous drug use.*

*I do realize, however, that you may not choose to do what I feel you should. I know sometimes you disagree with me and with what our church teaches is best for you. I know I can't always be with you to talk things through and protect you from danger, and that is very hard for me to accept. I do want you to have all the information necessary so you will make intelligent choices. So, while it's difficult for me to do so, I want to talk to you about condoms.*

*Condoms do present a degree of safety from contracting AIDS and other STDs. They are not 100% safe; they will not guarantee that you won't get AIDS. However, they are a limited protection against disease. Because of this, I'm going explain to you the right way to use a condom. I want you to understand that I hope you will not use this information, because I hope you will wait till you are married before you engage in intercourse. But I love you very much, and I will not take a chance on risking your life because I failed to give you information that might have saved it. Besides, I have a lot of confidence in your ability to make good decisions, and I know you love God very much and you try to do the right things.*

My suggestion would then be to have a condom in your possession and proceed to show your teenager how to use it properly. You can use your fingers to show the proper way to roll the condom on. (See chapter 12 for detailed information in this regard.) Remember to advise your teen of the danger of oil-based lubricant. Be sure to give him/her the opportunity and encouragement to ask any questions about condom use, AIDS, or related issues that s/he wants to. Acknowledge embarrassment with reassurance that *you* want to be the one to give accurate information.

Remember also, questions do not always arise at the time a topic is discussed. Be sure to explain this to your teen and assure them they may bring this topic up again whenever they feel the need. Answer all questions nonjudgmentally and honestly. Gently but firmly restate your beliefs about intercourse and commitment. Once you have clearly stated your position, let the matter rest. You will not gain anything by beating them over the head with it.

Ignorance about AIDS can be very dangerous. Remember, your child may marry someone who is a hemophiliac or a health-care worker exposed frequently to AIDS infection. Your own child may become a health care worker who needs to protect his/her spouse from infection. The use of condoms may be a necessary safeguard to avoid disease transmission. We are not discussing a birth-control issue; we are discussing a *health* issue. Do not confuse the two. Condom use to prevent disease is *not* the same as condom use to prevent pregnancy.

Please do not leave this information to chance. *Giving information does not mean giving approval.* Your child knows very well when you are encouraging certain behaviors and when you are not.

At difficult times like these, I always remind myself that Jesus was very much in the same position as parents. He knew what was best for us and he came on this earth to save us. However, he was not overprotective, he did most of his teaching by example, not by lecturing, isolating us from outside influence, or reading long lists of rules. Nor did he beat people over the head with his suggestions.

When Jesus left, he left us in a world filled with temptations and attractions that clearly violate the divine law he wished us to follow. However, he *did* leave us in the midst of all this. He left us with information on the best way to lead our lives. He left us with hope that we would follow him to God. But he also left us with the ability to make *choices.* Jesus knew our choices would not always be wise. Still, he gave us the opportunity to make them. He modeled correct behavior for us.

Moreover, Jesus left us with the guidance of the Holy Spirit (to provide knowledge) and the sacrament of reconciliation. (The very essence of the sacrament of reconciliation implies that Christ knew we would sometimes fail and make unwise choices.) However, with reconciliation, Jesus left us secure in the knowledge that we would always be loved, always be forgiven, even when, in our human frailty, we failed to follow his example.

Can we do less for our children than Jesus did for us?

HERPES: The sign of this disease is a cluster of blisters on or near the sex organs about six days after contact with an infected person. These will erupt and become small sores that may be painful, tender, or itchy. There may also be fever, headaches, or "flu-like" feelings (sick all over). If the blisters form inside the vagina and are not painful, a woman can pass this disease to others unknowingly. Often the blisters, in both men and women, are very, very painful. They may last up to three weeks. Once they disappear, they may not surface again for sometime. Whenever they do, the infected person may infect others.

A mother who has herpes in the active stage may infect her infant during childbirth. More than half of the infected infants die. Those who survive often have permanent brain damage. The doctor may deliver the infant by Caesarean section if it is known that the mother is active at the time. Often, the mother is not aware she is infected. At this time there is no cure for herpes. However, when seen by a doctor, medications to reduce pain and soreness can be administered and infected persons can learn how to live better with the disease.

CHLAMYDIA: This is currently the most common of all STDs, and has reached epidemic portions. There are an estimated three to four million cases each year. Chlamydia can cause PID which increases the risk of ectopic pregnancy. Chlamydia is a major cause of infertility in women today. A woman who is infected with chlamydia may pass it on to her infant during childbirth. Adolescents have the highest rate of chlamydial infection and associated complications, such as pelvic inflammatory disease (PID), ectopic pregnancy, and infertility. [16]

PID: Many women experience no symptoms with this disease. Pelvic inflammatory diseases are very common in young women. They are a collection of various diseases that cause scar tissue to form in the woman's Fallopian tubes, ovaries, and uterus. This scar tissue can render a woman sterile. PID can also cause ectopic pregnancy, that is, a pregnancy that occurs in the Fallopian tubes. This is very dangerous to the woman and can be life-threatening. PID is usually the result of frequent sexual intercourse with many partners.

SYPHILIS: The rate of syphilis infection declined steadily between 1982 and 1986. Since then it has increased dramatically, by forty-six percent, reaching a rate of 16.6 per 100,000, the highest level in forty years. [17] The primary symptom of syphilis is a painless sore or chancre on the penis or in the vagina that appears anywhere from a few days up to a month after contact with an infected person. They may also appear other places such as in the mouth or rectum. If left untreated, the chancre will disappear.

The second stage will be a rash, which does not itch, somewhere on the body. There may be fever, sore throat, and aching body. Another symptom of syphilis is hair falling out in patches. These symptoms will disappear if untreated, but the disease will not. Untreated syphilis can result in death. Before the discovery of penicillin, thousands died of syphilis. Today the disease can be cured *if* it is treated.

Adolescents who are sexually active and suffer from genital ulcers associated with syphilis or genital herpes are probably at greater risk of acquiring HIV. Several studies have shown that genital ulcers facilitate transmission of HIV. [18]

GONORRHEA ("THE CLAP"): There are approximately between one and two million cases of gonorrhea each year. Even though the rates of gonorrhea have declined, many new penicillin-resistant strains have emerged. [19] Rates among adolescents have declined more slowly than any other group, and rates among black adolescents have actually increased.[20]

Eight-five percent of women infected with gonorrhea have no noticeable symptoms. However, infertility in both men and women can result from untreated gonorrhea. Some women will feel the frequent need to urinate and/or have painful burning sensations when urinating. Infected men experience a severe burning sensation at the tip of the penis and pain when urinating. There may also be a cloudy mucous discharge. The penis often becomes swollen and inflamed. If left untreated, gonorrhea will attack the joints and sex organs.

PUBIC LICE ("CRABBIES"): These are small insects that appear in pubic hair and hair around the anus. Taking a bath or shower will not remove them. They must be treated with a special medicated shampoo from a doctor. The primary symptom will be itching, especially at night. Crabbies travel through locker rooms and dorms with great speed!

GENITAL WARTS: These uncomfortable and often painful sores occur in the vagina and must be surgically removed. These warts can be passed on to the infants of infected women during childbirth.

Care should be taken when discussing STDs with young teens. Bacterial infections can cause many of the same symptoms as STDs, and adolescents need to be reassured that parents *will not assume* they are sexually active if they complain of symptoms similar to those listed above. If teens feel they will be accused and confronted with hostility, they will be too embarrassed to seek help from parents.

Parents should be clear in advising their children that STDs may be contracted from deep kissing and heavy petting as well as from intercourse. It is not our purpose to spread fear. Most STDs can be cured with proper treatment. We are trying to encourage careful decision making and develop critical thinking and discernment in our children. It is wise to keep these broader, long-term goals in mind, and not overreact when confronted with temporary problems that can be solved. We all need to remember that the future is created by the decisions we make today.

As parents, we also need to take care that we do not imply that STDs are some form of punishment from God for making a mistake. *This is not God's way of operating.* Ours is a loving God who created us for happiness, not a God of revenge or meanness.

# Chapter 12

. . . . . . . . .

# A Hundred Commonly Unknown/Misunderstood Facts that Every Person Should Know

L isted below are some facts that are frequently unknown or misunderstood by many people. Because many young teens get their information from their peers, these incorrect ideas are perpetuated over time, and continue to be recycled even in this age of sophisticated information. It is not surprising, then, that even many adults have lived under the shadow of this misinformation. This list is an attempt to clarify some of the more commonly mistaken or unknown facts.

1. A girl *can* become pregnant before she begins to menstruate. This is rare and uncommon, but it has happened.

2. A woman can become pregnant during her menstrual period.

3. It is not harmful to have intercourse when a woman is menstruating. The decision to have intercourse during this time should depend on the comfort level of the couple.

4. Having intercourse while standing up will not prevent pregnancy.

5. A woman can become pregnant without penetration. If the penis

is on or near the labia when ejaculation occurs, sperm can make their way to the uterus. Even very small amounts of semen, emitted prior to ejaculation, can enter the vagina if the penis is in or near the vaginal area.

6. Douching with a Coke will not prevent pregnancy.

7. Douching itself is not an effective or reliable method of contraception.

8. To be an effective method of birth control, the birth-control pill must be taken for about three months prior to the start of engaging in intercourse. Thus if a married couple want to use the pill to limit the size of their family, they must use an additional form of contraception for the first three months the wife is on the pill. The body has to build up the amount of hormones needed to prevent conception.

9. In order to be an effective contraceptive, the pill must be taken daily as directed. Taking the pill only the day before or after you engage in intercourse will not prevent pregnancy.

10. If you are using condoms to prevent the spread of AIDS and other STDs, you should be using latex condoms accompanied by a lubricant that contains nonoxynol-9. *Make sure your lubricant is water based* (K-Y Jelly, Astroglide). Oil-based lubricants (*Vasoline, baby oil*) will cause the condom to break within seconds. If you are using condoms to prevent pregnancy, you should use them with a foam or jelly that contains a spermicide.

11. Although condoms *are* helpful in preventing the spread of AIDS and other sexually transmitted diseases, they are *not* foolproof. Condoms have a fourteen percent failure rate: twelve percent due to human error, two percent to condom defect. Only consistent abstinence will guarantee complete protection against HIV infection through sexual activity. This means no oral sex, anal sex, or intercourse. Should you choose to engage in intercourse where transmission of disease may occur anyway, you are better off *with* a condom than without one, but you are still taking a risk.

12. There is a right and a wrong way to put on a condom. Condoms

should be applied with the lubricated side to the outside of the penis. If the condom is not rolling on easily, it may be on inside out. *Read the directions.* Be sure to leave space at the tip of the condom to hold the ejaculate if there is not a tip built into the condom itself. This can be done by holding the tip of the condom between the forefinger and thumb, and rolling the rest of the condom on the penis. Be sure to unroll the condom all the way to the top of the penis. For additional safety, one partner should be responsible for holding onto the top of the condom or checking the condom to prevent it from slipping off during intercourse. This can be done discreetly or playfully, without interfering with lovemaking.

13. When using a condom, the penis after ejaculation should be removed from the vagina *before* the penis becomes flaccid (soft). The condom should be removed from the penis well away from the vagina and thrown away. *Do not attempt to reuse a condom.* After removal of the condom, hands and penis should be carefully washed.

14. The earlier teenagers begin dating and the earlier they begin to go steady, the more likely they are to experience sexual intercourse before the age of eighteen.

15. There is less sexual activity among young people who are able to talk positively with their parents about sex.

16. Studies show that a very high percentage of teens engaging in sexual intercourse are doing so in the context of a caring relationship. Young women, in particular, state that they engage in sexual relations because they are in love with their partner. From the perspective of many teens, premarital sex is not morally wrong as long as there is love between the couple.

17. Premarital activity is not deterred by giving teens partial or preselected information. To be effective, abstinence education is best presented in the context of complete sexuality education.

18. Teens become pregnant due to lack of information, not from too much information. Premarital pregnancy results from ignorance,

irregular or misuse of contraceptives, drug/alcohol use, and/or a belief that they (teens) are immune to pregnancy.

19. According to a study done in 1981 by O'Connell and Moore, sixty percent of teenagers are pregnant at the time of marriage. Most of these pregnancies were not desired or planned.

20. A third of all teenage mothers have a second child before they are twenty.

21. The use of alcohol is significantly associated with premarital sexual activity, as is regular marijuana use.

22. There is an increase in anal sexual activity among young teens. It is thought this is due to an attempt to avoid pregnancy on the part of young girls.

23. On the whole, the female still seems to be responsible for how far the couple will go sexually and whether or not contraception will be used. This is unfair and irresponsible behavior on the part of young males.

24. Despite the AIDS crisis, the rate of teenage sexual involvement is still rising. In 1988, seventy-two percent of seventeen-year-old males said they had had sexual intercourse. In 1979 this response was fifty-six percent.

25. There are still specific gender differences in the way we educate and view adolescent sexual activity. For example, a girl "loses" her virginity, but a boy "becomes a man." These phrases reflect a clear difference in approval of boys and girls having a sexual experience.

26. The peer group is cited by most teens as their primary source of information about sex. This source is followed by literature, mothers, and school. Street talk and personal experience are cited before fathers, ministers, and physicians.

27. The pill has a six percent failure rate. The diaphragm has a sixteen percent failure rate. Rhythm has a sixteen percent failure rate. Spermicides have a twenty-six percent failure rate, and condoms have a fourteen percent failure rate.

28. You can get sexually transmitted diseases from having oral, anal, or genital sex with an infected person (they may not know they are infected). Some of them you may also get from deep (French) kissing. You do not get them from toilet seats or hugs.

29. Studies have found that teens who attend church regularly and who consider religion very important to them are less sexually active than their peers.

30. A condom is not effective unless it is fresh and used properly. Do not keep condoms in your wallet.

31. Pregnancy is most likely to occur when intercourse takes place fourteen days after the first day of menstruation.

32. Chlamydia is the fastest growing STD. It can cause PID (pelvic inflammatory disease), which in turn can increase the risk of an ectopic pregnancy. This is a dangerous pregnancy, when the embryo implants in the Fallopian tubes instead of the uterus. PID may also make it impossible for a woman to have children. Chlamydia has reached epidemic proportions in the United States.

33. Genital herpes is an STD for which there is no cure at this time. If your partner is infected with herpes and the sores are active, it is not safe for you to engage in intercourse. Use of a condom may help, but due to breakage or slippage, it is no guarantee against infection.

34. Genital warts, genital herpes, chlamydia, syphilis, gonorrhea (the clap, the drip), and lice (crabs) are all sexually transmitted diseases that infect millions of teens each year. There are twenty-five known STDs. Many of these have symptoms that can be passed on to newborn babies, resulting in serious consequences and even death. Some of these have symptoms that are not readily noticeable, and if ignored will disappear. *The disease itself does not unless treated with medication from a physician.* This is especially dangerous because the disease continues to live in the body even after the symptoms are no longer noticeable.

35. A teenager does not need parental consent to be treated for an STD. One may go to a local or state health center, VD clinic, or

private doctor and be treated in confidentiality. VD clinics test for STDs and offer treatment without charge. These are usually listed in the Yellow Pages of the phone book.

36. Ovulation occurs when the woman's body releases an egg for fertilization. It does not occur at the same time as menstruation. Ovulation occurs in the middle of a woman's menstrual cycle (for most women).

37. Taking a shower immediately after intercourse will not keep you from getting pregnant.

38. Wearing tight shorts may slightly reduce the production of sperm, but it *will not* stop production altogether. This is not a reliable method of birth control.

39. Going to the bathroom immediately after intercourse will not prevent pregnancy.

40. Having intercourse in the shower will not prevent pregnancy.

41. You will not harm children by telling them "too much." They can be harmed if you do not tell them enough.

42. Only four percent of unmarried teen mothers put their babies up for adoption.

43. Neither the size of the penis nor size of the breast has anything to do with sexual pleasure or ability to perform better.

44. Masturbation is not physically or emotionally harmful. Most people masturbate sometime during their life.

45. Wet dreams are perfectly normal. They are not sinful or harmful.

46. Simultaneous orgasm has nothing to do with getting pregnant.

47. Male breasts, like female breasts, are sensitive to touch and can produce pleasurable feelings when touched.

48. Small, short, less physical men can be just as good as lovers as

big, strong, athletic men. Physical size and strength do not make a good lover. Thoughtfulness, kindness, consideration, patience, and a willingness to please your partner make a good lover.

49. Women enjoy sex just as much as men do.

50. Alcohol is a depressant. It slows the body down.

51. Douching is unnecessary unless recommended by your doctor.

52. Babies born to teen mothers under age eighteen have higher rates of prematurity, mental retardation, death, and other health problems.

53. Sexual intimacy is desired and possible as long as we live.

54. Forty percent of those who get pregnant between the ages of fifteen and nineteen choose abortion.

55. Currently the highest-risk population for AIDS is adolescent girls and women, through heterosexual transmission.

56. Each year over one million American adolescents become pregnant.

57. Four of every ten females become pregnant before they reach the age of twenty.

58. In 1984 teens fourteen or younger gave birth to 9,965 babies.

59. Date rape is *forced* sexual intercourse with a party who does *not* give consent. Date rape is a crime.

60. Date rape is *never* justified. A person's being unconscious, passed out, or too drunk to say no, is never justification for intercourse. Saying "yes" to a drink does not mean saying "yes" to intercourse.

61. Every person has the right to say "no" to unwanted sexual behavior. Every person should have that right respected.

62. Young girls need to be taught from the earliest age to say "no"

clearly and forcefully when they mean no. They should not be given the impression that it is "more feminine" to speak indirectly.

63. Everyone should have the right to change their mind regarding sexual behavior.

64. A simultaneous orgasm is not necessarily a better orgasm.

65. A girl cannot get pregnant by kissing.

66. The male chromosome, carried in the sperm, determines the sex of the baby.

67. Only one sperm is needed to fertilize an egg. Usually, millions of sperm are ejaculated with each orgasm.

68. A girl is born with all the eggs she will ever have. Usually, about four hundred or five hundred of these will mature and be released, one at a time, during the monthly ovulation. Very few of these will be fertilized and develop into children.

69. A boy is not born with sperm. His body begins to produce sperm when he reaches puberty. This continues during the course of his entire life. During his lifetime, a man may produce billions of sperm. Very few of these will fertilize an egg and develop into a child. Masturbating will not cause him to run out of sperm.

70. If a girl has not begun her menstrual period by the time she reaches sixteen she should see a doctor.

71. It is normal for a boy to have one testicle larger than the other one.

72. A boy may have an erection even when he is not thinking about something sexual. Especially during puberty, a boy may have spontaneous erections for no apparent reason. He cannot make the erection go away simply by thinking about something else. Girls should not equate erections with having "dirty thoughts."

73. The Center for Population Options reports that TV portrays six times more extramarital sex than sex between spouses. Ninety-

four percent of the sexual encounters on soap operas are between people not married to each other.

74. Young men should not worry that their penis is too small for intercourse, or that if they marry, they will unable to please their spouse. When the penis is excited it becomes erect and will fit into the vagina. The vagina is a muscle that will adapt to the size of the penis.

75. A broken hymen does not mean a girl is not a virgin. If the hymen is tight and intercourse is painful when a woman becomes sexually active she should see a doctor. He may stretch the hymen or teach her how to do so. Intercourse should not be painful.

76. It is not always painful the first time a female has intercourse.

77. Having intercourse during pregnancy does *not* harm the baby.

78. Your brain is your most important sex organ!

79. Breasts come in all shapes and sizes; so does the penis.

80. Both men and women have male and female hormones.

81. A woman's desire for sexual pleasure does not stop after menopause.

82. Intercourse can bring the most satisfaction when you focus on giving pleasure to your partner. This is not something you will necessarily automatically know how to do. It is, however, something everyone can learn to do. Satisfying intercourse involves the mind as well as the body. There are many good books available for you to learn from.

83. AIDS is a disease that affects *all* people, heterosexual and homosexual. At the time of this writing it is over sixty percent heterosexual worldwide. Heterosexual transmission is consistently rising in the United States.

84. Withdrawal is *not* a reliable method of birth control. All it takes

is for one sperm to find its way to the uterus, and there's no way to be sure one hasn't escaped before you withdraw.

85. You can become pregnant even if you don't experience an orgasm.

86. Neither getting drunk nor taking a hot shower will have any effect on sperm. These are not useful methods of birth control.

87. Washing the vagina after intercourse *will not* keep you from getting pregnant.

88. Saran wrap is *not* a reliable method of birth control.

89. Natural Family Planning is a scientific method of birth control that works for many women. NFP, as it is commonly called, is *not* the same thing as practicing "Rhythm." This method places equal responsibility on both husbands and wives for limiting the family size. Many hospitals and/or churches give courses on how a young woman can learn to identify and pay attention to the vaginal mucus her body secretes during the monthly cycle, and look for changes in the mucus that may tell her if she is fertile or not. The couple then abstains from having intercourse during this fertile time.

    This information is useful for any woman, whether she is interested in using this method to postpone birth or not. It is a good idea to know about your body and all of its functions. It is also best if men participate with their spouse and learn to identify and understand changes in the monthly cycle. Men can be better lovers when they know and understand well the body of their spouse. This method is also very useful when a couple is trying to have a child. There are books available on this method in most bookstores.

90. Louis Sullivan, the former Secretary of the United States Commission on Health and Human Services, in a March 1992 report stated that here in the United States, someone is infected with HIV every thirteen minutes.

91. National STD hotline: 1-800-227-8922.

92. National AIDS hotline: 1-800-342-2437.

93. There are approximately twenty thousand scenes of suggested sexual intercourse, sexual comment and behavior, or innuendo in one year of prime-time television.

94. You are not abnormal if you do not masturbate.

95. Child abuse is committed most often by someone the child knows.

96. AIDS is *not* transmitted by casual contact, mosquito bites, kissing, hugging, coughing, sneezing, or sharing a drinking glass. *AIDS is transmitted through an exchange of body fluids.* This takes place:
    - through oral or anal intercourse;
    - when mothers with AIDS infect their child before, during, or after birth (through nursing);
    - when needles are shared for any purpose (ear-piercing, steroids, intravenous drug use, injections of any sort using contaminated needles, etc.) with an infected person;
    - when someone receives a transfusion of infected blood.

97. When being tested for HIV infection a person should wait six months after possible exposure for a valid test. A second test may be desired for accuracy.

98. A 1993 survey of 15,463 students in grades six, eight, ten, and twelve has found that clear relationships exist between unhealthy behaviors. The study found that there is a definite link between drug and alcohol abuse, violent behavior, suicide, and sexual behaviors.

99. Adolescents who have used drugs are more likely to report earlier sexual intercourse and multiple partners than those who have not used drugs.

100. Premarital intercourse in young women has risen from 32.3% (1970) to 51% (1988) in seventeen-year-olds and from 48.2% (1970) to 75.3% (1988) in nineteen-year-olds.

# Conclusion

Congratulations! If you have gotten this far, you have just begun to scratch the surface of learning about sexuality. Education in sexuality is a lifelong process. At every age and stage of development there is new and pertinent information that can increase your knowledge about yourself and enhance your ability to relate to others. Because we are sexual beings from the cradle to the grave, it's never too late to learn something new about ourselves. However, to do so, you must be willing to open your mind and heart to such learning.

I hope this book has begun that process for you, or that it has in some way contributed to your understanding of yourself as a sexual person. In particular, I hope it has increased your confidence in your ability to talk with your child about sexuality, no matter what age he or she may be.

Through your willingness to communicate about sexuality, you are giving your child a precious gift few others can give. Good luck as you continue on your journey of parenting. I wish you and your family the joy of many shared hugs!

# Notes

## 5 · Ages and Stages of Psychosexual Development

1. Krieger, 1979, 18–20, and Linn, Fabricant, and Linn, 1988, 27–31.
2. Freud, 1907, 36–44.
3. Kenny, 1988.
4. National Center for Health Statistics, 1988.
5. Sonenstein, Pleck, and Ku, 1989, 152–58.
6. Sweeney, 1991.

## 6 · Inviting Morality

1. Finkelhor, 1984.
2. "Childhood sexual abuse," 1990, 5.
3. American Humane Association, 1981.
4. U.S. Department of Justice, 1984, 13–15.
5. Bradshaw, 1988, 6.
6. Ooms, 1981.
7. Jessor and Jessor, 1977, 211–29.
8. Fox, 1980, 21–28.
9. Kahn, Smith, and Roberts, 1984.
10. Nolin and Petersen, 1992, 59–79.
11. Kahn, Smith, and Roberts, 1984.
12. Smith and Udry, 1985, 1200–1203.
13. Zelnik and Shah, 1983, 64–70.
14. Abernethy, 1974, 622–65.
15. Benson, Wood, and Johnson, 1984.
16. Hunter, 1985, 433–40.
17. Center for Disease Control, 1986, and National Council on Health Studies, 1988.
18. Bennett, 1988, 5–35.
19. Byrd, 1988, A2.
20. Resource Manual for Trainees, 1990.
21. National Conference of Catholic Bishops, 1991, 22–23, 25.
22. Ibid., 25.
23. Bouchard, 1993.
24. Nelson, 1978, 168.
25. National Conference of Catholic Bishops, 1991, 62.

26. Ibid., 62.
27. Kosnik, 1977, 229.
28. Conger and Peterson, 1984, 232.

7 · *Loving Your Gay or Lesbian Child*

1. Nugent, 1989, 25, 261.
2. Remafedi, 1987, 326–30.
3. Russel, 1986, 133.
4. Feinleib, 1989.
5. PRESEREC, 1989.
6. United States General Accounting Office, 1992.
7. Gallop, 1992, 100–103.
8. *SIECUS Report*, 1993, 19–20.
9. "Personal communication," 1993.
10. Fairchild and Hayward, 1989.
11. Nugent, 1989, 5–6.
12. Money, 1988, 123 (Emphasis mine).
13. National Conference of Catholic Bishops, 1976, 52.
14. Congregation for the Doctrine of the Faith, 1986.
15. Department for Studies, 1993, 15–16.
16. Dinter, 1987, 3–7.
17. Powell, 1978, 66–68.

8 · *Do As You Say*

1. Van De Polder, 1980, 78.
2. Ibid., 89.
3. National Conference of Catholic Bishops, 1991, 71.
4. National Conference of Catholic Bishops, 1993.

9 · *The Reality of Sexual Abuse*

1. Finkelhor, 1979, 53.
2. Haffner, 1992, 11.
3. Crime Victims Research and Treatment Center, 1992.
4. Kirkendall and Jarvis-Kirkendall, 1989, 12.
5. Baisden, 1978.
6. Faria and Belohlavek, 1984, 465–71.
7. Russel, 1983, 133.
8. Kempe, et al., 1962, 17–24.
9. Rush, 1980.
10. *SIECUS Report*, 1991, 11.
11. Peters, 1988, 101–17.
12. Miller, 1989.

10. · *Avoiding the Tragedy of Date Rape*

1. Abarbanel, 1986, 100–105.
2. Signorielli and Gerbner, 1988.

3. Doyle, 1989, 184.
4. Ibid., 185.
5. Burgess, 1988, 196.
6. Ibid., 197.
7. Pleck, 1981, 146.
8. Doyle, 1989, 187.
9. De Angelis, 1989, 12–13.
10. Fagot, 1985, 471–76.
11. Worth, Matthews, and Coleman, 1990, 250–54.
12. Macooby and Jacklin, 1974, 191–226.
13. McCormick and Jones, 1989, 271–82.
14. Schechter, 1982, 33–35.
15. Cohen, et al., 1990, 480.
16. Burgess, 1988, 199.
17. Ibid.
18. Doyle, 1983, 193.
19. Russel, 1982, 190–205.
20. Ehrhart and Sandler, 1985.
21. Ibid.
22. Griffin, 1971, 26–35.
23. Yegidis, 1986, 51–55.
24. Brownmiller, 1975.

*11 · AIDS and Sexually Transmitted Diseases*

1. Division of STD/HIV Prevention 1989.
2. Bennett, 1988, 5–35.
3. "Mortality Attributable," 1991, 41–46.
4. Chu and Buehler, 1990, 225–29.
5. *Contemporary Sexuality*, 1993, 7.
6. *Contemporary Sexuality*, 1990, 11.
7. *Contemporary Sexuality*, 1994, 5.
8. Capuzzi and Gros, 1989, 234.
9. Melchert and Burnett, 1990, 294.
10. Davidson, 1990, 11.
11. National Conference of Catholic Bishops, 1991, 65.
12. Ibid., 66.
13. National Conference of Catholic Bishops, 1989, 8.
14. National Conference of Catholic Bishops, 1987, 18.
15. "Can you rely on condoms?" 1989, 134–41.
16. Randolph and Washington, 1990, 545–550.
17. "Progress toward Achieving," 1990, 53–57.
18. Quinn, et al., 1988, 197–203.
19. Division of STD/HIV Prevention, 1989.
20. Whittington and Knapp, 1988, 202–10.

# Bibliography

Abarbanel, Gail. "Rape and Resistance." *Journal of Interpersonal Violence 1* (1986): 100–105.

Abbott, Walter, M., ed. *The Documents of Vatican II.* New York: America Press, 1966.

Abernethy, Virginia. "Illegitimate Conception among Teenagers." *American Journal of Public Health 64/7* (1974): 622–65.

"Adolescent Sexuality and the Media." *The Facts.* Washington, D.C.: Center for Population Options (January 1987).

American Humane Association. "The National Study of Child Neglect and Abuse." Denver, 1981.

Avasthi, Surabhi. "Study Reveals Girls Lose Self-Esteem as Adolescents." *Guidepost 33/12* (February 1991): 1, 10, 13.

Avvento, Gennaro P. *Sexuality.* Mystic, Conn.: Twenty-Third Publications, 1984.

Baisden, M. "The World of Rosaphrenia: The Sexual Psychology of the Female." Sacramento, Cal. Quoted in H. Giarretto, "The Humanistic Treatment of Father-Daughter Incest." *Journal of Humanistic Psychology 18/4* (Fall 1978): 57–76.

Baldwin, J. D., et al. "The Effect of Ethnic Group on Sexual Activities Related to Contraception and STD." *Journal of Sex Research 29* (May 1992): 189–205.

Bennett, William J. *AIDS and the education of our children.* Washington, D.C.: U.S. Department of Education, 1988.

———. "Sex and the Education of Our Children." *American* (February 14, 1987): 120–25.

Benson, P. L., P. K. Wood, and A. L. Johnson. "Early Adolescents and Their Parents: Highlights from the National Study." *Momentum* (February 1984).

Bernstein, Anne C. "How Children Learn about Sex and Birth." *Psychology Today* (January 1976): 31–35.

Biehler, Robert F. and Jack Snowman. *Psychology Applied to Teaching.* Boston: Houghton Mifflin Company, 1986.

Bishop, Paul D. and Angela Lipsitz. "Sexual Behavior Among College Students in the AIDS Era: A Comparative Study" (Paper presented at the meeting of the Society for the Scientific Study of Sex, San Francisco, November 1988).

Bouchard, Charles E. "Sexual Morality: Wholeness and Holiness." *Liguorian 80* (October 1992): 56–60.

———. Interview by author, St. Louis, Mo., June 14, 1993.

—— and James R. Pollock. "Condoms and the Common Good." *Second Opinion* 12 (November 1989): 98–106.

Bradshaw, John. *Bradshaw on: The Family*. Deerfield Beach, Fla: Health Communications, 1988.

Brooks-Gunn, Jeanne and Frank F. Furstenberg Jr. "Adolescent Sexual Behavior." *American Psychologist* 44/2 (February 1989): 249–257.

Brown, Larry, et al. "HIV Prevention for Adolescents." *AIDS Education and Prevention* 3/1 (Spring 1991): 50–59.

Brownmiller, Susan. *Against Our Will: Men, Women, and Rape*. New York: Simon and Schuster, 1975.

Bruner, Jerome S. *Actual Minds, Possible Worlds*. Cambridge, Mass.: Harvard University Press, 1986.

——. *In Search of a Mind*. New York: Harper and Row, 1983.

Burgess, Ann Wolbert. *Rape and Sexual Assault II*. New York: Garland Publishing, Inc., 1988.

Byrd, R. "10 or More Sex Partners a Year Puts Thousands of Men at Risk." *Corvallis Gazette-Times*, September 23, 1988.

Cahill, Lisa Sowle. "Catholic Sexual Ethics and the Dignity of the Person: A Double Message." *Theological Studies* 50 (1989): 120–50.

——. "Reuniting Sexuality and Spirituality." *Christian Century* (February 25, 1987): 187–90.

"Can You Rely on Condoms?" *Consumer Reports* (March 1989): 134–41.

Capuzzi, Dave, and Douglas R. Gross. *Youth at Risk*. Alexandria, Va.: American Association for Counseling and Development, 1989.

Carrol, Leo. " Concern with AIDS and the Sexual Behavior of College Students." *Journal of Marriage and the Family* 50/2 (1988): 405–411.

Carroll, J. L., et al. "Differences between Males and Females in Motives for Engaging in Sexual Intercourse." *Archives of Sexual Behavior* 14/2 (1985): 131–40.

Centers for Disease Control. "Youth Suicide in the United States, 1970–1980." Atlanta: U.S. Department of Health and Human Service, Public Health Service, 1986.

"Childhood sexual abuse." *National Catholic Educators Accent* 2/4 (Spring 1990): 5.

Chu, Susan, et al. "Impact of the Human Immunodeficiency Virus Epidemic on Mortality in Women of Reproductive Age, U.S." *Journal of American Medical Association* 264/20 (1990): 225–29.

Citizens Commission on AIDS for New York City and Northern New Jersey, Carol Levine, Executive Director. "AIDS Prevention and Education: Reframing the Message." *AIDS Education and Prevention* 3/2 (Summer 1991): 147–63.

Cohen, M. L., et al. "The Psychology of Rapists," quoted in Janet Shibley Hyde, *Understanding Human Sexuality*. New York: McGraw-Hill, Inc., 1990, 480.

Conger, John J., and Ann Peterson. *Adolescence and Youth*. New York: Harper and Row, 1984.

Congregation for the Doctrine of the Faith. *Letter to the Bishops of the Catholic Church on the Pastoral Care of Homosexual Persons*. Rome: Vatican Press, 1986.

*Contemporary Sexuality; Monthly Newsletter of the American Association of Sex Educators, Counselors, and Therapists* 22/6 (June 1990): 7.

——. 27/9 (September 1993): 11.

——. 28/3 (March 1994): 5.

Crime Victims' Research and Treatment Center. "Rape in America: A report to the Nation." National Institute on Drug Abuse (April 23, 1992).

Davidson, J. K., et al. "Multiple Sex Partners among College Women and Men: Influences on Sex Behaviors, Intimacy Attitudes, and Sexual Satisfaction." (Paper presented at the meeting of the Society for the Scientific Study of Sex, San Francisco, November 1988).

———. "Multiple Sex Partners at College." *Medical Aspects of Human Sexuality* (January 1990): 11.

De Angelis, Tori. "Men's Interaction Style Can Be Tough on Women." *Monitor* (November 1989): 12–13.

Denney, N. W., et al. "Sex Differences in Sexual Needs and Desires." *Archives of Sexual Behavior 13/3* (1984): 233–46.

Department for Studies, Division for Church in Society of the Evangelical Lutheran Church in America. *The Church and Human Sexuality: A Lutheran Perspective*, First Draft of a Social Statement. (1993): 15–16.

DiGiacomo, James J., and Edward Wakin. "How to Talk about Sex with Your Teens." *Understanding Teenagers: A Guide for Christian Parents*. Allen, Tex.: Argus Communications, 1983, 5–8.

Dinter, Paul E. "Getting Some Respect." *Church* 3 (Fall 1987): 3–7.

Division of STD/HIV Prevention, *Annual Report*. Atlanta: Centers for Disease Control, 1989.

Doyle, James A. *The Male Experience*. Dubuque, Iowa: Wm. C. Brown Publisher, 1983.

Drane, James. "Condoms, AIDS and Catholic Ethics." *Commonweal* 22 (March 1991): 188–92.

Dwyer, Johanna, and Jean Mayer. "Psychological Effects of Variations in Physical Appearance during Adolescence." *Adolescence 3* (1968–69): 353–80.

Ehrhart, J. K., and B. R. Sandler. *Myths and Realities about Rape*. Washington, D.C.: Project on the Status and Education of Women, 1985.

Erikson, Erik. *Childhood and Society*. New York: Norton, 1963.

———. *Identity, Youth and Crisis*. New York: Norton, 1968.

———. *Insight and Responsibility*. New York: Norton, 1964.

———. "Our Children's Self-Esteem." *Family Life Educator* (Summer 1983): 5–7.

Fagot, Beverly I. "A Cautionary Note: Parents' Socialization of Boys and Girls." *Sex Roles 12 5/6* (1985): 471–76.

Fairchild, Betty, and Nancy Hayward. *Now That You Know*. New York: Harcourt Brace Jovanovich, 1989.

Faria, Geraldine, and Nancy Belohlavek. "Treating Female Adult Survivors of Childhood Incest." *Social Casework 65/8* (1984): 465–71.

Feinleib, Marcia R. "Gay Male and Lesbian Youth Suicide." *Report of the Secretary's Task Force on Youth Suicide*, U.S. Department of Health and Human Services, 1989.

Finkelhor, David. *Child Sexual Abuse*. New York: Free Press, 1984.

———. *Sexually Victimized Children*. New York: Free Press, 1979.

Fox, G. L. "The Mother-Adolescent Daughter Relationship as a Sexual Socialization Structure: A Research Review." *Family Relations* 29 (1980): 21–28.

Freud, Sigmund. "The Sexual Enlightenment of Children" (an open letter to Dr. M. Furst, editor of *Soziale Medizin und Hygiene*) in *Collected Papers, Volume II*. London: Hogarth Press, 1907, 36–44.

Furstenberg, Frank Jr. "National Survey of Children in 1981." *Psychology Today* (June 1986): 10.

Gallagher, Ralph. "Understanding the Homosexual." *The Furrow* (September 1979): 555–69.

Gallop, George Jr. *The Gallop Poll.* Wilmington, Del: Scholarly Resources Inc., 1993, 100–103.

Gasiorowski, John. *Adolescent Sexuality and Sex Education.* Dubuque, Iowa: Brown ROA, 1988.

Gilligan, Carol. *In a Different Voice.* Cambridge, Mass.: Harvard University Press, 1982.

Griffin, Susan. "Rape: The All-American Crime." *Ramparts* 10 (1971): 26–35.

Guild, Pat Burke, and Stephen Garger. *Marching to Different Drummers.* Alexandria, Va.: Association for Supervision and Curriculum Development, 1985.

Guindon, Andrew. *The Sexual Language.* Ottowa: University of Ottawa Press, 1977.

Haffner, Debra. "Youth Still at Risk, Yet Barriers to Education Remain." *SIECUS Report* 21/6 (October/November 1992): 11–12.

Heise, Robin G., and Jean A. Steitz. "Religious Perfectionism versus Spiritual Growth." *Counseling and Values* 36/1 (October 1991): 11–18.

"Heterosexuals See Growing Risk of AIDS." *St. Louis Post Dispatch* (February 1992).

Hochhauser, Mark. "Moral Development and HIV Prevention among Adolescents." *Family Life Educator* 10/3 (Spring 1992): 9–12.

Horney, Karen. *The Neurotic Personality of Our Time.* New York: Norton, 1937.

Humm, Andrew J. "Homosexuality: The New Frontier in Sexuality Education." *Family Life Educator* 10/3 (Spring 1992): 13–18.

Hunter, F. T. "Adolescents' Perception of Discussions with Parents and Friends." *Developmental Psychology* 21/3 (1985): 433–40.

Jessor, Shirley L., and Richard Jessor. *Problem Behavior and Psychosocial Development.* New York: Academic Press, 1977, 211–29.

Kahn, J., K. Smith, and E. Roberts. *Familial Communication and Adolescent Sexual Behavior.* Final report to the Office of Adolescent Pregnancy Programs. Cambridge, Mass.: American Institutes for Research, 1984.

Keane, Philip. *Sexual Morality: A Catholic Perspective.* New York: Paulist Press, 1978.

Kempe, C. H., F. N. Silverman, B. F. Steele, William Droegemueller, and Henry K. Silver. "The Battered Child Syndrome." *Journal of the American Medical Association* 181/1 (1962): 17–24.

Kennedy, Eugene. *Free to Be Human.* New York: Image Books/Doubleday, 1987.

———. *Sexual Counseling: A Practical Guide for Non-Professional Counselors.* New York: Continuum Books, 1980.

Kenny, James. *Making Family Matter.* Cincinnati, Ohio: St. Anthony Messenger Press, 1988.

Kirby, Douglas, et al. "Reducing the Risk: Impact of a New Curriculum on Sexual Risk-Taking." *Family Planning Perspectives* 23/6 (November/December, 1991): 253–63.

Kirkendall, Jeffery, and Carol Jarvis-Kirkendall. *Without Consent.* Scottsdale, Ariz.: Swan Press, Inc., 1989, 11–12.

Kosnik, Anthony, et al. *Human Sexuality: New Directions in American Catholic Thought.* New York: Paulist Press, 1977.

Krieger, Dolores. *The Therapeutic Touch.* Englewood Cliffs, N.J.: Prentice-Hall, Inc., 1979.

Linn, Matthew, Sheila Fabrican, and Dennis Linn. *Healing the Eight Stages of Life.* N.Y./ Mahwah: Paulist Press, 1988.

Macooby, Eleanor E. and Carol N. Jacklin. *The Psychology of Sex Differences.* Stanford: Standford University Press, 1974.

Martin, Lloyd. Los Angeles Police Department, 1981; A. Nicholas Groth, 1983; Quoted in Carol and Jeffery Kirkendall's *Without Consent.* Scottsdale, Ariz.: Swan Press, Inc., 1989, 11.

Masters, William H., and Virginia E. Johnson. *Human Sexual Response.* New York: Little, Brown and Company, 1966.

————. *Sex and Human Loving.* Boston: Little, Brown and Company, 1986.

————, Virginia E. Johnson, and Robert C. Kilodny. *Heterosexuality.* New York: Harper Collins, 1994.

McConnell, James V. *Understanding Human Behavior.* 6th ed. New York: Holt, Rinehart and Winston Inc., 1989.

McCormick, Naomi B., and Andrew J. Jones. "Gender Differences in Nonverbal Flirtation." *Journal of Sex Education and Therapy* 15/4 (1989): 271–82.

McCorry, Frank. *Preventing Substance Abuse.* Washington, D.C.: National Catholic Education Association, 1990.

McNaught, Brian. *A Disturbed Peace.* Washington, D.C.: Dignity, 1981.

Melchert, Tim, and Kent F. Burnett. "Attitudes, Knowledge, and Sexual Behavior of High-Risk Adolescents: Implications for Counseling and Sexuality Education." *Journal of Counseling and Development* 68 (1990): 294.

Miller, Patricia F. *In God's Image: Male and Female.* Video and print series produced by Franciscan Communications, "Your Right to Respect," 1989.

Money, John. *Gay, Straight, and In-Between.* New York: Oxford University Press, 1988.

"Mortality attributable to HIV infection/AIDS-United States, 1981–1990." *Morbidity and Mortality Weekley Report* 40/3 (January 1991): 41–46.

Nassar, Carine Mokbel, et al. "Self-Concept, Eating Attitudes, and Dietary Patterns in Young Adolescent Girls." *School Counselor* 39/5 (May 1992): 338–43.

National Center for Health Statistics. *National Survey of Family Growth 1988,* special tabulations for the National Institute of Child Health and Human Development, Bethesda, Md., 1988.

National Conference of Catholic Bishops. *Called to Compassion and Responsibility: A Response to the HIV/AIDS Crisis.* Washington, D.C.: USCC Office for Publishing and Promotion Services, 1989.

————. *Education in Human Sexuality For Christians.* Washington, D.C.: USCC Office for Publishing and Promotion Services, 1981.

————. *Follow the Way of Love: Pastoral Message to Families.* Washington, D.C.: USCC Office for Publishing and Promotion Services, 1993.

————. *Human Sexuality: A Catholic Perspective for Education and Lifelong Learning.* Washington, D.C.: United States Catholic Conference, 1991.

————. *The Many Faces of AIDS.* Washington, D.C.: USCC Office for Publishing and Promotion Services, 1987.

————. *To Live in Christ Jesus.* Washington, D.C.: United States Catholic Conference, 1976.

National Council on Health Studies. *Vital Statistics Mortality Data, Multiple Cause-of-Death Detail* (machine-readable public-use tape). Hyattsville, Md.: U.S. Department of Health and Human Services, Public Health Service, Centers for Disease Control, 1988.

National Guidelines Task Force. *Guidelines for Comprehensive Sexuality Education.* Washington, D.C.: Sex Information and Education Council of the United States, 1991.

Nelson, James B. *Embodiment.* Minneapolis, Minn: Augsburg Publishing House, 1978.

Newcomb, Michael D., and Peter M. Bentler. "Substance Use and Abuse Among Children and Teenagers." *American Psychologist 44/2* (February 1989): 242–48.

Nolin, M. J., and K. K. Petersen. "Gender Differences in Parent-Child Communication about Sexuality: An Exploratory Study." *Journal of Adolescent Research 7/1* (January 1992): 59–79.

Nugent, Robert, ed. *A Challenge to Love.* New York: Crossroad Publications, 1989.

————, and Jeannine Gramick, eds. *A Time to Speak.* Mt. Rainier, Md.: New Ways Ministry, 1982.

Ooms, Theodora, ed. *Teenage Pregnancy in a Familly Context: Implications for Policy.* Philadelphia: Temple University Press, 1981.

"Parents and Sexuality Education." *The Facts.* Washington, D.C.: Center for Population Options (January 1987).

Pennington, Sylvia. *But Lord They're Gay.* Hawthorne, Cal.: Lambda Christian Fellowship, 1982.

"Personal Communication." Gay and Lesbian Anti-Violence Project, February 1993.

Peters, Stefanie Doyle. "Child Sexual Abuse and Later Psychological Problems." In *Lasting Effects of Child Sexual Abuse,* ed. Gail Elizabeth Wyatt and Gloria Johnson Powell, 101–117. London: Sage Publications, 1988.

Piggins, Ann Carol. "The Silent Crime." *Momentum* (November 1991): 56–60.

Pleck, Joseph H. *The Myth of Masculinity.* Cambridge: MIT Press, 1981.

Powell, John. *Unconditional Love.* Allen, Tex.: Argus Communications, 1978, 66–68.

"Premarital Sexual Experience among Adolescent Women—United States, 1970–1988." *Morbidity and Mortality Weekly Report 39: 51/52* (January 4, 1991): 929–32.

PRESEREC. *Preservice adjustment of homosexual and heterosexual military accessions: Implications for security clearance suitability* (January 1989).

"Progress toward Achieving the 1990 Objectives for the Nation for Sexually Transmitted Diseases." *Morbidity and Mortality Weekly Report 39/4* (Feb. 2, 1990): 53–57.

Puls, Joan. *A Spirituality of Compassion.* Mystic, Conn.: Twenty-Third Publications, 1988.

Quinn, John R. *Pastoral Letter on Homosexuality.* A Pastoral Statement by the Archbishop of San Francisco. The Chancery Office, 1980.

Quinn, T. C., et al. "Human Immunodeficiency Virus Infection among Patients Attending Clinics for Sexually Transmitted Diseases." *New England Journal of Medicine 318/4* (January 1988): 197–203.

Randolph, A. G., and A. E. Washington. "Screening for Chlamydia Trachomatis in Adolescent Males: A Cost-based Decision Analysis." *American Journal of Public Health 80/5* (May 1990): 545–50.

Ranke-Heinemann, Uta. *Eunuchs for the Kingdom of Heaven.* New York: Penguin Books, 1990, 9–20.

Reinisch, June M. *The Kinsey Institute New Report On Sex.* New York: St. Martin's Press, 1990.

Remafedi, Gary. "Adolescent Homosexuality: Psychosocial and Medical Implications" *79/3* (1987): 331–37.

———. "Male Homosexuality: The Adolescent's Perspective." *Pediatrics* 79/3 (1987): 326–30.

*Resource Manual for Trainees.* Missouri Coalition Against Domestic Violence, 1990.

Riordan, Richard J., and Anne C. Verdel. "Evidence of Sexual Abuse in Children's Art Products." *School Counselor* 39/2 (November 1991): 116–21.

Rodin, Judith. "Body Mania." *Psychology Today* (January/February 1992): 56–60.

Rush, Florence. *The Best Kept Secret: Sexual Abuse of Children.* Englewood Cliffs, N.J.: Prentice-Hall, 1980.

Russel, Diana E. H. "The Incidence and Prevalence of Intrafamilial and Extrafamilial Sexual Abuse of Female Children." *Child Abuse and Neglect 7* (1983): 133.

———. *Rape in Marriage.* New York: Macmillan, 1982.

———. *The Secret Trauma: Incest in the Lives of Girls and Women.* New York: Basic Books, 1986.

Sacred Congregation for the Doctrine of the Faith. *Declaration on Sexual Ethics.* Washington, D.C.: United States Catholic Conference, 1976.

Sanday, P. R. *Female Power and Male Dominance: On the Origins of Sexual Inequality.* Cambridge: Cambridge University Press, 1981.

Santrock, John W. *Adolescence.* 4th ed. Dubuque, Iowa: Wm. C. Brown, 1990.

Schechter, Susan. *Women and Male Violence.* Boston: South End Press, 1982.

Schmidt, Alvin John. *Veiled and Silenced.* Macon, Ga: Mercer University Press, 1989.

"Sexuality Education." *The Facts.* Washington, D.C.: Center for Population Options (January 1987).

Shelton, Charles M. *Adolescent Spirituality.* New York: Crossroad Publishing Co., 1983.

———. *Morality of the Heart.* New York: Crossroad Publishing Co., 1990.

*SIECUS Report.* "Sexual orientation and identity." (Fact Sheet). Sex Information and Education Council of the United States (February/March 1993): 19–20.

———. "When Children's Sexual Behaviors Raise Concern." 19/6 (August/September 1991): 11.

Signorielli, Nancy and George Gerbner, eds. *Violence and Terror in the Mass Media: An Annotated Bibliography.* Westport, Conn: Greenwood Press, 1988.

Smith, E. A., and J. R. Udry. "Coital and Non-coital Sexual Behaviors of White and Black Adolescents." *American Journal of Public Health 75* (1985): 1200–1203.

Sonenstein, F. L., J. H. Pleck, and L. C. Ku. "Sexual Activity, Condom Use and AIDS Knowledge among Adolescent Males." *Family Planning Perspectives 21/4* (Jul/Aug. 1989): 152–58.

Sullivan, Susan K., and Matthew A. Kawiak. *Parents Talk Love.* New York: Paulist Press, 1985.

Sweeney, Richard. *Sexuality, Loneliness and Intimacy.* Cassette. Cincinnati, Ohio: St. Anthony Messenger Press, 1991.

Switzer, David K., and Shirley Switzer. *Parents of the Homosexual.* Philadelphia: Westminster Press, 1980.

"Talking to Your Children about AIDS." *Psychology Today* (October 1989): 62–63.

"Teenage, Sexuality, Pregnancy, and Parenthood." *The Facts.* Washington, D.C.: Center for Population Options (April 1987).

Timmerman, Joan H. *Sexuality and Spiritual Growth.* New York: Crossroad Publishing Co., 1992.

Todres, Rubin. "Effectiveness of Counseling in the Transmission of Family Planning and

Sexuality Knowledge." *Journal of Sex Education and Therapy* 16/4 (Winter 1990): 279–85.

United States Department of Justice. *Uniform crime reports: Crime in the United States.* Washington, D.C.: U. S. Government Printing Office, 1984.

United States General Accounting Office Report to Congressional Requesters. "Defense force management: DOD's policy on homosexuality" (June 1992).

Van De Polder, Jean. "Why Parents' Sexual Warnings to Adolescents Backfire." *Medical Aspects of Human Sexuality* (April 1980): 78–89.

Von der Osten-Sacken, Peter. "The Pauline Gospel and Homosexuality." *Theological Digest* 33/3 (Fall

Walf, Knut. "Hom                                                            33/3 (Fall 1986): 309–12.

Weakland, Rembert                                                            Milwaukee on the Topic of H

Westley, Dick. Mo                                                            lications, 1984.

Whitehead, James,                                                            k: Image Books/Doubleday,

———. Seasons of                                                            k: Image Books/Doubleday,

Whittington, W. L.                                                            orrhoeae to Anitmicrobial                                                            ases 15/4 (1988): 202–10.

Worth, Denise, Pam                                                            ffiliation, Family Backgroun                                                            of College Student Developme

Wurtele, Sandy K.,                                                            Genital Terminology." Jou                                                            15–22.

Yegidis, B. L. "Date                                                            lege Stu- dents." *Journal of*

"Young Men and Tee                                                            Popula- tion Options (July

Zelnik, Melvin and                                                            ." *Family* Planning Perspectiv

Zukowski, Angela A                                                            February 1991): 79.